SAVAGE ENERGIES

SAVAGE ENERGIES
Lessons of Myth and Ritual
in Ancient Greece

WALTER BURKERT

Translation by Peter Bing

THE UNIVERSITY OF CHICAGO PRESS
Chicago & London

WALTER BURKERT is emeritus professor of classics at the
University of Zurich. He is the author of a number of books,
most recently *The Orientalizing Revolution: Near Eastern
Influence on Greek Culture in the Early Archaic Age* and
Creation of the Sacred: Tracks of Biology in Early Religions.

THE UNIVERSITY OF CHICAGO PRESS, CHICAGO 60637
THE UNIVERSITY OF CHICAGO PRESS, LTD., LONDON
© 2001 by The University of Chicago
All rights reserved. Published 2001

Printed in the United States of America

10 09 08 07 06 05 04 03 02 01   5 4 3 2 1

ISBN (cloth): 0-226-08085-4

Originally published as *Wilder Ursprung: Opferritual und
Mythos bei den Griechen*, © 1990 Verlag Klaus Wagenbach,
Ahornstraße 4, 1000 Berlin 30

Chapters 1 and 3 are published from original English-language
versions, with editing. Chapters 2, 4, and 5 were translated from
the German edition by Peter Bing. The foreword is
a translation by Glenn W. Most of his foreword to the
German edition.

Library of Congress Cataloging-in-Publication Data

Burkert, Walter, 1931–
    [Wilder Ursprung. English]
    Savage energies : lessons of myth and ritual in ancient
Greece / Walter Burkert ; translation by Peter Bing.
        p.   cm.
    Includes bibliographical references.
    ISBN 0-226-08085-4 (cloth : alk. paper)
    1. Mythology, Greek.   2. Rites and ceremonies—Greece.
I. Title.

BL785 .B8513   2001
292.08—dc21

                                                00-046717

CONTENTS

v

RIGOROUS RESEARCH INTO
SAVAGE ENERGIES: WALTER BURKERT
ON MYTH AND RITUAL
Glenn W. Most

> The human being, in its highest and noblest powers, is wholly nature and
> bears within itself nature's uncanny double character. The human's fright-
> ful capabilities, the ones which are considered inhuman, are indeed perhaps
> the fertile soil from which alone can grow all humanity, in impulses, deeds,
> and works. So it is that the Greeks, the most humane human beings of
> ancient times, have within themselves a trait of cruelty, of tiger-like joy
> in destruction. . . .
> —F. Nietzsche, *Five Prefaces to Five Unwritten Books*[1]

Not only for us, but already for the Greeks there was something uncanny
about their own myths—and not only about this one or that one, which
told how some god was castrated or torn apart, or how some hero went
mad or committed atrocities, but about the category of myth itself, as a
narrative of the deeds and sufferings of characters both superhuman and
all too human, designed to render the conditions of human existence intelligible, and hence, perhaps, somewhat less intolerable.[2] Every Greek poet,
starting with Homer, had to face the delicate challenge posed by an often
bizarre or enigmatic legend—because of a single woman, an enormous
army besieged a mighty city for ten years and then mercilessly destroyed
it; a king saved his city, murdered his father, and married his mother—
and every time it was retold it had to be shaped in a new way for a new
audience, neither reiterated so unimaginatively that it seemed stale and bor-
ing nor altered so radically that it contradicted the tradition and seemed
implausible. Every historian who chose not to limit himself to his own period had to deal with the embarrassing contradictions and improbabilities
of the myths, for these were his only sources for the events of prehistory:
he had to collect, select, reshape, and combine them—astonishingly, almost
no one dared simply to do without them, and even if Ephorus excluded
the mythic period from his universal history on the grounds that accurate

knowledge of it was unobtainable, nonetheless he did not hesitate to assume as the secure starting point for his own work of history the wanderings of the sons of Herakles.[3] And every philosopher, even if entirely convinced of the inferiority of mythic thought, had to deal with the traditional myths, either by circumstantially refuting them (not least in order to create room for the new ones he invented himself) or by painstakingly demonstrating that his own truths had already been expressed in the most ancient legends under an allegorical veil that could be entirely lifted by the proper exegesis. In the end, no ancient philosophical school managed to do entirely without allegorical interpretation, and even Aristotle justified it[4] and Lucretius applied it.[5]

Poetic plausibility, historical reduction, philosophical allegoresis: these were the three most important stopgap remedies that the Greeks employed in their millennial effort to come to terms with their indispensable but indecipherable myths. If we measure the difficulty of this challenge in terms of their repeated efforts to meet it, we will be less astonished that the Greek myths were constantly exposed to assaults and reinterpretations than that they retained their validity for as long as they did. Of course, they were protected to a certain extent by their anchors in civic religion and elementary instruction: but why did these anchors, too, not come loose with time? There can be little doubt that these three strategies were crucial to the survival of the myths, not only in all of ancient Greek culture but also beyond it: whether as an inexhaustible source of literary inspiration, as a lasting document of the earliest epochs of human history, or as an enigmatic hint at sublime physical or moral doctrines, the myths achieved rescue from the shipwreck of antiquity and survival beyond the Middle Ages into the modern period.[6] Indeed, so successful was this rescue that not even the development of autonomous national literatures and of new historical sciences and philosophies in the course of the early modern period could break the spell of the Greek myths altogether: even if the traditional forms of Baroque poetry, of Euhemerism, and of allegorical interpretation went into decline during the eighteenth century,[7] the myths themselves, which originally had been assumed to depend upon just such vehicles for rescue, turned out in fact to have long since ceased to need them and went on frolicking gaily. In the nineteenth century almost every Romantic poet was able to make free use of classical myths, while at the universities, in the proud new pseudo-scientific discipline of mythology, the ancient ghosts of Euhemerism and of various forms of philosophical allegoresis returned to haunt the rising discipline of classical philology in the forms, respectively, of K. O.

Müller's theory of the myths as tribal legends and of Creuzer's *Symbolism and Mythology of the Ancient Peoples* and Max Müller's *Comparative Mythology*.[8]

In practice, all such interpretative strategies proceed by detaching the myth from its original functional context in order to insert it into new systems, literary, historical, or philosophical. But only very rarely indeed do any of these interpretative modes have the honesty, or the effrontery, to admit this: instead, they claim to be restoring to the myth precisely the same original meaning it had but, long ago (when? how? why?), had lost. Upon the stage of new cultural needs, the myth enters in a costume designed to make it seem ancient and entirely original: its putative content, however meager it may sometimes be, is always enriched by a luxuriant archaic pathos, and rhetorically this pathos contributes far more than does the content toward legitimating the new system. For a myth is not the same thing as a fiction: even if detaching it from its original context comes close to aestheticizing it, it nevertheless retains as an intrinsic part of itself an inextinguishable reference to its remote, original context: "Dorther kommt und zurück deutet der kommende Gott" ("Thence comes, and back thither points, the coming god," F. Hölderlin, "Brod und Wein" [Bread and Wine]). What makes the myth so uncanny is precisely this tension between originality and detachability, between religion and art, between what is lost forever and what is rescued over and over again. For the myth has always survived itself, and every survivor is uncanny.

Walter Burkert's studies of the history of Greek religion represent the most important approach to understanding the uncanniness of Greek myth that has appeared in the German-speaking countries since World War II.[9] The central methodological step in his approach is the assumption that originally the narrative myth on the one hand and the ritual actions of the cult on the other belonged together functionally. For the colorful fables on which ancient and (at least until recently) modern children were raised made up only one aspect of Greek religiosity: besides these, the Greek world was full of temples and sanctuaries, in which rituals were performed in honor of the particular divinity according to ancient custom on regularly recurring occasions. Every community had its own cults that were intimately bound up with its members' understanding of their own political identity. Greek religion was essentially a civic religion: the regulation of offices, ceremonies, and the religious calendar comprised the most important duties of a community and grounded its political identity; and within the sphere of the citizens' obligations, religious and political actions very often coincided—indeed, even the conceptual distinction between politics and religion, which seems so self-evident to us, can apply to the Greeks only in a highly qualified sense.

Now, many Greek myths are transmitted to us in the familiar form given them by the great poets of antiquity; but for information about most rituals we must depend upon the much drier texts of ancient scholarship—travelers' reports, monographs, commentaries, lexica—and only the rarest of good fortunes provides us with archaeological finds to complete or correct their lacunose, contradictory, or misleading information. What is more, however alien the Greek myths may sometimes seem, nonetheless they certainly appear to us (and already to most authors of classical times and late antiquity) to be far more readily intelligible than most Greek rituals. What is the significance of the ritual in Brauron, for example, according to which girls between five and seven years of age were called "female bears" and performed sacrifice to the goddess Artemis in saffron-colored robes; or why is it that in the sacrificial procession at the great festival of Dionysus in Athens not only an image of the god and a bull, but also a large number of oversized phalloi were ceremoniously carried in parade? It is hardly surprising that mythological handbooks preceded by many centuries the first scholarly collections of the evidence for ancient cult practices.

Exactly a century ago, the so-called "Cambridge school of anthropology"—W. Robertson Smith, Jane Ellen Harrison, James George Frazer[10]—thought that they had discovered the solution for such riddles by tracing the myths back to rituals and explaining these latter through comparison with the customs early anthropologists had observed among "primitive" peoples. Thus, for Harrison, the myth was the spoken counterpart to the action performed in the ritual: the one could not be understood without the other. In the English-speaking world this idea exerted a lasting influence on the ways in which ancient Greek culture was understood, but in German classical studies it never really took root, partly out of a not-unjustified skepticism with regard to forced parallels and inadequately supported generalizations, partly because of a less commendable resistance to the very notion that the ancient Greeks, those putative paradigms of ideal humanity, could be compared in any significant respect with "savage" tribes. The result, in the German-speaking countries, was for a long time an almost insuperable division between research into myths on the one hand and research into rituals on the other: the former was subordinated to the study of the poets, since these were supposed to have freely invented the fables

x

(Wilamowitz: "The myths are not holy: poets have narrated them, poets reinvent them in different ways"),[11] and was excluded from the handbooks of the history of Greek religion, which limited themselves for the most part to providing systematic presentations of the results of the latter. Religious word and religious act were artificially separated from one another—and so were the poet who once invented the fable and the populace who repeatedly performed the rituals.

Closing this gap has been one of the central aims of Walter Burkert's work. For him, myth and ritual illuminate one another: the fact that the one takes place as a paradigmatic narrative, the other as a paradigmatic action, does not in the least exclude a reciprocal connection between the two but rather permits both sides all the more successfully to complete and support one another. To this extent Burkert is certainly an heir of the Cambridge school. But what separates him from its members in the end is his universalistic claim to be able to go beyond specific local genetic connections between individual myths and rituals and to arrive at fundamental—and that means, for him, at original—structures of human social life. For in Burkert's eyes the message of myth and the message of ritual are the same: in Nietzsche's words, "The terrible energies—what people call Evil—are the cyclopic architects and pathfinders of humanity."[12] On this view, the order that is indispensable for the survival of every lasting human community presupposes not only the repression of the destructive violence of inborn aggressive impulses but also the constructive liberation of their energies: violence is not only the opposite of order, but also its premise and its constitutive energy. Burkert's central questions—How can order draw upon the energies of violence without being sacrificed to it? How can civilization survive without barbarism?—have been shaped on the basis of the theories of Nietzsche and Freud and the anthropology of the last fifty years,[13] but they have been sharpened by the catastrophes of the twentieth century. Each of the articles reprinted here treats a specific critical point in the life of human societies—sacrifice, initiation, renewal, purification, legitimation— and demonstrates that without ritual and myth the particular crisis could not have been overcome and the endangered society could not have survived. To be sure, Burkert does seem to have a decided, and perhaps somewhat exaggerated, preference for origins (especially for paleolithic ones); but his admiration for the accomplishments of Greek culture, which managed to combine durability with humanism, leads him to an entirely practical and contemporary anxiety: Is it too late for us to learn from the Greeks?

These early writings of Burkert have a peculiar charm; after a quarter century they still seem fresh and have not been superseded by later scholarship, even if many of the themes announced here have been treated with greater depth and subtlety in his own more recent publications.[14] A partial explanation may be that in general the study of classical antiquity in the German-speaking countries has not yet benefited in full from the fundamental insight into the reciprocal relation between myth and ritual that has long since proliferated in such countries as the United States,[15] France,[16] and Switzerland,[17] where the structuralist anthropology of Lévi-Strauss has also exerted a strong influence. But Burkert's early writings may still seem fresh because an authentically literary tension is clearer than in his more exhaustive later studies. For on the one hand the tone of these essays is entirely cool and sober. Their style is objective, their argumentation subtle; Burkert demonstrates an extraordinary mastery over the whole repertory of the ancillary disciplines of classical scholarship—archaeology, numismatics, epigraphy, Indo-European linguistics—and knows how to apply them tactically and tactfully. But on the other hand the preferred object of these studies is blood, death, madness, disgust, terror. Over and over again Burkert leads the reader from the bright daylight of Greek humanity back into the frightful night of uncontrolled aggression, of destructive and self-destructive impulses, which preceded that daylight, constantly besieged it, and incessantly threatened to annihilate it. Burkert's Apollonian analysis of Dionysian phenomena, his scholarly observation of abominable dangers, is itself capable of exerting an uncanny effect.

NOTES

1. F. Nietzsche, *Kritische Studienausgabe*, ed. G. Colli and M. Montinari (Munich and Berlin, 1988), vol. 1, p. 783; hereafter this edition is cited as *KSA* with volume and page number. All translations from this and other foreign language texts are my own.

2. On the category of myth and the history of ways in which it has been understood, cf. W. Burkert, "Mythos—Begriff, Struktur, Funktion," in F. Graf, ed., *Mythos in mythenloser Gesellschaft. Das Paradigma Roms* (Stuttgart and Leipzig, 1993) 9–24, and "Antiker Mythos—Begriff und Funktion," in H. Hofmann, ed., *Antike Mythen in der europäischen Tradition* (Tübingen, 1999) 11–26; and my "From Logos to Mythos," in R. Buxton, ed., *From Myth to Reason? Studies in the Development of Greek Thought* (Oxford, 1999) 25–47.

3. *Fragmente der griechischen Historiker* 70 T 8 Jacoby.

4. Aristotle, *Metaphysics* xii.8.1074a38–b14.

5. Lucretius, *De rerum natura* 2.600–660, 3.978–1023. His master Epicurus, on the other hand, seems to have had no interest in the traditional myths.

6. For a classical account, superseded only in details, of the role of allegorical interpretation in this process, cf. J. Seznec, *The Survival of the Ancient Gods* (New York, 1953). A recent

xii

collection of essays illustrating a variety of contemporary approaches is provided by H.-J. Horn and H. Walter, eds., *Die Allegorese des antiken Mythos* (Wiesbaden, 1997).

7. On the connection between the crisis of traditional allegorical interpretation and the rise of the modern concept of the genius, see my "The Second Homeric Renaissance: Allegoresis and Genius in Early Modern Poetics," in P. Murray, ed., *Genius: The History of an Idea* (Oxford, 1989) 54–75.

8. On the history of scientific mythology in the nineteenth and twentieth centuries, see W. Burkert, "Griechische Mythologie und die Geistesgeschichte der Moderne," in W. den Boer et al., *Les Etudes classiques aux XIXᵉ et XXᵉ siècles: Leur place dans l'histoire des idées*, Fondation Hardt Entretiens sur l'antiquité classique 26 (Geneva, 1980) 159–207. A useful anthology of texts is provided by B. Feldman and R. D. Richardson, *The Rise of Modern Mythology 1680–1860* (Bloomington and London, 1972).

9. On at least two occasions, Burkert himself has sketched out his own development for a general public and in this process has criticized certain aspects of his early writings: "Burkert über Burkert. 'Homo Necans': Der Mensch, der tötet," *Frankfurter Allgemeine Zeitung*, 3 August 1988, no. 178, 29–30; and "An Interview with Walter Burkert," *Favonius* 2 (1988) 41–52.

10. W. R. Smith, *Lectures on the Religion of the Semites* (Edinburgh, 1889); J. E. Harrison, *Mythology and Monuments of Ancient Athens* (London, 1890), *Prolegomena to the Study of Greek Religion* (Cambridge, 1903), *Themis. A Study of the Social Origin of Greek Religion* (Cambridge, 1912), *Epilegomena to the Study of Greek Religion* (Cambridge, 1921); J. G. Frazer, *The Golden Bough* (London, 1890; thereafter many expanded and abridged editions). Other scholars later associated with the Cambridge school included A. B. Cook, F. M. Cornford, and G. Murray. See W. M. Calder III, ed., *The Cambridge Ritualists Reconsidered* (Atlanta, 1991).

11. U. von Wilamowitz-Moellendorff, *Der Glaube der Hellenen* (Darmstadt, 1976⁵), vol. 2, p. 95. See A. Henrichs, " 'Der Glaube der Hellenen': Religionsgeschichte als Glaubensbekenntnis und Kulturkritik," in W. M. Calder III, H. Flashar, and T. Lindken, eds., *Wilamowitz nach 50 Jahren* (Darmstadt, 1985) 263–305.

12. *KSA* vol. 2, p. 205.

13. Especially important influences on Burkert: K. Meuli, "Griechische Opferbräuche," in *Phyllobolia. Festschrift für Peter von der Mühll* (Basel, 1946) 185–288=K. Meuli, *Gesammelte Schriften*, ed. T. Gelzer (Basel, Stuttgart, 1975), vol. 2, 907–1021; and K. Lorenz, *Das sogenannte Böse. Zur Naturgeschichte der Aggression* (Vienna, 1963)=*On Aggression*, trans. M. K. Wilson (New York, 1966).

14. See especially W. Burkert, *Homo Necans. Interpretationen altgriechischer Opferriten und Mythen* (Berlin, New York, 1972)=*Homo Necans: The Anthropology of Ancient Greek Sacrificial Ritual and Myth*, trans. P. Bing (Berkeley, 1983); *Griechische Religion der archäischen und klassischen Epoche* (Stuttgart, Berlin, Cologne, Mainz, 1977)=*Greek Religion*, trans. J. Raffan (Cambridge, MA, 1985); *Structure and History in Greek Mythology and Ritual* (Berkeley, Los Angeles, London, 1979); "Glaube und Verhalten: Zeichengehalt und Wirkungsmacht von Opferritualen," in *Le Sacrifice dans l'antiquité=Fondation Hardt Entretiens sur l'antiquité classique* 27 (Vandoeuvres, Geneva, 1981) 91–125; and the contributions and discussions in R. G. Hammerton-Kelly, ed., *Violent Origins: Walter Burkert, René Girard and Jonathan Z. Smith on Ritual Killing and Cultural Formation* (Stanford, 1987).

15. See, for example, F. I. Zeitlin, *Playing the Other: Gender and Society in Classical Greek Literature* (Chicago, 1996); C. Segal, *Tragedy and Civilization. An Interpretation of Sophocles* (Cambridge, MA, and London, 1981), *Dionysiac Poetics and Euripides' Bacchae* (Princeton, 1982), *Interpreting Greek Tragedy: Myth, Poetry, Text* (Ithaca, NY, and London, 1986); H. P. Foley, *Ritual Irony. Poetry and Sacrifice in Euripides* (Ithaca, NY, and London, 1985).

16. See, for example, J.-P. Vernant, *Mythe et pensée chez les Grecs* (Paris, 1965)=*Myth and Thought among the Greeks* (London and Boston, 1983), *Mythe et société en Grèce ancienne* (Paris, 1974)=*Myth and Society in Ancient Greece,* trans. J. Lloyd (New York and Cambridge, MA, 1988), and now especially J.-P. Vernant, *Mortals and Immortals: Collected Essays,* ed. F. I. Zeitlin (Princeton, 1991); J.-P. Vernant and P. Vidal-Naquet, *Mythe et tragédie en Grèce ancienne* (Paris, 1972)=*Myth and Tragedy in Ancient Greece,* trans. J. Lloyd (New York and Cambridge, MA, 1988); M. Detienne, *Dionysos mis à mort* (Paris, 1977)=*Dionysus Slain,* trans. M. and L. Muellner (Baltimore, 1979); P. Vidal-Naquet, *Le Chasseur noir: Formes de pensée et formes de société dans le monde grec* (Paris, 1981)=*The Black Hunter: Forms of Thought and Forms of Society in the Greek World,* trans. A. Szegedy-Maszak (Baltimore, 1986); M. Detienne and J.-P. Vernant, *La Cuisine du sacrifice en pays grec* (Paris, 1979)=*The Cuisine of Sacrifice among the Greeks,* trans. P. Wissing (Chicago, 1989).

17. See, for example, J. Rudhardt, *Notions fondamentales de la pensée religieuse et actes constitutifs du culte dans la Grèce classique* (Geneva, 1958), "Les Mythes grecs relatifs à l'instauration du sacrifice: Les Rôles corrélatifs de Prométhée et son fils Deucalion," *Museum Helveticum* 27 (1979), pp 1–15; C. Calame, *Les Choeurs de jeunes filles en Grèce archaïque* (Rome, 1977)=*Choruses of Young Women in Ancient Greece: Their Morphology, Religious Role, and Social Functions,* trans. D. Collins and J. Orion (Lanham, MD, 1997), *Thésée et l'imaginaire athénienne: Légende et culte en Grèce antique* (Lausanne, 1996), *Mythe et histoire dans l'Antiquité grecque: La Création symbolique d'une colonie* (Lausanne, 1996); P. Borgeaud, *Recherches sur le dieu Pan* (Rome, 1979)=*The Cult of Pan in Ancient Greece,* trans. K. Atlass and J. Redfield (Chicago, 1988).

GREEK TRAGEDY AND SACRIFICIAL RITUAL

The proliferation of theses and hypotheses, of reconstructions and constructions on the subject of the origin of tragedy leads to reflection on a basic problem of philological statements.[1] Evidently we ought not to expect that we can reduce so complex a phenomenon as Greek tragedy to one single formula of origin. Every statement is necessarily one-sided. When we are dealing with an evolution, with *pollai metabolai* (numerous transformations; Aristotle *Poetics* 1449a14), there will be in each case persistence as well as differentiation, yet it is difficult to describe both pertinently at the same time. So, following his own inclinations, a scholar will be apt either to praise the creative achievement of a unique poet, be it Thespis or Aeschylus, or to insist on the primeval elements, with the ritual still preserved. We may collect exact information or formulate precise hypotheses as to the external organization of the Dionysia in the Polis Athens in the sixth century B.C.: temple and theater, chorus of citizens and choregos, *poiētēs* (poet), *didaskalos* (director), *hupokritēs* (actor), masks and actors' dress, musical instruments, figures of dancing, musical and literary technique in the tradition of choral lyric and the iambos. But whoever tries to grasp the unique *kairos*, that "critical moment" in the history of the human mind which brought forth tragedy, to understand the intellectual, psychological, and social motives involved, enters a field of basic ambiguity. On the precarious balance and the conflict of tradition and emancipation, individual and society, religion and the profane, myth and reason, not even Thespis himself could have given final elucidation. It is left to us to attempt again and again to form a comprehensive picture of man and his world out of the testimonies of the past. In each individual case, we shall not be able to grasp more than some of the possible aspects, a few strands in a complicated pattern. But we ought to keep in mind just this to avoid the danger that traditional or contemporary prejudices may unduly narrow the possibilities of approach.

It is a single aspect that shall be considered here, the question why tragedy is called *tragōidia*—a word that seems to impose the animal on the development of high human civilization, the primitive and grotesque on sublime literary creations. If we seek an explanation of the word, we cannot avoid going back to earlier strata, to the religious basis of tragedy and indeed to Greek cult in general. Whether this has any bearing on fully developed Attic tragedy cannot be determined in advance. The theory most prevalent today, going back to Welcker and owing its popularity to Wilamowitz, who claimed Aristotle's authority for it, understands *tragōidia* to mean "song of goats," sc., of dancers dressed as goats. Scholars more concerned with the history of religion, however, still uphold the ancient etymology, "song at the sacrifice of a goat."[2] It will be necessary to establish first that philological criticism of the sources does not lead to a decision. When, however, the essence of sacrificial ritual is studied, a new perspective seems to emerge in which, eventually, even plays of Aeschylus, Sophocles, and Euripides may reveal a ritual background.

I

There are so many learned, subtle, and exhaustive discussions of Wilamowitz's theory of the origin of tragedy that it may suffice here to point out the well-known difficulties involved. The only ancient evidence is a gloss in the *Etymologicum Magnum, s.v. tragōidia* (764.5), which says, after three other explanations, ἢ ὅτι τὰ πολλὰ οἱ χοροὶ ἐκ σατύρων συνίσταντο, οὓς ἐκάλουν τράγους (because the choruses mostly were composed of satyrs, whom they called goats). The statement that tragic choruses "mostly" consisted of satyrs is clearly wrong. Yet modern scholars have combined this with a passing remark of Aristotle's that tragedy developed *ek saturikou* (*Poetics* 1449a20, cf. 22); this may mean that tragedy originated "from the satyr play," as Chamaeleon, one of Aristotle's pupils, explained *expressis verbis.*[3] The notice in the *Etymologicum Magnum* has therefore been regarded as a somewhat corrupt reproduction of the "Peripatetic theory of the origin of tragedy": that the proto-tragedy was the satyr-play—or, since Aristotle derives tragedy from the dithyramb, a "Satyrdithyrambos"—and this was called "song of the goats." The first difficulty arises from the tradition that names Pratinas of Phlius, the slightly older contemporary of Aeschylus, as the inventor of the satyr-play. This piece of information is supported in a remarkable way by the pictorial tradition: scenes that un doubtedly come from satyr-plays begin to appear in vase paintings after about 520 B.C., considerably after the first production of tragedy by Thespis. The scholar who has done the most fundamental work on the pictorial representations of satyr-plays, Frank Brommer, therefore concluded as long ago as 1937 that the satyr-play was "keine Vorform der Tragödie, sondern eine neue Erfindung" (no primitive form of tragedy, but a new invention).[4] So in order to save the theory it becomes necessary to postulate a proto-satyr-play existing before Pratinas; this turns Pratinas's achievement into a mere reform of satyr-play. Insofar as the type of the satyr undoubtedly existed long before Pratinas, this is a possible way out of the difficulty; whether the Peripatetics could know anything about this proto-satyr-play is another question.

The other difficulty is more disturbing. The satyrs of the satyr-play and the even earlier satyrs that we know from vase paintings and sculpture are not "goats," but wild men with animal ears and horses' tails; only in the Hellenistic period did they acquire horns. A satyr may on occasion be called *tragos*, and when on vase paintings satyrs and goats are depicted together, their physiognomy becomes remarkably similar;[5] but still they are not *tragoi* themselves, as a satyr-play never could be called *tragōidia*. The theory necessitates a further step backwards. It is argued that the home of the proto-satyr-play, or rather goat-play, was not Athens, but the Peloponnese; Pan belongs to Arcadia, and in Corinth, about 600 B.C., Arion developed the dithyramb that Aristotle connects with tragedy. Wilamowitz unhesitatingly assumed that Arion's chorus consisted of *tragoi* (86). Now Corinthian vases of this period offer countless variations on the retinue of Dionysus, but no singing goats. Most frequently one finds the grotesque padded dancers; it is possible that they were called *saturoi*, but surely they are much less *tragoi* than the satyrs of Attic satyr-play. There also appear shaggy creatures with hairy bodies, but they lack any characteristic that would allow us to assign them to a definite species. Only someone who is determined to produce *tragoi* at all costs for the sake of *tragōidia* will call them "goats."[6] The expression *mallōtos chitōn* (coat of fleece) would rather suggest sheepskins. Only the same fixed prejudice in favor of goats explains why the *tragikoi choroi* in the cult of Adrastus at Sicyon (Herodotus 5.67) have so often been understood to be "choruses of goats."[7]

There remains what has been thought to be the supreme piece of evidence for the singing goats, an archaic bronze from Methydrion in the Peloponnese, more than a century earlier than Arion. It is so primitive that experts doubted whether the four dancing figures were goats or rams until recently when Roland Hampe, referring to similar bronzes found at Olympia, established that neither goats nor rams are represented but quite simply men. What had been taken to be horns are a primitive attempt at ears.[8] There are, of course, goatlike demons even beside Pan. Terracotta statuettes, mostly from Boeotia, represent an ithyphallic goatman with a cornucopia. His name is unknown,[9] whereas the horned dancers on the so-called Anodos-scenes may with some probability be identified as *Panes* (gods Pan); they seem to be confined to this special occasion.[10]

So still there is no evidence for choruses of singing goats from which *tragōidia* could have derived its name. And at any rate there would remain the deeper question—whatever could be the relation between satyr-like gaiety and the high seriousness of tragedy? Did *tragōidia* originally lack the "tragic" element (so Wilamowitz 93)?

We also have to consider a simple but decisive linguistic fact: the primary word formation is not *tragōidia* at all, but *tragōidoi*, or rather *tragōidos*. This word is used in official inscriptions as well as in colloquial speech until well into the fourth century, where we should expect to find *tragōidia: en tois tragōidois* (among the *tragōidoi*), *theasasthai tragōidous* (watch the *tragōidoi*), *nikān tragōidois* (to win a victory with *tragōidoi*). *Tragōidoi*—that is, the chorus with its strange masks and splendid robes, as it stood before the eyes of the Athenians.[11] Now the laws of Greek word formation show that *tragōidos* cannot mean "singing goat"; nor indeed does the word *kōmōidoi* imply "singing *kōmoi*" (revels), but "singers on occasion of the *kōmos*."[12] To be exact, we are dealing with a determinative compound, in which regularly the first part determines in some way the area of operation of the second. It can be either purely nominal, like *aulōidos*, *kitharōidos:* the "singer" who has something to do with a "goat," "flute," "cithara"; or *-ōidos* can be verbal, "he who sings the goat," like *linōidos* (who sings the Linus song), *melōidos* (who sings the song), *thrēnōidos* (who sings the lament). At any rate, *tragōidoi* are "singers," one particular group out of different kinds of singers. There is at least one exact parallel: Dionysios of Argos, fourth or third century B.C., has preserved what he states to be an earlier name for rhapsodes, *arnōidos*, explaining the word unhesitatingly *tou de athlou tois nikōsin arnos apodedeigmenou* (from the prize offered the victors: a ram, *arnos*).[13]

To this corresponds the explanation of the name *tragōidia*—the only one current in antiquity—as "song for the prize of a goat" or "song at the sacrifice of a goat"; the two interpretations are identical, for naturally the goat won as a prize was sacrificed to Dionysos. The earliest evidence for the *tragos* (goat) as *athlon* (prize) in the tragic agon is the Parian Marble, then an epigram of Dioskorides; Eratosthenes, in his *Erigone,* certainly treated Icarius's sacrifice of a goat as the *aition* of *tragōidia: Ikarioi tothi prōta peri tragon ōrchēsanto* (tragedy: the Ikarians then first danced for a goat). The most familiar descriptions are those in the Augustan poets. Particularly detailed are the accounts given in two late Latin writers, Diomedes—whose source is supposed to be Suetonius—and Euanthius; both use the same Greek material, which may come from Didymos, *Peri poiētōn* (On the poets). The same tradition survived in the Scholia to Dionysius Thrax, in the Johannes Diaconus published by Rabe, and in Tzetzes; the intermediate source appears to be the *Chrestomathy* of Proclus.[14] A great deal was written in the Hellenistic period on matters of literary history, and what survives is absurdly scanty. Kaibel was nevertheless able to show in the case of the rather fuller literature *peri kōmōidias* (on comedy) that even in the Byzantine excerptors there are traces of a theory of the fourth century B.C., a theory that did not know the comedy of Menander. Even the latest sources may preserve excellent tradition. It is worth noting that some fragments of Aristotle, from the *Peri poiētōn,* have survived in this way.[15]

Among modern scholars the derivation of *tragōidia* from the sacrifice of a goat has not enjoyed much success. "Spielend ersonnene αἴτια," "Konstruktionen, keine Überlieferung" (strikes the note of playing *aitia,* a fabrication, not a tradition)—this was the judgment of Wilamowitz (63), who maintained that the whole thing was a fabrication of Eratosthenes; incidentally, he had overlooked the Parian Marble. Pohlenz tried to correct this oversight while retaining the result: he argued that the theory was earlier than Eratosthenes, but still post-Aristotelian, early Alexandrian. The secondary fabrication, according to him, gives itself away by its bias: while Aristotle's evidence about dithyramb and *saturikon* points toward the Peloponnese, the autochthonous origin of tragedy in Attica is here defended. Pohlenz's argument has found wide acceptance.[16] Yet it evidently depends on two assumptions: that Attic local patriotism did not start to consider tragedy until after Aristotle, and that it could contribute nothing but invention, no facts of any sort. But the Atthidographers were at work before Aristotle: Cleidemus wrote ca. 350, Phanodemus about a decade later. They were keenly interested in the Attic cults. A fragment of Cleidemus on the lesser Dionysia is extant (*FGrHist* 323 F 27). Phanodemus displays a marked Athenian bias (325 F 14, F 27). Are we to suppose that the earlier Atthidographers wrote nothing about the Great Dionysia? This festival was certainly treated by Philochorus (328 F 171; cf. F 5, F 206), who took special interest in sacrificial rites (F 178, F 194) and gave an explanation of the word *rhapsōidos* (F 212). In view of the general inflexibility of Greek cults, it is hard to maintain that even a post-Aristotelian Atthidographer would present sheer invention in matters of sacrifice.

Aristotle, however, says quite explicitly that the dispute between Athenians and Dorians for the glory of the "invention" of tragedy and comedy had been going on for some time: διὸ καὶ ἀντιποιοῦνται τῆς τε τραγῳδίας καὶ τῆς κωμῳδίας οἱ Δωριεῖς . . . ποιούμενοι τὰ ὀνόματα σημεῖον. αὐτοὶ μὲν γὰρ κώμας τὰς περιοικίδας καλεῖν φασιν, Ἀθηναίους δὲ δήμους, ὡς κωμῳδοὺς οὐκ ἀπὸ τοῦ κωμάζειν λεχθέντας ἀλλὰ τῇ κατὰ κώμας πλάνῃ ἀτιμαζομένους ἐκ τοῦ ἄστεως . . . (This is how the Dorians lay claim to tragedy and comedy . . . taking the names of these for evidence. They assert that they use the name *kōmai* for outlying villages, whereas the Athenians call them *dēmoi* with the implication that they are not called *komōdoi*, "comedians," from their reveling [*kōmazein*] but from their wanderings about to the villages [*kōmai*] because they were held in low esteem by the city (*astu*) . . . *Poet*. 1448a29 ff.). This presupposes two things: a derivation of *kōmōidia* from *kōmē* (village) in the form of an anecdote—some people, for lack of appreciation, leave the city and wander around in the villages; the song that they sing is the *kōmōidia*—and an inference from this derivation: the word *kōmē* is Doric, therefore *kōmōidia* itself must be of Doric, not Attic, origin. Now it is unlikely that both, etymology and inference from it, were produced at the same time. The word *antipoiountai* (make an opposing claim) presupposes two parties to the dispute, and therefore Athenian counter-claims. Polemic is most effective when it can take the arguments of an opponent and turn them against him. The derivation of *kōmōidia* from *kōmē* is so far-fetched, that from *kōmos* (revel) so obvious, that it would have been quite idiotic for the Doric partisans to introduce the *kōmē*-argument into the debate if it had not already been accepted by the Athenians themselves. This means that the etymology, together with the *kōmē*-anecdote, was first advanced at Athens; this is supported by the specifically Attic word *astu*; and indeed *kōmē* is an Attic word, too.[17] So Aristotle's statement presupposes at least two stages in the discussion about the origin of comedy: an Attic etymology based on a "village" custom, and a counter-attack by the Dorian party.

The Attic etymology that Aristotle rejects lived on in Greek literature; though the anecdote varies, the derivation of comedy from *kōmē* is the prevailing explanation of the name in Diomedes and Euanthius, in the trea-

6

tises *Peri kōmōidias* (On comedy), in the Scholia to Dionysius Thrax and in Tzetzes[18]—in fact, in precisely those authors who offer "song over the goat" as the etymology of *tragōidia*. Thus in the case of *kōmōidia* we are dealing with a pre-Aristotelian Attic etymology that survives in the later tradition. If we may assume something analogous for *tragōidia*, this squares very well with the tradition about the *tragos*-prize. And whether this tradition really is contradicted by and incompatible with Aristotle's testimony is by no means certain.[19] So it is quite possible, though it cannot be proved, that the tradition of the goat-sacrifice is pre-Aristotelian. Even this possibility, however, is enough to destroy Pohlenz's argument: he has not succeeded in proving by *recensio* of the evidence that the tradition of the goat-sacrifice is secondary and therefore to be rejected. The *recentiores* are not necessarily the *deteriores*. Before rejecting it, we ought to try at least to make sense of the tradition.

Was a goat sacrificed in connection with the *tragōidoi* performances at the Great Dionysia? Oddly enough, this question is seldom clearly put. Ziegler (1926) thought that the answer is definitely no; in all extant tragedies and comedies, there is "nie mit einem Sterbenswort von einem Bock als Preis die Rede."[20] This clearly is an *argumentum ex silentio*, which is contradicted by the literary-historical sources, beginning with the Parian Marble. The evidence of the Latin sources is most detailed: Diomedes—*hircus praemium cantus proponebatur, qui Liberalibus die festo Libero patri ob hoc ipsum immolabatur, quia, ut Varro ait, depascunt vitem;*[21] Euanthius—*incensis iam altaribus et admoto hirco id genus carminis quod sacer chorus reddebat Libero patri tragoedia dicebatur.* In view of this testimony, the burden of proof lies with those who deny that a goat was sacrificed at the Great Dionysia.

The sacrificial victim as prize in an agon occurs as early as the *Iliad* (22.159).[22] Most important was the bull as prize and sacrificial victim in connection with the dithyramb. By chance we have unimpeachable early evidence in this case: Pindar (*O.* 13.19) speaks of the *boēlatas dithurambos* (bull-driving dithyramb) that originated in Corinth; the Scholia explain, as if it were a matter of course, "because a bull was *epathlon* (prize) for the winner." This is confirmed by an epigram of Simonides (79 D.), who boasts that he has won "56 bulls and tripods." *Boēlatas dithurambos*—the bull was led along in solemn procession; vase paintings show the bull, adorned by the victorious Phyle and ready for sacrifice, beside the tripod.[23] Why should we not suppose that the goat was similarly connected with tragedy? Plutarch sets the two, the prize of bull and goat, victory with dithyramb 7 and tragedy, in vivid proximity when, in his essay *De gloria Atheniensium*, he describes the triumphal procession of the poets: he has the Nikai themselves, the "Victories," march up, *boun epathlon helkousas ē tragon* (leading an ox as prize or a goat; 349c). This is allegory, influenced by the pictorial tradition (n. 23), but the experience of Greek sacrificial festivals lies behind it. In the church of Aghios Eleftherios, the "Little Mitropolis" at Athens, there is an ancient frieze depicting the months of the Attic year. Elaphebolion is represented by the figure of a comic actor pulling along a goat: comedy and tragedy as the epitome of the Great Dionysia, the main festival in Elaphebolion.[24] Are we to suppose that this representation, too, owes its existence to early Hellenistic speculation based on a stupid etymology? No one denies that the *tragos*-sacrifice played a special part in the cult of Dionysus. The earliest evidence are vase paintings of the sixth century, especially Attic black-figure vases: they show again and again the he-goat together with Dionysus or satyrs, sometimes *ductus cornu* (Verg. *Georg.* 2.395).[25] To which of the Dionysus festivals the *tragos* belongs can be seen from Plutarch (*De cupid. div.* 527D): ἡ πάτριος τῶν Διονυσίων ἑορτὴ τὸ παλαιὸν ἐπέμπετο δημοτικῶς καὶ ἱλαρῶς, ἀμφορεὺς οἴνου καὶ κληματίς, εἶτα τράγον τις εἷλκεν, ἄλλος ἰσχάδων ἄρριχον ἠκολούθει κομίζων, ἐπὶ πᾶσι δ' ὁ φαλλός (The ancestral festival of the Dionysia was a simple and cheerful procession, there was a large jar of wine with vine, then someone led a goat, another followed carrying a basket of figs, the whole thing completed by the phallus). On account of the word *patrios* (ancestral), this description is usually connected with the *Dionusia kat' agrous* (rural Dionysia).[26] The combination of fig-basket and goat recurs, however, in the Parian Marble (A 39; 43) and Dioskorides (*AP* 7.410) with reference to comedy and tragedy, performed together at the Great Dionysia; so it is probable that Plutarch's source is referring to the same festival. Indeed a sixth-century institution was *patrios* (ancestral) already in the fifth century. Nevertheless it is usually assumed that the *Dionusia en astei* (city Dionysia) were modeled on the Dionysia *kat' agrous;* so the *tragos* will not have been missing in either of the festivals, any more than the phallus.

The sacrifice of a *tragos* is quite an unusual event;[27] one finds only one *tragos* in a herd, perhaps in a village; he is the *dux pecoris,* Tibullus (2.1.58) says. Nor is the appetizing smell of roast meat the idea primarily associated with the *tragos;* a kid, an *eriphos* (young goat) would be better; *tragos,* that implies lewdness and foul smell.[28] Nevertheless the *tragos* is sacrificed—because his procreative power is coming to an end. A five-year-old *tragos* is no longer fit for use, Columella (7.6.3) tells us. So at least every four years the old he-goat must be removed. To get rid of the old and risk a fresh start may have been an exciting course for the farmer and goatherd. Now there follows the *ocheia* (impregnating) of the she-goats in late autumn, that the kids may be born in spring (Varro *RR* 2.3.8; Columella 7.6.6); then the *tragos* has done his duty. It is still necessary to wait for a little while until it is certain that the she-goats are pregnant—then we come to January-February, the month *Posideōn*, the month of the *Dionusia kat'* agrous.[29] These simple facts of husbandry are, however, embedded in very ancient religious customs by no means confined to Greece.[30] But to follow them up seems to lead from *obscurum* to *obscurius*.

One piece of evidence, however, is unambiguous: characteristic of the Dionysiac orchestra, perhaps the very center of the circle, is the *thumelē* (altar). Already Pratinas makes the chorus conquer *Dionusiada polupataga thumelan* (the tumultuous Dionysiac *thumelē*).[31] What exactly the *thumelē* was like, was a matter of dispute even in antiquity: *eite bēma ti eite bōmos* (either some kind of rostrum or altar).[32] Most probably it was a kind of platform or flat table, as it is depicted on vase paintings amid Dionysiac scenes: perhaps it was used as an altar when this was required in the play. But *thumelē* cannot be separated from *thuein* (to sacrifice). Is it in origin the block or bench on which the victim was slaughtered and divided up? The memory of sacrifice stands in the center of the Dionysiac performance. And since the *boēlatas dithurambos* was introduced in Athens later than tragedy,[33] there remains for the original festival in the precinct of *Dionusos Eleuthereus* just the sacrifice of the *tragos;* and the *tragōidoi*.

II

In fact, it was not critical caution in the face of late testimony or unprejudiced *recensio* of the tradition that has nearly expelled from modern discussions the explanation of the name *tragōidia* most favored in antiquity, but the seeming triviality and pointlessness of the etymology. What has the *vilis hircus* to do with tragedy? What would be the point of the sacrifice of a goat? But this is in fact the fundamental question: what is the sense of animal sacrifice, and, in particular, of a goat sacrifice in the cult of Dionysus? The slaughter of animals for sacrifice ceased in the West with the victory of Christianity (cf., however, n. 37); practically no feature of ancient religion is so alien to us as the *thusia* (burnt offering), which for the ancients was the sacred experience par excellence: *hieron, hiereus, hiereion, hiereuein* (sacrificial victim, priest, sacrificial offering, to sacrifice). Perhaps this is the reason why we find it so difficult to accept the explanation of the word *tragōidia* that seemed almost self-evident in antiquity.

Greek sacrificial practice[34] is of course a complex phenomenon; different elements may have been amalgamated in the course of time. We can still observe a change in terminology. As Aristarchus rightly observed,[35] in Homer *thuein* still means, in accordance with its etymology, "to burn so as to provide smoke"; later it is the technical term for "sacrificial slaughter," for which Homer uses *hiereuein* and *rhezein*. *Thuein* in a narrower sense is quite often contrasted with *enagizein*, the term appropriate to hero-cults; in accordance with this it is customary to distinguish as the two basic forms of Greek sacrifice the "Olympian feast-sacrifice" and the "chthonic holocaust." This convenient dichotomy must, however, not be overestimated; it is by no means all-pervasive, there are more and other differences of equal importance.[36] But as the words *hiereon*, *hiereuein* and, in the classical period, *thuein* cover all forms of sacrifice, we ought to keep the whole complex in view.

We are best informed on the "Olympian" feast-sacrifice.[37] It seemed puzzling as early as Hesiod. The thighbones, the tail, the fat, and the gallbladder are burnt for the god in whose honor the sacrifice is held; the pious congregation appropriates almost all the rest. The phrase *en thusiēisi te kai eupatheiēisi* (in sacrifices and merriment) in Herodotus (8.99) is revealing. Hesiod can only explain this as the result of a trick by Prometheus. This amounts to an admission that these sacrifices could not be understood as a gift to the divinity, at any rate not as the gift of a meal. But the theory adopted by Wilamowitz and Nilsson, following Robertson Smith, that the sacrifice was a common meal of men and gods,[38] also is impossible in view of the "Promethean" division. Certainly, there were *theoxenia* (feasting of the gods)—in which the menu was largely vegetarian, corresponding to the normal diet—and there were, as in the Orient, *trapezai* (tables) for the gods. But the sacral center of the *thusia* is the *mēria kaiein*, the "burning of the thighbones." When Nilsson supposes that some pieces of meat were sent to the gods by fire and the inedible parts were immediately consumed by the same "convenient medium" (*Griech. Rel.*[2] I.144 f.), he supplies his own *reductio ad absurdum:* homage and garbage-disposal combined?

It was Karl Meuli's article "Griechische Opferbräuche" (n. 34) that provided a decisive advance.[39] He pointed out the evident connection with the "Schädel- und Langknochenopfer" practiced by Siberian hunting people and attested as early as the paleolithic period. When an animal is caught and slaughtered, the skull and the bones, above all the thighbones are presented to the god; they may be buried, or hung on a sacred tree, or set up in a sanctuary. Meuli also offered an explanation: the hunter wishes to save from complete destruction the animal he has killed, his source of food. The thighbones, as it were the marrow of its existence, remain preserved. In mythical terms, the life of the animal is restored to the lord of life. "If we should not do this, we would never catch animals again," the hunters explained. Meuli is right in interpreting this concern about the continuity of life as a deep-rooted human respect for life as such, which prevents man from utterly destroying other beings in an autocratic way. In the situation of killing, man feels guilty, and he has to overcome this reluctance by means of a complicated ritual pattern, which Meuli pertinently calls "comedy of innocence" (*Unschuldskomödie*), though we must not forget that this "comedy" has a very serious basis. At the center of the sacrifice stands neither the gift to the gods nor fellowship with them, but the killing of the animal,[40] and man as its killer. As Meuli put it: "the Olympian sacrifice is simply ritual slaughter" ("nichts anderes als ein rituelles Schlachten," 223). The definition must be expanded only a little to cover all kinds of sacrifices involving bloodshed: sacrifice is ritual killing.[41] In the sacrificial ritual man causes and experiences death.

Thus in the sacrificial feast the joy of the festival and the horror of death interpenetrate. The Greek sacrificial rites represent in vivid detail human aversion to killing and the feelings of guilt and remorse caused by the shedding of blood. Adorned for the festival, garlanded like the celebrants, sometimes with gilded horns,[42] the animal was led along. Many legends tell how the victims have pressed forward voluntarily to the sacrifice, *theēlatou boos dikēn* (just like an ox led to the god; A. *Ag.* 1297).[43] The beginning of the rite was emphatically harmless: a vessel containing water and the basket with the sacrificial barley, brought to the place by a virgin, were carried round the altar; a line is drawn that separates the sacred from the profane.[44] Then the participants wash their hands—their first common action—and the victim has its share, too: it is sprinkled with water; *seiou* (sprinkle!), Trygaios exclaims (Ar. *Pax* 960): the animal was supposed to express its consent by bowing its head, *hekousion kataneuei.*[45] The meaning of the *oulai* (barleycorns) has been much discussed,[46] though the Greek expression is quite clear: *cherniba t' oulochutas te katarchesthai* (to make a start with the basket and strewing of barley)—it is the act of beginning. The participants take the barley out of the basket as if they were to prepare for a vegetarian meal; but beneath in the basket there is a knife, which is now

11

uncovered. There is a prayer, a moment of silence and concentration; then all participants throw the *oulai* "forward" at the victim and the altar. Throwing together at a common object is the primeval gesture of aggression: lapidation, transformed into something harmless, as in the *phullobolia* (throwing of leaves). Indeed, instead of the barley, leaves can be used and, at least in one instance, stones. Everyone takes part, is guilty and innocent at the same time. There is still a last delay: the *hiereus* cuts off a few hairs from the victim's forehead and throws them in the fire. With extraordinary obstinacy, scholars have looked for daemons who demanded hair,[47] though the Greek expression again is both clear and simple: this, too, is *archesthai*, the "beginning." The first cut does no harm, does not yet draw blood, but the victim is no longer physically inviolate. This step is irreversible. Now the fatal stroke follows. At this moment, the women scream, *ololuzousin* (*Od.* 3.450); this is the *Hellēnikon nomisma thustados boēs* (the peculiar Greek custom of the sacrificial cry; A. *Septem* 269);[48] this marks the emotional climax of the *thusia*; this is *rhezein* (sacrificing). The blood is caught in a vessel and poured out at the altar:[49] the most appalling element is set first of all within the divinely appointed order. Then the thighbones are cut out, and small pieces of meat from each limb laid with them on the altar—*ōmothetein*,[50] and they are burnt. Wine is poured over the flames, the music of the flute and song accompany the action. Along with the burning of the *mēria* (thighbones), the *splangchna*—heart, lungs, liver, kidneys—are roasted on the altar and eaten at once.[51] The slightly uncanny "vitals," the internal organs that come to light only now and may seem to contain the "life," which sometimes cause disgust and sometimes are regarded as rather a delicacy, must be disposed of first of all. No wonder that *susplangchneuein* (sharing the vitals) is the firmest foundation of fellowship. The shudder dies away in a feeling of physical well-being. When the *splangchna* have been eaten and the fire has died down, the preparation begins for the main meal, which was generally of a quite secular character.[52]

We see, then, that the ritual of a Greek sacrifice is designed to display the destruction of life as the sacral center of the action. The many complicated preparations stress how unnatural and shocking this is. There are some special cases in which the representation of the feelings of guilt, the "comedy of innocence" seems quite excessive. Above all, the Buphonia at Athens: the ox must himself be responsible for his own death; he is induced to eat barley cakes from the altar of Zeus, and then punished for sacrilege with the axe. But the sacrificing priest immediately throws the axe away and flees, a trial follows the sacrificial meal, in which the responsibility is passed from one to another, until finally a knife is pronounced guilty and thrown into the sea. But the ox is stuffed and harnessed to a plough—he is, as it were, resurrected.[53] The goat-sacrifice to Dionysus is in fact another example of making the victim responsible for its own death: the goat, it is said, has gnawed the vine and must therefore die. In Corinth, at the festival of Hera Akraia, the she-goat was made to dig up for herself the knife with which she is slaughtered (n. 71).

Most characteristic of all these rites is the ambivalence of feeling displayed in the ceremony. Man, sacrificing according to the will of the god, still has to overcome or even to outwit his reluctance to kill. Expressing his feelings of guilt and remorse, man shows his deeply rooted respect for life. Prevalent, however, is a higher necessity, which commands him to kill.

"Das Opfer ist die älteste Form der religiösen Handlung" (sacrifice is the oldest form of religious action; Kühn [*supra* n. 34] 17). From this fact, the inference has been drawn that there was some kind of "Urmonotheismus," a primordial revelation of the idea of God. The "Promethean" division and the horrible fascination of bloodshed are perhaps less comforting. It could seem advisable to resign completely, considering the fact that we are led back well into paleolithic times. We shall never have direct evidence for religious belief in this period; and even if we had, as modern ethnologists were in a position to ask hunters living under similar conditions about their motives, it would still be a question whether primitive man could give a more lucid explanation of his ritual than the Greeks, who are so often said to have misunderstood their own cults completely. But we must not overestimate the importance of beliefs and explanations in religion. Down to the beginnings of Christianity and even farther on, the justification of religion is tradition. Rites are performed *kata ta patria* (according to ancestral custom), and this is the reason why so little change took place in these rites between paleolithic times and the Greeks, during tens of thousands of years. So the essential matter cannot have been what a hypothetical *heuretēs* (inventor) came to feel or believe, owing to his private experience or associations, but rather it was the effect of the rite on society according to the structure of the human psyche. Instead of asking which incident could bring forth some special form of religion, we should ask why it succeeded and was preserved. The answer can be seen in its function in human society. We may still speak of "ideas" inherent in the rites, but we must discard the rationalistic preconception as if there had been, first, a concept or belief, which led in a second step to action. Behavior is primary, but its form is correlated to typical human situations and, therefore, understandable. In

13

this respect, rites may make sense. To some extent, even biology can contribute to understanding; animals, too, have their rites that control mutual recognition and cooperation. The contrast of man and animal will emerge immediately.

Indeed carnivorous animals show no sign of ambivalent feeling when eating their animal of prey; the cat has neither reluctance nor repentance while killing the mouse. But even in animals there are psychological antagonisms as regards their behavior toward animals of the same species. Here the impulses of intraspecific aggression come to work, the impulses to fight. Konrad Lorenz[54] has brilliantly shown the social importance of this instinct. But it is inhibited and controlled by contrary impulses, fear above all, but often also by a special reluctance to kill, especially important in dangerous animals. Man, by his physical endowment, is neither carnivorous nor particularly dangerous; the other primates are rather innocent creatures. Man, however, starting from the earliest times came to be a hunter, a hunter even of big animals. This presupposes the use of tools, of weapons, and social cooperation. So it is safe to say: in the center of the earliest human society, the earliest "Männerbund," there is common killing, killing the prey. The very problem of human civilization arose at the same time: his instincts will not tell man what he has to do with his weapons; instead of killing the bear or bison he can as well slay a man; it is even easier. No wonder cannibalism is attested in the oldest strata of human civilization; and man has continued killing man to an extent that no carnivorous animal has done. In the Bible there is at the very beginning of human civilization the story of the sacrifice combined with the murder of Abel; man is the descendant of Cain. Sigmund Freud[55] went still farther with his hypothesis that human society arose with the brothers killing and eating their father; since then, they are compelled to repeat again and again this primordial crime in the sacrificial slaughter. I think Freud is basically right in describing the psychic impulses underlying sacrifice, though he is wrong in assuming that this crime must have occurred as one historical fact. Generally man has been living on animals; but the hunter is always at the same time a warrior, animated by the impulses of aggression. Human sacrifice, therefore, is a possibility that, as a horrible threat, stands behind every sacrifice. This is the reason why sacrificial ritual has this complicated pattern, the "comedy of innocence."

On the other hand, more sympathetic forces too have been developing in man's psyche; the respect for life has grown universal. The hunter may imagine the animal that he is going to kill as his "brother";[56] he recognizes death in all its manifestations. So the feelings of guilt and remorse crystallize into symbolic acts through which man tries to restore the equilibrium disturbed, to stress the continuity of life through death. Man alone among living beings buries his dead. In a similar way, he restores at least the remains of the animals he had to kill to some superhuman order, on which in fact the continuity of his own civilization depends.

Society is built on the impulses of aggression controlled by ritual, as Konrad Lorenz has shown. So precisely in communities familiar with agriculture, in which meat is of secondary importance as a source of food, rites involving bloodshed become the center of religion. They stir the depths of the soul, the fear of death, the frenzy of killing. *Hierōn metechein* (participation in the sacra)—the community is knit together in the common experience of shock and guilt. All participate, but one stands at their head, the sacrificer, *thutēr*, the *pater familias* or the king. To him belongs the *vitae necisque potestas*, and he demonstrates this power of his in the sacrifice. In reality, of course, there is only a *necis potestas*, but by exercising it the *thutēr* claims and seems to reestablish *e contrario* his *vitae potestas*. There is a curious ambivalence in *thuesthai*, which is already Indo-European: the same expression means "to sacrifice on one's own behalf" and "to be sacrificed."[57] Sacrificer and victim are so correlated as to be nearly identified. Self-asserting life presupposes death. So sacrificial festivals are the traditional means to overcome all sorts of social crisis. Extraordinary situations of emergency, famine, disease may again and again lead to human sacrifice. More firmly established are the customs that deal with the recurrent crises of society, the succession of the young to the old: no initiation without sacrifice. The continuous renewal of the year, too, is given dramatic accents by sacrifices, which celebrate the destruction of the old for the sake of the new.

The myths, too, are concerned with sacrificial ritual. They clearly tell of the mutual substitution of man and animal: the animal dies instead of the man,[58] be it Isaac or Iphigeneia. The equivalence of man and animal may also lead to successive interchange, as in the cult legend of Artemis of Munichia: to atone for the killing of a bear belonging to the goddess, a girl is supposed to be sacrificed, but a she-goat is substituted—man for animal and animal for man. Greek mythology also knows the horrible converse, the sacrificial slaughter of a human instead of an animal; at the *hestia* (altar) at Delphi, Neoptolemus was cut up with sacrificial knives. Such scenes are not mere phantasy. Phainias of Eresus (fr. 25 Wehrli) gives an account of the preparations for the battle of Salamis which seems intrinsically probable: in full view of the enemy, the *sphagia* (victims) are slaughtered, blood is flowing, the altars are burning with fire. In this moment, by chance, three captured Persians are led along. The fire blazes up, and suddenly the seer and then the whole crowd of warriors, greedy of blood and death, demand that these three enemies be killed as *sphagia;* and they were. On one occasion, even Caesar sacrificed insurgents.[59] The Catilinarians were supposed to have sealed their conspiracy by eating human *splangchna.*[60] Classical Rome betrays an almost paleolithic imagination.

III

Perhaps the larger context has made clearer what the significance of the sacrifice of a *tragos* at the *thumelē* may be. The rites of sacrifice touch the roots of human existence. In the ambivalence of the intoxication of blood and the horror of killing, in the twofold aspect of life and death, they hold something fundamentally uncanny, we might almost say tragic. Our information about the goat-sacrifice to Dionysus is scanty. Whether we are entitled to see in the goat Dionysus himself impersonated, or to understand both goat and Dionysus as representing an "eniautos-daimon" or even the dying king, is difficult to assess.[61] The ancient texts call the goat the enemy of Dionysus, making his death a triumph of aggression. When Domitian tried to restrict viticulture, the epigram of Euenus (*AP* 9.75) was turned against him as an almost deadly weapon (Suet. *Dom.* 14.2): people readily associated the dying goat with the emperor they hated. On the other hand, there is the "comedy of innocence," making the vine-gnawing goat responsible for his own death. And perhaps there was even a kind of mock resurrection, analogous to the Buphonia: the *tragōidoi* are said to have received a wineskin full of wine[62]—*askoi* (wineskins) were made of goatskin. So we are reduced again to the basic ambivalence of sacrifice, and perhaps this ambivalence is the most essential feature.

It is possible to establish, though by conjecture only, some striking connections between the situation of sacrifice and tragedy. One form of the "comedy of innocence" is lament at the sacrifice. There seem to be no immediate parallels in the Greek world for lamentation over the victim, but the practice is found elsewhere, e.g., in Egypt.[63] In the center of the developed tragedy (*akmēn pros autēn ērmenēs tragōidias,* Tz. *De trag.* 63) stands the kommos. Sacrifice was usually accompanied by the music of the flute, and while the cithara is the normal instrument for choral lyric otherwise, the aulos is used predominantly in tragedy.[64] There is a more important point: there is a form of the "comedy of innocence" in which masked, disguised men have to kill the animal.[65] The *tragōidoi* too hide their identity; no tragedy without masks. By preference, the choruses of tragedy wear the masks of foreigners or of women; if they represent Athenians, they can only be very old men (S. *OC* 112), hardly ever the young citizens of Athens they really are. And whereas the Greeks were so fond of names that they even made catalogues a form of poetry, no member of the tragic chorus ever seems to be called by an individual name (cf. Freud [*supra* n. 34] 187).

All this would fit the following hypothesis: the *tragōidoi* are originally a troop of masked men who have to perform the sacrifice of the *tragos* that falls due in spring; they perform with lamentation, song, and mumming, and in the end they may feast on the goat. It is possible that the custom was at home in Icaria; seriousness and "satyr-like" fun may have interpenetrated in a curious way. Rudiments of an agon, competition between several groups could arise at an early date. The transformation to a high level of literature, the adaptation of the heroic myth remains, of course, a unique achievement. Nevertheless, it is based on pre-existing elements: the use of masks, song, and dance at the *thumelē*, lamentation, the music of the flute, the name *tragōidia*, all combined in the basic situation of sacrifice: man face to face with death.

We may ask why it was *tragōidia* in particular which became tragedy, not a hypothetical *boōidia* (song at ox sacrifice) or *kriōidia* (song at ram sacrifice). By comparison with the ox and the ram, the goat is the least attractive. But this may be just the reason. The victim has only a representative function: he is used for the fulfilment and discharge of an inevitable threat in the human soul which is really directed against man. In the sacrifice of the goat, these psychological forces are least absorbed by the symbol on which they concentrate; matter and form are never perfectly adjusted, and thus there arises the continual need for new forms of expression. The sacrifice of the bull especially had long ago become an official, civic affair; it was an immutable and established part of the ritual of the *polis*. But in the sacrifice of the goat, village-custom still allowed an element of *autoschediazesthai* (improvisation); there were changes and additions. Because it was not too serious, the mummers' play could evolve. The *thumelē* provoked what would have been impossible at an ordinary altar. This was the reason why *tragōidia* could come to depict the "tragic" *condition humaine*.

Tragōidia emancipated itself from the *tragos*. And yet the essence of the sacrifice still pervades tragedy even in its maturity. In Aeschylus, Sophocles, and Euripides, there still stands in the background, if not in the center, the pattern of the sacrifice, the ritual slaying, *thuein*. A few instances may

17

suffice. I deliberately pass over those tragedies in which the whole plot is concerned with human sacrifice—*Iphigeneia at Aulis, Iphigeneia in Tauris, Bacchae;* Sophocles wrote a *Polyxena,* Aeschylus a *Pentheus.* Euripides used the motif of human sacrifice in many variations—*Heracleidae, Hecuba, Phoenissae, Erechtheus, Phrixus.* He made even Alcestis's death a sacrifice, Thanatos a sacrificial priest, *hiereus thanontōn* (25), whereas Aegisthus is slain by Orestes with the sacrificial knife at the sacrifice.[66] What is more general and more important: any sort of killing in tragedy may be termed *thuein* as early as Aeschylus, and the intoxication of killing is called *bakcheuein,* a word for Dionysiac frenzy.[67] In earlier choral lyric, these metaphors do not occur. This imagery, however, is not something superficial: if tragedy draws on heroic myth, every hero has his cults, i.e., his sacrifices.[68] The situation of the sacrifice may be just the point where heroic myth and Dionysiac *tragōidia* meet each other.

Three examples will illustrate these interrelations. First, Sophocles' *Trachiniae.* Herakles must sacrifice before returning (287); so Deianeira sends him the garment of Nessus with express instructions to put it on for the first time when he is sacrificing a bull to Zeus, *hēmerai taurosphagōi* (609); he shall present himself to the gods, a "sacrificer, new in a new garment" (613, cf. 659). So it happens: Herakles is sacrificing to Zeus at Cape Cenaeum in Euboea (750 ff.), he stands there in his new garment, he slaughters the bulls. But "when the bloody flame of the solemn rites blazed up," *hopōs de semnōn orgiōn edaieto phlox haimatēra* (765 f.), at that moment the garment of Nessus too begins to burn and destroys Herakles. Priest and victims, Herakles and the bulls suffer the same fate in the same *orgia* (ritual). The myth of the death of Herakles is based on a sacrifice, a holocaust offered on Mount Oeta; the site of the *pura* (pyre/altar) has been excavated. Nilsson interprets the custom as an annual fire (Jahresfeuer), although the literary evidence on this festival states that it was penteteric.[69] It is not the nature-symbolism that is primary, but human actions and passions. Fascinated by their own fire-controlling power, men celebrate the destruction of the old, originally perhaps the old king's death. The myth elucidates the sacrificial rite, which still pervades tragedy.

Second, Euripides' *Medea:* at the climax of the famous soliloquy is an echo of the language of sacrificial ritual (1053 ff.):[70]

ὅτῳ δὲ μὴ
θέμισ παρεῖναι τοῖς ἐμοῖσι θύμασιν,
αὐτῷ μελήσει . . .

[Whomsoever the law
forbids to be present at my sacrifice,
let him look to it.]

So this killing of the children is a secret sacrifice, an *aporrhētos thusia*.
Mere metaphor? Vase paintings constantly show Medea killing her children
at an altar. By chance we are fairly well informed about the ritual in the
temple of Hera Akraia at Corinth, which underlies the Corinthian saga of
Medea: seven Corinthian boys and seven girls were interned for a year in
the sanctuary of Hera, where the tombs of Medea's children were shown.
They wore black clothes. The climax and conclusion of their service was a
sacrifice at the festival of Akraia, the sacrifice of a black she-goat. It was a
holocaust, an *enagizein*, and it was combined with that special form of the
"comedy of innocence" which was already mentioned: the goat had to dig
up for itself a knife or sword, *machaira*, with which it was killed. Then the
sword was buried again, as it was said until next year.[71] Once a year the
instrument of destruction emerged from the darkness of the earth, to remain buried there and almost forgotten for the rest of the year. It is clear
that the black she-goat died as a substitute for the black-clad children; they
were then free from their obligation. The myth told that the children of
the Corinthians suffered this penalty to atone for the children of Medea,
who had died and were buried there in the temenos of Hera Akraia. The
mysterious sword, which year by year was dug up and then reburied, was
said to be the very sword with which Medea killed her children. We need
not here go into the question of how far the ritual along with the myth is
to be understood as an initiation ceremony. At all events, the metaphor of
the *thuma* (sacrifice) at the climax of Euripides' play leads back to a sacrificial ritual that comprises the mystery of death.

Lastly, the *Agamemnon* of Aeschylus: through it the language of sacrificial ritual runs like a leitmotiv. The choral song begins with the portent
of the two eagles tearing in pieces the pregnant hare, *thuomenoi* (sacrificing;
137); to this corresponds the goddess's "demand for another sacrifice," *speu-
domena thusian heteran* (151). So Agamemnon becomes the "sacrificer" of
his own daughter, ἔτλα δ᾽ οὖν θυτὴρ γενέσθαι θυγατρός (224, cf. 215),
and now one evil generates another. When the news comes of Agamemnon's victory and imminent return, Clytaemestra prepares a great sacrifice
(83 f., 261 ff., 587 ff.); does the sacrificial fire burn on the altar in the orchestra? In the palace herds of sheep stand ready *pros sphagas* (for slaughter,
1056 f.). Yet instead of the smell of sacrifice, Cassandra scents murder   19

(1309 f.). She calls for *ololugē* (a sacrificial cry) (1118) at the unprecedented *thuma* that is going to happen here: he who commits it deserves lapidation.[72] Later Clytaemestra boasts that she has slain her husband "for Ate and Erinys," that is, as a sacrifice (1433, cf. 1415 ff.). Then she tries to disclaim responsibility: the Alastor of Atreus himself has killed, or rather sacrificed, Agamemnon, has slain him as the full-grown victim after the young animals, *teleon nearais epithusas* (adding a perfect sacrifice to the young ones, 1504). Even so, at the great sacrificial festivals, first the lesser, then the full-grown victims fell. Cassandra is another sacrifice. With full knowledge she goes to her destruction, "like a heifer driven on by a god, you go unafraid to the altar" (1297 f.). One sacrifice leads to another: finally Orestes is the victim of the Erinyes—ἐπὶ δὲ τῷ τεθυμένῳ τόδε μέλος (this song is sung over the sacrificial victim, *Eu.* 329 ff., cf. 305) runs the binding-song.

This again is more than a mere metaphor, a stylistic ornament. Agamemnon dies ὥς τίς τε κατέκτανε βοῦν ἐπὶ φάτνῃ (as one would kill a bull at the manger, *Od.* 4.535, 11.411); to be more exact, Clytaemestra throws a net over him and strikes him down with the axe, *pelekus, bouplēx.* This is in fact how a bull was killed; the famous gold cup from Vaphio shows the bull struggling in the net—the table decoration of some Mycenaean prince who had himself celebrated as a victor over the bull. So Cassandra in her vision sees Agamemnon as the *tauros* (bull), caught in the "black-horned device," the net.[73] A *lebēs* (basin) receives his blood (1129, cf. 1540)—even this a feature of the ritual.

We have very little information about the Argive cults. But it is not mere fancy to conjecture that the myth of the death of Agamemnon was connected with a sacrificial ritual, a bull-sacrifice—*bouphonia*—in a similar way as the myth of the death of Medea's children was connected with the Corinthian sacrifice of a goat at the Akraia festival. The bull as a symbol of the king must have played a very important part in the Mycenaean-Minoan world, and this bull-symbolism concentrates on the major sanctuary of the Argive plain, the Heraion that was called Argos itself. Here we have herds of sacred cows, Zeus as a bull, Io as a cow, Epaphos, their common son, again as a bull, Cleobis and Biton drawing the sacred chariot as substitutes for oxen. Most remarkable is Argos Panoptēs, slain by Hermes, apparently the eponym of sanctuary and city. Argos was clad in bull's hide, having conquered the bull, and was in his turn killed by Hermes, the *bouphonos* (bull slayer). As was seen long ago, the epithet Panoptēs makes him a duplicate of Zeus himself; and how the community of Argos arose and

got its name from the primordial crime of Argos's death may now be understandable. It was a *thusia leusimos* (a sacrifice worthy of stoning). Incidentally, Pausanias mentions *aporrhētoi thusiai* (forbidden sacrifices, 2.17.1) at
the Heraion.[74] They may have preceded the main festival of Heraia, as in
Athens the Buphonia are due in the last month of the year, to be followed
by the new year festival, the Panathenaia.

Not all the problems can be solved. It was not the intention of this paper
to show *the* origin of tragedy, but only to investigate the clue offered by
the word *tragōidia*. It has emerged that the tradition of a goat-sacrifice deserves to be taken seriously; it leads back to the depths of prehistoric human
development, as well as into the center of tragedy. This will do no damage
to the originality of the Greeks. Indeed the uniqueness of their achievement
emerges most clearly when we compare what in other civilizations sprang
from similar roots: ceremonial hunting and warfare, human sacrifice, gladia-
tors, bullfights. It may be that the sublimation and transformation performed by the Greek poets are so fundamental as to reduce to nothingness
any crude "origins." Or do the greatest poets only provide sublime expression for what already existed at the most primitive stages of human development? Human existence face to face with death—that is the kernel of
tragōidia.

NOTES

This chapter originally appeared in *Greek, Roman, and Byzantine Studies* 7, no. 2 (1966): 87–
121. Reprinted by permission of Duke University Press.

1. I had the opportunity to discuss this paper at the Oxford Philological Society and at
the University Seminar in Classical Civilization at Columbia University, New York, and I
wish to thank all participants for their suggestions and criticism. I am especially indebted to
Mrs. Stephanie West, Oxford, for most of the translation. Of course I am fully responsible
for any defects in style or contents.

2. The derivation of τραγῳδία from σάτυροι=τράγοι was advanced by F. G. Welcker,
*Nachtrag zu der Schrift über die Aeschylische Trilogie nebst einer Abhandlung über das Sa-
tyrspiel* (Frankfurt, 1826), 240; cf. U. v. Wilamowitz-Moellendorff, *Euripides Herakles* I [here-
after, Wilamowitz] (Berlin, 1889, repr. Darmstadt, 1959); with different pagination: *Einleitung
in die griechische Tragödie* (Berlin, 1907) 82 ff.; *Kleine Schriften* I (Berlin, 1935) 372;
K. Ziegler, in *RE* VI A (1937) 1917 ff. [hereafter, Ziegler]; M. Pohlenz, *Die griechische Tragödie*[2] [hereafter, Pohlenz] I (Göttingen, 1954) 18 ff.; A. Lesky, *Die tragische Dichtung der Hellenen*[2] [hereafter, Lesky] (Göttingen, 1964) 15 ff. H. Patzer, *Die Anfänge der griechischen
Tragödie* [hereafter, Patzer] (Weisbaden, 1962) 131 f. upholds the same etymology, though
rejecting any connection with the dithyramb and differentiating satyrs from goats (52 ff.). The
theory of the goat-prize was defended by E. Reisch, *Festschrift Th. Gomperz* [hereafter, Reisch]
(Vienna, 1902) 466 ff.; R. C. Flickinger, *The Greek Theater and Its Drama* [hereafter, Flick-
inger] (Chicago, 1918; 4th ed., 1936) 1 ff.; W. Schmid, *Geschichte der griechischen Literatur* I.2

21

(Munich, 1934) 46 ff.; A. W. Pickard-Cambridge, *Dithyramb, Tragedy and Comedy* [hereafter, Pickard-Cambridge, *Dith.*[1]] (Oxford, 1927) 164 ff., whereas T.B.L. Webster in the rev. ed. of this book [Webster's additions are hereafter quoted as Webster only] (Oxford, 1962) 123 f. is inclined to follow Welcker/Wilamowitz. G. F. Else thinks the word τραγῳδός, while deriving from the goat-prize, to be "clearly jocose or sarcastic," i.e., devoid of significance: *Hermes* 85 (1957) 42, cf. *The Origin and Early Form of Greek Tragedy* [hereafter, Else, *Origin*] (Cambridge, MA, 1965) 69 f. M. P. Nilsson, *NJbb* 27 (1911) 609 ff.=*Opuscula* I (Lund, 1951) 61 ff., combined goat-sacrifice and singers dressed as goats, cf. *infra* n. 61. A. B. Cook, *Zeus* [hereafter, Cook] (Cambridge, 1914–1940) I.665 ff. assumed the sacrifice to have been a σπαραγμός performed at the Lenaea; the τραγῳδοί, however, belong to the Dionysia, not the Lenaea. Further comments on the goat-sacrifice: F. Robert, *Mélanges Ch. Picard* II (Paris, 1949) 872–80; K. Kerényi, *Streifzüge eines Hellenisten* (Zurich, 1960) 40 ff.; R. Merkelbach, "Die *Erigone* des Eratosthenes," in *Miscellanea di Studi Alessandrini in memoria di A. Rostagni* (Turin, 1963) 496 ff.

3. Fr. 38 Wehrli, together with Plut. *Q. Conv.* 615a. There was an extensive Peripatetic literature on the history of tragedy; cf., besides Chamaeleon, Heracleides fr. 179 W., Aristoxenus fr. 113 ff., Hieronymus fr. 29 ff. W. On account of the Arabic translation, Gudeman, followed by Lesky 16, emended Arist. *Poet.* 1449a20 ἐκ ⟨τοῦ⟩ σατυρικοῦ; the emendation is not accepted by R. Kassel (OCT, 1965), cf. Patzer 53. G. F. Else, *Aristotle's Poetics: The Argument* (Cambridge, MA, 1957) 164 ff. thinks a19 ἔτι–a21 ἀπεσεμνύνθη to be an interpolation, but hesitates himself (*Origin* 16) to draw conclusions from this hypothesis. A vase painting from the fifth century represents ΤΡΑΓΩΙΔΙΑ being awakened by satyrs: Chous Oxford 534=J. D. Beazley, *Attic Red-figure Vase-painters*[2] [hereafter, *ARV*[2]] (Oxford, 1963) 1258,1; cf. bell-crater Compiègne 1025=*ARV*[2] 1055,76; chous Leipzig T 527=*ARV*[2] 1258,2; H. Herter, *RE* VIᴀ (1937) 1897. Dionysus, satyrs, tragedy still belong together.

4. F. Brommer, *Satyroi* (Würzburg, 1937) 36, cf. *Satyrspiele*[2] (Berlin, 1959); Patzer 128 ff. Pratinas as inventor of satyr-play: Suda *s.v.* Pratinas, Ps.-Acr. *in* Hor. *AP* 216 (*Cratini Cd., Pratinae* Pohlenz), cf. Dioskorides, *AP* 7.37, 707; M. Pohlenz, *Das Satyrspiel und Pratinas von Phleius* (*Gött. Nachr.* 1926) 298–321=*Kleine Schriften* II (Hildesheim, 1965) 473–96.

5. On satyrs, goats, and horses, cf. A. Furtwängler, *Kleine Schriften* I (Munich, 1912) 134 ff., 190 ff.; Wilamowitz 83 f.; Ziegler 1920 ff.; Lesky 23 ff.; Patzer 57 ff.; Else, *Origin* 15 ff. Satyrs sometimes wear goatskins (E. *Cyc.* 80), but Pollux (4.118) also mentions νεβρίς, παρδαλῆ, θήραιον, χλανὶς ἀνθινή as satyr's dress, whereas girls wore goatskins in some Dionysiac ritual, Hsch. τραγηφόροι. More important are A. fr. 207 Nauck=455 Mette, *S. Ichneutai* 357 f., Hsch. τράγους· σατύρους . . . (where the accusative shows that the lemma comes from a quotation); together with the vase paintings (n. 25), these texts show that satyr and goat formed a current association, whereas there seems to be no evidence for a satyr called ἵππος. Webster 301 no. 6 affirms that the ΣΙΛΕΝΟΙ on the François Vase (Florence 4209) have legs of goats; on the reproduction (A. Furtwängler/K. Reichhold, *Griechische Vasenmalerei* [Munich 1904–32] pl. 11/12) I am unable to see any difference between the silens' and the mule's legs.

6. Webster 114, arguing that these dancers surely are not horses. Μαλλωτὸς χιτών of silens: D.H. 7.72.10. On the subject of the Corinthian dancers, cf. Webster 100 f., 113 ff., 169 ff.; L. Breitholz, *Die dorische Farce im Griechischen Mutterland vor dem 5.Jh.* (Göteborg, 1960); Patzer 114 ff., who, following Buschor, calls them σάτυροι. One Corinthian vase has a τράγος amid the Dionysiac revelers, Webster no. 37, cf. n. 25.

7. E.g., Wilamowitz 84, Pohlenz II.10, Ziegler 1919 f.; *contra*, Nilsson, *Opuscula* I.93 f.; C. del Grande, ΤΡΑΓΩΙΔΙΑ[2] (Milan, 1962) 40 ff.; Else, *Origin* 17 f.; Patzer 19 f., 59 f. The only natural way to express "chorus of goats" in Greek would be τράγων χορός. A sufficient reason

for Herodotus or his source to call these choruses "tragic" could have been that they wore masks and sang on πάθη; but a goat-sacrifice is entirely possible (Flickinger 13 ff., combining the date given by Eusebius's and Jerome's *Chron.*, Ol. 47,2). One ought to take seriously the tradition about Epigenes of Sicyon (the evidence: *RE* VI [1909] 64), considering the fact that there was a relatively old Σικυωνίων ἀναγραφή (*FGrHist* 550) dealing especially with the history of literature and music.

8. The bronze of Methydrion, Athens Nat.Mus. 13789, was found and published in 1911 by F. Hiller von Gaertringen and H. Lattermann, *AbhBerl* 1911, 4, pl. 13; "vier widderartige aufrechte Gestalten" p. 24; "rams" Pohlenz I.18, M. P. Nilsson, *Geschichte der griechischen Religion* I² (Munich, 1955) pl. 50, 2; identified as "goats" by F. Brommer, *Satyroi* (Würzburg, 1937) 10, cf. Patzer 64 f., 124. *Contra*, R. Hampe, *Gymnasium* 72 (1965) 77 ff. Lead figurines from the sanctuary of Artemis Orthia in Sparta represent standing he-goats; Brommer *supra* concluded they were "mythische Wesen oder deren menschliche Nachahmer," cf. Patzer 65. The standing goat, however, is an iconographic type since Sumerian times, cf. n. 30.

9. F. Winter, *Die Typen der figürlichen Terrakotten* I (Berlin, 1903) 220; P. Baur, *AJA* 9 (1905) 157 ff.; Cook I.704 f. Webster no. 73 refers to a bronze statuette of similar type, as it seems, from Samos.

10. Reisch 456 ff.; Patzer 62 ff.

11. Τραγῳδοί in the Attic *Fasti*, A. W. Pickard-Cambridge, *The Dramatic Festivals of Athens* (Oxford, 1953) 104; ἐν τοῖσι τραγῳδοῖς Ar. *Av.* 512, cf. *Pax* 531; *IG* II/III² 956, 34; Aeschin. 3.41,45; D. 21.10; ἐνίκα τραγῳδοῖς *IG* II/III² 3091; cf. And. 4.42; τραγῳδοῖς χορηγεῖν Lys. 21.2, cf. 19.29, 24.9; D. 21.59; Is. 5.36; τεθέασαι τραγῳδούς Men. *Epit.* 149. In light of these well-established usages of τραγῳδοί, it is very improbable that the word should be "Rückbildung" (Lesky 22 n. 3), secondary to τραγῳδία, cf. Ziegler, Else *Origin* 25 f. Else, however, holds that τραγῳδός was the actor-poet (*Hermes* 85 [1957] 20 ff.). In this case it would be difficult to account for the constant plural νικᾶν, χορηγεῖν τραγῳδοῖς; χορηγῶν ἐνίκα τραγῳδοῖς *IG* II/III² 3091: there is only one poet for each χορηγός. The parallelism ἀνδρῶν—παίδων—κωμῳδῶν—τραγῳδῶν in *IG* II/III² 2318 is revealing, too. Whereas "no one of the ὑποκριταί ever danced" (Περὶ τραγῳδίας ed. R. Browning, ΓΕΡΑΣ G. Thomson [Prague, 1963] 70 line 74), dancing is characteristic of the τραγῳδός, Ar. *V.* 1476 ff. Τραγῳδοί and ὑποκριτής are contrasted in the vita of Aeschines, *P.Oxy.* 1800 fr. 3 col. ii 47 ff.: ἐτριταγωνίστει τραγῳδοῖς ὑποκρινόμενος.

12. The first to stress this fact was Reisch 467, followed by Pickard-Cambridge, *Dith.*¹ 164 f. They could not apply the more exact rules of word-formation developed by linguistics since then; cf. E. Risch, *Wortbildung der homerischen Sprache* (Heidelberg, 1937); *IGForsch* 59 (1944/9) 1 ff., 245 ff.; E. Schwyzer, *Griechische Grammatik* I (Munich, 1950) 428 ff.; W. H. Willis, *Studies Presented to D. M. Robinson* II (Saint Louis, 1953) 553 ff.; I am indebted to A. Heubeck (*Erlangen*) for advice. There are very few exceptions among the determinative compounds where the second part determines the first, e.g., ἱπποπόταμος, αἴγαγρος. In an attempt to refute Pickard-Cambridge, Patzer (132) adduces, besides κωμῳδός, χορῳδός, and μονῳδός; this word, however, is found only in Tzetzes, χορῳδός seems not to be attested at all. Lesky (22 n. 3) refers to E. Kalinka, *Commentationes Aenopontanae* 10 (1924) 31, who, however, shows his unawareness of Greek word-formation by referring to ῥοδοδάκτυλος: this, the *bahuvrihi*-type, is exocentric, i.e., used as adjective, Schwyzer 429, 454; ῥαψῳδός belongs still to another, the τερψίμβροτος-type. Del Grande (*supra* n. 7) 56 ff., 354 ff., thinks τραγῳδός has nothing at all to do with τράγος, "goat." If, however, a goat was sacrificed at the Dionysia in the time of Thespis, it is difficult to believe that the Athenians would keep τραγῳδοί and τράγος apart.

13. *FGrHist* 308 F 2=Schol. *in* Pi. *N.* 2.1; Eust. p. 6.25; *EM*, Hsch. *s.v.* ἀρνῳδός, Phot.   23

s.v. ῥαψῳδός. The *Lex sacra* of Coresus, *SIG*³ 958.36 assigns κρεῶν μερίδα to the rhapsode. So there is no reason to look for another etymology of ἀρνῳδός as Welcker (*supra* n. 2) 241 did.

14. Marm.Par. *FGrHist* 239 A 43, cf. Euseb./Hieron. *Chron. Ol.*47,2; Dioskorides, *AP* 7.410, cf. 411; Eratosth. fr. 22 Powell=Hygin. *Astr.* p. 35.4 ff. Bunte, cf. F. Solmsen in *TAPA* 78 (1947) 270 ff.; K. Meuli, *MusHelv* 12 (1955) 226 f.; Merkelbach (*supra* n. 2) 496 ff. Patzer 33 f. thinks Eratosthenes is referring to the ἀσκώλια rather than to tragedy, though admitting that περὶ τράγον ὀρχεῖσθαι does not suit the jumping on the goatskin. Eratosthenes' theory, however, seems to have been that both tragedy and comedy sprang from the same root, the τρυγῳδία understood as "vintage-song," to which the ἀσκώλια too are said to have belonged, cf. Paus. *Gr.* ed. Erbse α 161=Eust. p. 1769.45 ff. (Erbse is not right in leaving out the phrases on κωμῳδεῖν and τραγῳδοί; the word κωμῆται in Paus. *Gr.* clearly points to κωμῳδία, cf. Meuli [*supra* 226 n. 4]); other texts gathered by Meuli *supra*. It seems impossible to accept Eratosthenes' theory in this respect, because the Dionysia was not a vintage-festival; but the falsity of the combination does not invalidate the single pieces of information Eratosthenes could use, e.g., on τραγῳδοί and τράγος. Verg. *Georg.* 2.380 ff. with Serv. Auct. 383, Prob. 380/4, Schol.Bern.; Hor. *AP* 220 with Ps.-Acr.; Tib. 2.157 f. Diomedes, *Grammatici Latini* I.487=Suetonius p. 5.16 ff. Reifferscheid (cf. *infra* n. 21); Euanthius in *Aeli Donati q.f. commentum Terenti* ed. P. Wessner, I (Leipzig, 1902) 13=*CGF* p. 62. Diomedes and Euanthius present nearly the same material in different arrangement; Euanthius does not use Diomedes (-Suetonius), since he has some more Greek material (*Apollo* Νόμιος, Ἀγυαῖος p. 13.16 Wessner), but—except the obvious reference to Vergil—not the Latin quotations (Varro, Lucilius) found in Diomedes (-Suetonius). Didymos, Περὶ ποιητῶν, is quoted by Orion p. 58.7 ff., Sturz for an etymology of ἔλεγος which recurs in Diomedes p. 484 K. and Procl. *Chr.* 319в6 ff. Proclus in his *Chrestomathy* must have dealt with tragedy and comedy, but nothing is extant in the excerpts of Photios; from Proclus, however, seem to be derived the excerpts of Iohannes Diakonos ed. Rabe, *RhM.* 63 (1908), 150, Schol. *in* Dionys.Thr. p. 18.3 ff.; 172.20, 306.27, 475.3 Hilgard; Tz. *ad* Lyc. p. 2.21, 3.1 Scheer; Tz. *Diff. Poet.* 100, 124 (*CGF* pp. 37 f.). Cf. G. Kaibel, *Die Prolegomena* ΠΕΡΙ ΚΩΜΩΙΔΙΑΣ (*AbhGött.* II.4 1898), a study of basic importance for the evaluation of the later sources. Else, *Origin* 17, declaring Iohannes Diakonos "worthless," ignores these affiliations. Patzer, affirming that the explanation "τραγῳδία= 'Gesang beim Bocksopfer'" was "in der Antike nirgends als Namensdeutung versucht" (34 n. 1), is overlooking Vergil and Euanthius. Vergil and Euanthius agree with the tradition of the goat as a prize as to the fact that the τραγῳδοί sang while the goat was still alive; cf. *infra* n. 68 at the end.

15. Fr. 676 Rose=Schol.Bob. *in* Cic. *Pro Arch.* p. 358 Orelli, on elegists; fr. 677= Procl. *Chr.* 320л31, on Arion; Rose included both fragments among the *dubia*, conjecturing Ἀριστοκλῆς instead of Ἀριστοτέλης. He could not yet know Iohannes Diakonos p. 150 Rabe (*infra* n. 19) and Schol. *in* Dionys.Thr. p. 306.9 Hilgard, on Susarion.

16. Pohlenz, *Gött. Nachr.* 1927, cf. Pohlenz II.8 ff., accepted by Ziegler 1925, Lesky 20 ff., Patzer 24. Pohlenz, referring to Jacoby, stated the source of the Parian Marble to be an early-third-century Atthis. Surely Eratosthenes in his *Erigone* was drawing on the Atthidographers, as did Callimachus in his *Hecale*. Jacoby, however, thought of Ephorus, Περὶ εὑρημάτων, too, as a possible source for the Parian Marble, *FGrHist* II D 668, cf. II C 42. It is the merit of Solmsen, Meuli, Merkelbach (*supra* n. 14) to have revived the interest in the "Eratosthenian" theory of the drama.

17. Else, *Aristotle's Poetics* (*supra* n. 3), pointed out the Attic setting of the anecdote and the Attic word ἄστυ (121 n. 101). He thinks the pro-Dorian party to consist of Artistotle's own pupils, Dicaearchus and Aristoxenus (123); "the whole idea of a competition between

Dorian and Athenian claims to the origination of the drama could only have arisen in the fourth century and in the context of Aristotle's school" (Else *Origin* 23)—as if the question of the εὑρετής were not already present in Pi. *O.* 13.18, Hdt.1.23, cf. Jacoby, *FGrHist* II C p. 42.25 on Ephorus Περὶ εὑρημάτων. On κώμη, Swoboda in *RE* Suppl. IV (1924) 951.

18. Diom. p. 488 quoting Varro; Euanthius p. 13 f. Wessner; Donatus p. 23.1 ff. Wessner; *CGF* p. 6, p. 14 col. b 39; Schol. *in* Dionys.Thr. p. 18.15 ff., 172.26, 306.16, 450.30 Hilgard; *EM* p. 764.13 ff.; Tz. *ad* Lyc. p. 2.32 Scheer; Iohannes Diakonos p. 149f. Rabe; Schol. *in* Pl. *Remp.* 394c.

19. Aristotle had little interest in etymology: φύσει τῶν ὀνομάτων οὐδέν ἐστιν (*Int.* 16a27); therefore it is quite doubtful whether in his remarks on σατυρικόν he was thinking of the word τραγῳδία and hypothetical Peloponnesian τράγοι. Of course, even satyrs could sacrifice a goat, cf. the vase paintings (*infra* n. 25, esp. no. 17). The Iohannes Diakonos passage p. 150 Rabe contains, together with the much-discussed testimony of Solon on Arion as inventor of tragedy, the statement ἄμφω δὲ (i.e., tragedy and comedy) παρ᾿ Ἀθηναίοις ἐφεύρηνται, καθάπερ Ἀριστοτέλης φησίν. There is no methodological reason why we should accept the testimony of Solon and reject the testimony of Aristotle. Aristotle, however, knew and quoted Solon's elegies (cf. e.g., *Ath.* 5, 12); so he will not have overlooked so ancient an authority on tragedy, and still he is said to have maintained its Attic origin. So the question comes up again what Solon really said. There is a well-established tradition that Arion "invented" the dithyramb (Hellanikos, *FGrHist* 4 F 86; Hdt. 1.23; Arist. in Procl. *Chr.* 320a31; Dicaearchus fr. 75 Wehrli; Schol. *in* Pi. *O.* 13.26 b; Schol. *in* Pl. *Remp.* 394c; Tz. *ad* Lyc. p. 2.15 Scheer; alluded to in Pi. *O.* 13.18). Aristotle thought dithyramb to be the ἀρχή of tragedy (*Poet.* 1449a9 ff.); whatever he meant by this statement and whether or not he was right, it must be noted that ἀρχή in his terminology implies that dithyramb was itself not tragedy, but an "ontologically" earlier step. His followers and epitomators, however, would not always keep to these subtle distinctions. The result was some confusion between dithyramb and tragedy. As Philoxenus is said to have been διθυραμβοποιὸς ἢ τραγῳδοδιδάσκαλος (Schol. *in* Ar. *Pl.* 290), *a fortiori* Arion came to be considered the first tragic poet (Suda *s.v.* Arion, Tz. *ad* Lyc. p. 3.7 Scheer). If Solon only spoke of Arion's κύκλιος χορός (κύκλιον ἤγαγε χορόν—a somewhat unusual word order—Schol. *in* Pi. [*supra*], cf. Procl., Tz. [*supra*]), this could develop into the statement of Iohannes Diakonos: the author's name and the title of his work are preserved, but instead of the text we have a questionable interpretation. So the quotation of Solon in Iohannes Diakonos may be similar to the quotation of Hesiod in Diog. Laer. 8.48: Hesiod there is said to have taught the sphericity of the earth, because Zenon (*SVF* I no. 276) read it into his text.

20. "In Ikaria und bei vielen anderen Dionysosfesten" there were goat-sacrifices, according to Ziegler 1926, but not at the Dionysia when tragedy was performed. Even so it would be less far-fetched to derive τραγῳδοί from Icaria than from hypothetical Peloponnesian τράγοι. Patzer (24) thinks the goat-prize to be a mere "inference" from the wrong etymology. Lesky (20) is more circumspect: "Man berief sich dabei gewiss auf alten attischen Dorfbrauch."

21. Diomedes—who is quoting Varro (*De scaenicis originibus* fr. 304 Funaioli) only for the *quia* phrase, as the change in number seems to indicate—explicitly refers to the Attic Dionysia, p. 488: *Liberalibus apud Atticos, die festo Liberi patris, vinum cantatoribus pro corollario dabatur* (cf. Philochoros, *FGrHist* 328 F 171); Serv. Auct. *in Georg.* 2.383 states that the Dionysiac goat-sacrifice originated at the Attic Dionysia. For the myth of Icarius and the first goat-sacrifice, there is no incontrovertible evidence prior to Eratosthenes. Attic black-figure vases represent a man receiving Dionysus (amphora BM B 149=J. D. Beazley, *Attic Black-figure Vase Painters*, hereafter, *ABV* [Oxford, 1956] 245,60 and B 153=*ABV* 243,45); the man is traditionally called Icarius, but Amphictyon and Semachus, too, are possible names. 25

The story of Icarius in Porph. *Abst.* 2.10 was reluctantly attributed to Theophrastus by J. Bernays, *Theophrastos' Schrift über Frömmigkeit* (Berlin, 1866) 61 and, with less hesitation, by W. Pötscher, *Theophrastos* ΠΕΡΙ ΕΥΣΕΒΕΙΑΣ (Leiden, 1964) 22ff. This, however, can be refuted: according to Theophrastus, the sanguinary sacrifice was caused by λιμὸς ἤ τινος ἄλλης δυστυχίας περίστασις (Porph. *Abst.* 2.9 first sentence)—which is neither "unglücklicher Zufall" nor "Missgeschick" (Pötscher 16, 153), but something like "inescapable impact of calamity" (cf. Theophrastus's definition of tragedy as ἡρωικῆς τύχης περίστασις Diom. p. 487). Introduced by αὐτίκα τῶν κατὰ μέρος . . . there follow in Porphyry the Attic anecdotes about the first sacrifice of a pig, a goat, a bull, which make ἤ ἀγνοίας ἤ ὀργὰς ἤ φόβους the origin of sacrifice; this is not δυστυχίας περίστασις. In the middle of chapter 10 (p. 141.3 Nauck; fr. 6 Pötscher), the κατὰ μέρος- examples come to an end, and suddenly the motive of λιμός reappears: this is Theophrastus again, the stories before are ἐμβεβλημένοι μῦθοι of Porphyry (*Abst.* 2.32). Nevertheless, the non-Theophrastean anecdotes may still be very old popular tradition, perhaps again preserved by Atthidographers. Later testimonies on the Dionysiac goat-sacrifice: Varro, *RR* 1.2.19; Ov. *Met.* 15.111 ff.; *Fast.* 1.349 ff.; Serv. *in Aen.* 3.118; *Prob. in Georg.* 2.380/4; above all Leonidas of Tarentum, *AP* 9.99, and Euenus of Ascalon, *AP* 9.75, an epigram that is also inscribed on a Pompeian wall-painting, *MonInst.* 10 (1876) T.36, cf. *infra* p. 114. Hellenistic and Roman representations of the goat-sacrifice are collected by O. Brendel, *RömMitt.* 48 (1933) 153 ff. A choregus paid 30 minas for one tragic agon (Lys. 21.1), the price of a goat in Erchia (*SEG* 21 [1965] no. 541) is 10 to 12 drachmas, i.e., less than ½ percent—*vilis hircus* indeed.

22. Cf. the foundation of Kritolaos in Amorgos, *IG* XII 7, 515.80: the meat of a sacrificed ram is to be used as ἔπαθλα for the victors in an athletic agon. Cf. also Schol. *in* Theocr. 7.106/8d.

23. On these "dithyrambic vases" cf. G. E. Rizzo, *RivFC.* 30 (1902) 471ff.; E. Pfuhl, *Malerei und Zeichnung* II (Munich, 1923) §617; esp. the neck-amphora BM E 298=*ARV²* 1581, 20, *CVA* pl. 51,1, with the inscription ΑΚΑΜΑΝΤΙΣ ΕΝΙΚΑ ΦΥΛΕ; the calyx-crater Bologna PU 286=*ARV²* 1158, with Dionysus, seated, expecting the sacrifice of the bull led by Nike. On later representations of bull-sacrifices, O. Brendel, *RömMitt.* 45 (1930) 196 ff. Further testimonies on the dithyrambic bull-sacrifice: Chamaeleon fr. 34 Wehrli explaining Simonides fr. 69 Diehl; Dionysus ταυροφάγος, S. fr. 607 Nauck=668 Pearson; Schol. *in* Pl. *Remp.* 394c; the expression θύσων διθύραμβον Pi. fr. 86a.

24. L. Deubner, *Attische Feste* (Berlin, 1932) 252 and pl. 38.

25. Surprisingly little attention has been paid to these unimpeachable τράγοι in the retinue of Dionysus. My collection (surely incomplete):

1. Amphora BM B 168=*ABV* 142,3 (satyr riding on goat)
2. Amphora New York, Metr.Mus. 06.1021.68=*ABV* 289 (Dionysus, satyr, goat)
3. Amphora Oxford 213=*ABV* 340,1 (maenad and satyr, Dionysus, maenad and goat)
4. Amphora E. Gerhard, *Auserlesene Vasenbilder* (Berlin, 1840–58) pl. 54=*ABV* 370,127 (Dionysus and Ariadne in a chariot drawn by goats)
5. Amphora ibid. pl. 32=*ABV* 372,155 (satyr, Dionysus with goat, satyr)
6. Oinochoe Cambridge 162=*ABV* 385,28 (man, maenad, winejug, man riding on a goat, amphora, dancing man)
7. Stamnos Bruxelles R 251=*ABV* 388,2 (on the neck: man between goats, goat between men; main picture: chariot race and dancing men, surrounded by vines and grapes)
8. Pelike Oxford 563=*ABV* 396,21 (satyrs with goat)
9. Amphora BM B 178=*ABV* 396,27 (Dionysus with goat, two satyrs)

10. Amphora BM B 258=*ABV* 402,9 (Ariadne with panther, Apollo with cithara, Dionysus with cantharus and goat)
11. Oinochoe *ABV* 431,11 (maenad riding on goat)
12. Lekythos Berlin=*ABV* 518,3 (goats, satyrs, a goat with human face, caught at the horn by a satyr)
13. Skyphos Agora P 1544=*ABV* 518,47 (procession with flute-player, youth carrying a wine-amphora, old man with ivy-wreath, other comasts, goat)
14. Skyphos Agora P 1547=*ABV* 518,49 (procession with flute-player, man catching a goat at the horn)
15. Skyphos Bruxelles R 283=*ABV* 627,2 (youth holding goat at horn; vines with grapes)
16. Amphora BM B 265=*CVA* pl. 66 (Great Britain 211) 1 (return of Hephaestus, goat beside the mule)
17. Amphora Gerhard *supra* pl. 37 (Dionysus with goat)
18. Skyphos Bologna C 44=*CVA* 2 pl. 42 (Italia 341) (goat, satyr, Hermes; suspended, a knapsack containing the head of a goat)
19. Skyphos Baltimore, *CVA* 1 pl. 22 (USA 155) (Dionysus in a chariot, goat, man)
20. Skyphos Athens 820 *bis*, A. Frickenhaus, *Lenaeenvasen*, Winckelmannsprogramm 72 1912) no. 2 (Dionysus-idol with women; under the handle, goat)
21. Amphora Warsaw 199184=*CVA* 4 pl. 17 (Pologne 146) 2/3 (Dionysus with goat)
22. Amphora Philadelphia L 64.259=*ABV* 285,6 (satyr and maenad, Dionysus with goat, satyr)
23. Oinochoe Paris, Cab. des Méd. 276, A. de Ridder, *Catalogue des vases peints de la Bibliothèque Nationale* (Paris, 1902) fig. 28 (silen with flute, goat, wineskin)

A goat is depicted on the altar of Dionysus on the cup of Makron, Acr. 325=*ARV*² 460,20, Frickenhaus (*supra*) p. 22. There is also a goat on a Boeotian cotyle in the BM, *JHS* 31 (1911) 4 ff. (together with satyr) and on one Corinthian kothon, Würzburg no. 118 (Webster no. 37). Similar representations recur in Attic red-figure, e.g., the cup of Gorgos, Agora P 24113=*ARV*² 213,242. It seems the vase painters felt some equivalence of he-goat and satyr (nos. 3, 12) and an intimate connexion of Dionysus and τράγος (nos. 5, 9, 10, 15). The sacrifice of an ἔριφος is represented on a South Italian vase (Naples H 2411, L. R. Farnell, *The Cults of the Greek States* V [Oxford, 1909] pl. 41); otherwise, the act of sacrifice to Dionysus is not represented in classical vase-painting (H. Metzger, *Recherches sur l'imagerie athénienne* [Paris, 1965] 113).

26. Deubner (*supra* n. 24) 136; Pickard-Cambridge (*supra* n. 11) 41; Else, *Hermes* 85 (1957) 18 n. 3: "in any case not the Greater Dionysia"; Patzer 36: "ohne jede Rücksicht auf die Tragödie." Pohlenz, however, pointed out the connection with the Parian Marble and Dioskorides, *Gött. Nachr.* 1927, p. 304 n. 1.

27. The *Leges Sacrae* make a distinction between the sacrifice of an ἔριφος and a τράγος, cf. F. Sokolowski, *Lois sacrées de l'Asie Mineure* (Paris, 1955) no. 67в.3, 10; id., *Lois sacrées des cités grecques* (Paris, 1962) no. 104: Διονύσῳ τράγον . . . The Erchia-inscription (*SEG* 21 [1965] no. 541) distinguishes οἶς from κριός (ε 52); it has 11 times the sacrifice of an αἴξ, no τράγος (cf. also S. Dow, *BCH* 89 [1955] 199ff.).

28. Hor. *Epod.* 10.23; Mart. 3.24 (cf. *infra* n. 62).

29. The αἴτιον of the goat gnawing the vine, however, fits Elaphebolion, the month of the Greater Dionysia: the goat "invented" the pruning of the vine (Hygin. *Fab.* 274.1), which takes place ὑπ' αὐτὴν τὴν βλάστησιν (Thphr. *CP* 3.13.1), i.e., about April.

30. The goat eating from a tree, endangered by carnivorous beasts, is an iconographic type down from Sumerian times; cf. the gold-silver-statuettes from Ur, J. B. Pritchard, *The Ancient Near East in Pictures* [hereafter *ANEP*] (Princeton, 1954) nos. 667/668; a seal from

Uruk, Berlin VA 10537, *ANEP* no. 672; H. Frankfort, *Cylinder Seals* (London, 1939) 21 f., pl. 3a (cf. pl. 3b, 4j, 17c): a man, standing beside a block (altar?), feeding goats (or a kind of sheep?) with a (stylized) twig; he is probably to be called Dumuzi-Tammuz: A. Moortgat, *Tammuz* (Berlin, 1949) 3 ff., 29 f.; a relief from Assur, first half of second mill. B.C., *ANEP* no. 528: a god with grapes, on each side a goat gnawing the grape-vine; a relief-vase, W. Andrae, *Kultrelief aus dem Brunnen des Assurtempels zu Assur* (Berlin, 1931) 10, pl. 7d: goat gnawing grapes, threatened by beastlike demons. Some connection of Dionysus-cult and Tammuz-cult is entirely possible, considering esp. the equation βάκχον· κλαυθμόν. Φοίνικες (Hsch.) and Ἰκάριος—Accadian *ikkaru* "farmer, planter" (M. C. Astour, *Hellenosemitica* [Leiden, 1965] 174 f.; 194 n. 6).

31. Fr. 708 Page; cf. Pohlenz, *Gött. Nachr.* 1927, and E. Roos, *Die tragische Orchestik im Zerrbild der altattischen Komödie* (Lund, 1951) 209 ff.

32. Pollux 4.123. To make the problem more complicated, the Tholos in Epidaurus was called θυμέλα (*IG* IV.1² 103), a Delian inscription mentions τὴν θυμέλην τοῦ βωμοῦ (*IG* XI.2 161A95), whereas Pherecrates (*CAF* I.204, fr. 214) is said to have used the word instead of θυηλαί. The tragic poets use θυμέλη as a kind of equivalent to ἑστία, A.S.F. Gow, *JHS* 32 (1912) 213 ff., F. Robert, *Thymélè* (Paris, 1939) 259 ff., Hsch. *s.v.* θυμέλη . . . οἱ δὲ τὸ ἐπίπυρον; E. *Supp.* 64 δεξίπυροι θυμέλαι—but E. *Ion* 114 θυμέλαν=δάπεδον 121; therefore Pickard-Cambridge concluded that there was an altar in the center of the orchestra, the upper part of which was the θυμέλη (*Dith.*¹ 175, 177; *The Theatre of Dionysus in Athens* [Oxford, 1946] 9 f.). Metzger (*supra* n. 25) 101 f. calls the round altar amid the Dionysiac thiasos on a vase painting θυμέλη (calyx crater Athens 12255=*ARV*² 1435, Metzger pl. 44). C. Robert had vigorously contested that there could have been an altar in the orchestra (*Hermes* 32 [1897] 438 ff., followed by F. Schmidt, *De supplicum ad aras confugientium partibus scenicis* [Diss. Königsberg, 1911]); his derivation of θυμέλη from the root θη-, θεμέλιον must however be discarded on linguistic grounds; on the suffix -μελ-, H. Frisk, *Eranos* 41 (1943) 51, and *Griechisches etymologisches Wörterbuch* (Heidelberg, 1960) *s.v.* θύω 2. Other testimonies point to θυμέλη=βῆμά τι: Orion p. 72.8 Sturz (~*Et.Gen.*, *EM* 458.32 ff.) *s.v.* θυμέλη: τράπεζα δὲ ἦν . . . ἐφ᾿ ἧς ἑστῶτες ἐν τοῖς ἀγροῖς ἦδον, μήπω τάξιν λαβούσης τραγῳδίας (cf. Pollux 4.123 on ἐλεός); *EM* 743.35 μετὰ δὲ τὴν ὄρχηστραν (meaning "stage" here) βωμὸς ἦν τοῦ Διονύσου, τετράγωνον οἰκοδόμημα κενὸν ἐπὶ τοῦ μέσου, ὃ καλεῖται θυμέλη. This rectangular platform was discovered by G. Löschcke (in E. Bethe, *Prolegomena zur Geschichte des Theaters im Alterthum* [Leipzig, 1896] 76 f.; cf. A. Frickenhaus, *Die altgriechische Bühne* [Strassburg, 1917] 83 ff.; M. Bieber, *Denkmäler zum Theaterwesen im Altertum* [Berlin, 1920] 8 ff.; *History of the Greek and Roman Theater*² [Princeton, 1961] 55, fig. 48) on the Brygos-cup BM E 65=*ARV*² 370,13, in a scene of a satyr-play; the same platform on calyx crater Bologna 329=*ARV*² 1410,21, in a Dionysiac scene. Musicians are often represented performing on similar platforms, so the later concept of θυμελικοὶ ἀγῶνες (J. Frei, *De certaminibus thymelicis* [Diss. Basel, 1900]) is easy to explain (Bieber, *Denkmäler, supra*). Pollux 4.123 mentions an altar ἐπὶ τῆς σκηνῆς. In the theater of Priene, there is an altar at the rim of the orchestra opposite the stage, accessible from the orchestra (M. Schede, *Die Ruinen von Priene*² [Berlin, 1964] 70 ff.); a similar altar in a theater on Cos (*Enciclopedia dell'arte antica* II [1959] 799). That the choreuts (of dithyramb and tragedy?) in strophe and antistrophe were dancing round the altar is stated by the Hellenistic scholar Ptolemaios (*RE* XXIII [1959] 1862–63 *s.v.* no. 78) in Schol. *in* Pi. III p. 311 Drachmann, cf. *EM* 690.44 ff., Byz.Schol. *in* E. *Hec.* 647 (ed. Dindorf; not in Schwartz), cf. F. Robert (*supra* n. 2) 874 ff.; L. B. Lawler, *The Dance of the Ancient Greek Theater* (Iowa City, 1964) 11 ff.

33. 510/508 B.C. according to Marm.Par. A 46; Pickard-Cambridge, *Dith.*¹ 15, 22 f.; it was organized by Lasos of Hermione, who therefore was sometimes called "inventor" of dithy-

28

ramb. There is no reason to assume earlier performances of dithyrambs in Athens at the time of Peisistratos, as, e.g., Patzer 93 does.

34. Only sanguinary sacrifices are studied here, not σπονδαί, ἀπαρχαί, etc. One of the most important contributions to the question is still W. Robertson Smith, *Lectures on the Religion of the Semites*[2] (London, 1894), though his theory of totemism has been abandoned. He vitally influenced S. Freud, *Totem und Tabu* (Vienna, 1913)=four essays in *Imago* 1/2 (1912/13)=*Gesammelte Schriften* 10 (Leipzig, 1924). There is the sociological approach: H. Hubert and M. Mauss, "Essai sur la nature et la fonction du sacrifice," *Année sociologique* 2 (1898) 29 ff., Engl. transl.: *Sacrifice, Its Nature and Function* (Chicago, 1964); their definition: "sacrifice is a religious act which, through the consecration of a victim, modifies the condition of the moral person who accomplishes it . . ." (13)—which leaves the question open why such advantage is gained by the destruction of life. They also define sacrifice as "establishing a means of communication between the sacred and the profane worlds through the mediation of a victim" (97)—basically the same definition as in E. O. James, *Sacrifice and Sacrament* (London, 1962), who gives a convenient survey of the material and literature. An original attempt at explanation: A. E. Jensen, "Über das Töten als kulturgeschichtliche Erscheinung," *Paideuma* 4 (1950) 23 ff.~*Mythos und Kult bei Naturvölkern* (Wiesbaden, 1951) 197 ff. (*infra* n. 55). On Greek sacrifice: P. Stengel, *Die Opferbräuche der Griechen* (Leipzig, 1910); *Die griechischen Kultusaltertümer*[3] (Munich, 1920); S. Eitrem, *Opferritus und Voropfer* (Oslo, 1915); F. Schwenn, *Gebet und Opfer* (Heidelberg, 1927); L. Ziehen, *RE* XVIII (1939) 579ff. *s.v.* Opfer, *RE* IIIA (1929) 1669 ff. *s.v.* σφάγια. Of special importance are: A. Thomsen, "Der Trug des Prometheus," *ArchRW* 12 (1909) 460 ff.; A. D. Nock, "The Cult of Heroes," *HthR* 37 (1944) 141 ff.; above all K. Meuli, "Griechische Opferbräuche," in *Phyllobolia, Festschrift P. von der Mühll* (Basel, 1946) 185 ff. [hereafter, Meuli], who established the connection of the Olympian sacrifice with the "Schädel- und Langknochenopfer," on which cf. A. Vorbichler, *Das Opfer auf den heute noch erreichbaren ältesten Stufen der Menschheitsgeschichte* (Mödling, 1956), and H. Kühn, *Das Problem des Urmonotheismus* (AbhMainz., 1950): 22. Unfortunately there is no exhaustive study of interrelations of Greek and ancient Near Eastern sacrificial rites (on which cf. B. Meissner, *Babylonien und Assyrien* II [Heidelberg, 1925] 73 ff.; G. Furlani, "Il sacrificio nella religione dei Semiti di Babilonia e Assiria," *MemLinc.* VI, 4 [1932] 103–370; F. Blome, *Die Opfermaterie in Babylon und Israel* [Rome, 1934]; K. Galling, *Der Altar in den Kulturen des alten Orients* [Berlin, 1925]; Y. Rosengarten, *Le Régime des offrandes dans la société sumérienne d'après les textes présargoniques de Lagaš* [Paris, 1960]; on the still very frustrating Ugaritic evidence, A. de Guglielmo, *CathBiblQuart.* 17 [1955] 196 ff.). It seems to be well established that, on the one hand, the Minoans and Mycenaeans had quite different sacrificial rites, because they had no altars of the Greek type (C. G. Yavis, *Greek Altars* [Saint Louis, 1949]), and, on the other hand, that the nearest relatives of Greek altars are to be found in Assur, 13th cent. (Galling [*supra*] pp. 46 ff.; *ANEP* nos. 576/577), and that Semitic (Phoenician and Hebrew) sacrificial rites offer the closest parallels to Greek ritual (R. K. Yerkes, *Sacrifice in Greek and Roman Religions and Early Judaism* [New York, 1952]). It is one of the paradoxes of our discipline that neither Nilsson nor Meuli, in their expositions of Greek sacrificial ritual, refer to the Old Testament, which contains the largest extant collection of ancient sacrificial rites.

35. Schol. A *in Il.* 9.219=K. Lehrs, *De Aristarchi studiis Homericis*[3] (Leipzig, 1882) 82 ff.; Schol. *in Od.* 14.446; Eust. p. 641.61; Frisk, *GriechEtymWörterb.* I.699. The more comprehensive use of θύειν is to be seen in the gloss Hsch. *s.v.* θῦμα· ἱερεῖον σφάγιον ὁλοκαύτωμα.

36. On "Olympic" and "chthonic" sacrifice, cf. Stengel, *Kultusaltertümer*[3] 105 ff.; Ziehen (*supra* n. 34); Meuli 201 ff.; the evidence for the contrast ἐναγίζειν—θύειν is most fully collected by F. Pfister, *Der Reliquienkult im Altertum* II (Giessen, 1912) 466 ff. In slaughtering,

the throat of the animal was sometimes turned to the sky, sometimes pressed to the earth (H. v. Fritze *JdI*. 18 [1904] 58 ff.; Schol. *in* Ap. Rh. 1. 587; *Et.Gen*. p. 115 Miller=*EM s.v.* ἔντομα). There are, besides the high "Olympian" altars, altars low and large for holocausts, but there are also ἐσχάραι just on the earth and βόθροι dug out (Yavis [*supra* n. 34] 91 ff.; Schol. *in* E. *Ph*. 274; Porph. *Antr*. 6; Serv. *in* Verg. *Buc*. 5.66 etc.). In fact ὁλοκαυτώματα were not very frequent, either in the cult of heroes or of those gods whom the Greeks called χθόνιοι (the evidence: Ziehen, *RE* III A [1929] 1674 ff.), and they occur also in cults of "Olympians" (cf. Meuli 209 ff.); the Erchia-inscription has Διὶ Ἐπωπετῆι χοῖρος ὁλόκαυτος (*SEG* XXI [1965] no. 541 Γ 23), i.e., for the god whose name seemd to designate the sky-god "looking down from above" (L. Preller and C. Robert, *Griechische Mythologie* I⁴ [Berlin, 1894] 117 n. 2). On the other hand, the sacrificial feast is quite common in the cult of heroes and χθόνιοι (Nock [*supra* n. 34] with 11 examples; the ram sacrificed to Pelops in Olympia was eaten, too, but not by participants in the festival, Paus. 5.13.2 f.). People even ate from καθάρσια, cf. οἱ σπλαγχνεύοντες Ath. 9.410B; only Porphyry's θεολόγοι tried to eliminate this custom (*Abst.* 2.44). At the oath-sacrifices, however, the victim was not eaten (*Il*. 19.266, Schol. *in Il*. 3.310, Paus. 5.24.10, 3.20.9), nor were, of course, the σφάγια proper, slain on the battlefield under the eyes of the enemy. The holocausts themselves usually have their place as a preliminary rite in a larger context: first the burnt sacrifice—χοῖρος or ἀρήν—for the hero, then the sacrificial feast—mostly βοῦς—in honor of the god: inscription from Cos, *SIG*³ 1027 (Herakles); Paus. 3.19.3 (Hyacinthus-Apollon); Paus. 2.11.7 (Alexanor-Euamerion). This goes along with the rhythm night-day in Greek time-reckoning: the new "day" begins at sunset, cf. Pi. *I*. 4.67 ff. c. Schol. In an analogous way, the "normal" sacrifice consists, first, in the burning of sacred parts; second, in the meal. In one case, the same animal was half burnt, half eaten (Paus. 2.10.1, Sicyon). There are many other special provisions in sacrificial ritual, each of which has its own function and meaning, e.g., about εὐνουχίζειν (*infra* n. 62), or οὐ φορά, i.e., the victim must be consumed at the spot: 22 times in the Erchia-inscription (*SEG* XXI no. 541); S. Dow, *BCH* 89 (1965) 210, thinks this to be a "purely secular matter," but cf. Ar. *Pl*. 1138 c. Schol.; Theopompus fr. 70 (*CAF* I.751); *SIG*³ 1004, 1024, 1025, 1026, 1041, Sokolowski, *Lois sacrées de l'Asie Mineure*, no. 34; L. Ziehen, *Leges Graecorum sacrae e titulis collectae* (Leipzig, 1906) no. 125; Paus. 2.27.1, 10.4.10, 10.38.8, 8.38.8; the same rule from the Old Testament (Ex. 12.8, Passover; cf. 29.31, 34) through Rome (Cato *Agr*. 83; *CIL* VI 1, 576) up to Alaska (A. Gahs, *Festschrift W. Schmidt* [Vienna, 1928] 251). The rite of drowning a victim in a spring or lake (D.S. 5.4: Cyane) is also attested as early as the paleolithic period (Kühn [*supra* n. 34] 22).

37. The most elaborate descriptions of sacrifice are in Homer *Il*. 1.447 ff., 2.410 ff., *Od*. 3.429 ff., 14.414 ff.; Hes. *Th*. 535 ff.; most detailed is Pherecrates, fr. 23 (*CAF* I.151): people burn τὼ μηρώ, τὴν ὀσφὺν κομιδῆ ψιλήν, τὸν σπόνδυλον. Menander mentions ὀσφὺν ἄκραν and χολήν *Dysc*. 447 ff., cf. fr. 264 Koerte. The comedians used to make fun of this ritual, cf. also Eubulus fr. 95 (*CAF* II.197) and 130 (*CAF* II.210), Adesp. fr. 1205 (*CAF* III.606). An interesting description of a sacrificial meal is given by Harmodios, *FGrHist* 319 F 1. Vase paintings containing sacrificial scenes are collected by G. Rizza, *ASAtene*. 37/8 (1959/60) 321 ff. and Metzger (*supra* n. 25) 107 ff.; they usually represent the altar with the fire and the tail of the victim, the σπλαγχνόπτης, wine-libations, flute-player. The cup of Brygos (*supra* n. 32) shows Iris, who came to fetch from the altar ὀσφὺν καὶ σπόνδυλον, attacked by satyrs. Most surprising survivals of sacrificial ritual were found until recent times among the Greeks of Pharasa, Cappadocia: there is a stone in the chapel opposite the altar, on which incense is burnt; it is called θάλι (< λιθάρι); the victim is led three times around the θάλι, pelted with leaves and flowers, slaughtered in the chapel so that the θάλι may receive its blood; the minister (παπᾶς) receives the right thigh, the hide, head, and feet of the victim: G. A. Megas,

Ἑλληνικαὶ ἑορταὶ καὶ ἔθιμα τῆς λαϊκῆς λατρείας (Athens, 1956) 15 f.; he also refers to similar customs in Thrace (17: the victim is slaughtered εἰς βόθρον in the churchyard) and at Lesbos (17 f.). Cf. also Cook III.1168 ff.

38. ἡγοῦντο γὰρ ὥσπερ συσσιτεῖσθαι τοῖς θεοῖς Schol. AT *in Il.* 3.310; U. v. Wilamowitz-Moellendorff, *Der Glaube der Hellenen* I (Berlin, 1931) 287; M. P. Nilsson, *Geschichte der griechischen Religion*² I (Munich, 1955) 144 f.; *contra*, Nock (*supra* n. 34) 150 ff., 156: "there was a conscious fellowship of the worshippers with one another, rather than of the worshippers with the deity honored." Wilamowitz thought the Promethean division was an "early" depravation of the original common meal; he could not know that this would lead back to times earlier than the paleolithic age. That μηρία really means "thighbones" is proved by Meuli 215 ff.

39. Nilsson (*supra* n. 38) objects to Meuli, stressing that "nur gezähmte Tiere, fast nie wilde geopfert werden"; but this, far from being a "durchschlagender Einwand," merely means that the neolithic farmers took over and transformed for their kind of civilization the rites of the paleolithic hunters. Another change took place when the Greeks (like the Western Semites) began to burn the sacred parts, establishing as it were fire as a means of communication with the divine, cf. n. 34. Whether the sacrificial rites presuppose from the start some kind of belief in god, even an "Urmonotheismus," is a question difficult to answer. Meuli wrote: "diese Jagdriten sind weder deistisch noch prädeistisch und sagen über Götterglauben überhaupt nichts aus . . . in der Beziehung von Mensch und Tier gehen sie vollständig auf" (249); *contra*, Kühn and esp. Vorbichler (*supra* n. 34); curiously enough, Freud's theory in this case comes to the same result as does P. W. Schmidt.

40. The Greeks were fully aware of this: ζωῆς δὲ διὰ θυσιῶν ἀπαρχόμεθα Sallust 16.1. Iamblichus turns the same idea into magic: by destruction (ἀνάλυσις) sacrifice provokes to action the higher principles (*Myst.* 5.24). In a very crude form, the same concept returns in a modern definition of sacrifice: "Mobilmachung von Kraftstoff zu Gunsten des Opfernden," A. Bertholet, *Der Sinn des kultischen Opfers* (*AbhBerl.* no. 2, 1942) 10.

41. As a reverse, every slaughter is a sacrifice. The Mosaic law was very outspoken about this, Lev. 17.2 ff. (Yerkes [*supra* n. 34] 147), but Josiah, concentrating the cult in Jerusalem, had to allow profane slaughter (Deut. 12.15), which had been common in the civilizations of Egypt and Mesopotamia. The Arabs still perform every slaughter "in the name of Allah" (*Die Religion in Geschichte und Gegenwart*³ IV [Tübingen, 1956 ff.] 1640); for the Siberian čukčes, every slaughter of a reindeer is a sacrifice (A. Gahs, *Festschrift P. W. Schmidt* [Vienna, 1928] 253); and in India, some temples still are slaughter-houses (H. Zimmern, *Eranos-Jb* 6 [1938] 180).

42. *Od.* 3.432 ff.; this was preserved in German and Slavic folk-custom down to modern times: a "Pfingstochse" with gilded horns led along through the streets of the town, to be slaughtered afterward; each family would buy part of his meat: U. Jahn, *Die deutschen Opferbräuche bei Ackerbau und Viehzucht* (Breslau, 1884) 137 ff., 315 ff.; a striking example in a festival at Lesbos: Megas (*supra* n. 37) 17.

43. Cf. Ael. *NA* 10.50 (Eryx), 11.4 (Hermione); Apollon. *Mir.* 13 (Halicarnassus); Arist. *Mir.* 844a35 (Pedasia); Plut. *Pel.* 21 (Leuktra), *Luc.* 24.6 f. (Persian Artemis=Anahita); Porph. *Abst.* 1.25 (Gadeira, Cyzicus); Philostr. *Her.* 17, p. 329 Kayser (Leuke), 8 p. 294 (Rhesus); Plin. *NH* 32.17 (Atargatis); the same is required for human sacrifice, Neanthes, *FGrHist* 84 F 16 (Epimenides), Serv. *in Aen.* 3.57 (Massalia), cf. Euripides' tragedies. Cf. also the lore of the haruspices, Serv. Auct. *in Georg.* 2.395, Macr. *Sat.* 3.5.8, and Lucan 7.165, D.C. 41.61; for India, cf. Hubert/Mauss (*supra* n. 34) 30. At the sacrifice of Poseidon Helikonios, on the contrary, the bull was expected to bellow fiercely, Schol.B *in Il.* 20.404, Cf. Paus. 4.32.3.

44. Cf., e.g., Ar. *Pax* 956 ff., E. *IA* 1568ff.; Eitrem (*supra* n. 34) 7ff.; *supra* n. 37.

45. Delphic oracle in Porph. *Abst.* 2.9=no. 537 in H. W. Parke and D.E.W. Wormell, *The Delphic Oracle* II (Oxford, 1956), cf. Meuli 254 ff., 266 f.; Schol. *in* Ar. *Pax* 960; Schol. *in* Ap. Rh. 1.425; Plut. *QConv.* 729 f., *DefOrac.* 435вс, 437а; *SIG*³ 1025.20 (Cos): θύεται δὲ (ὁ βοῦς), αἱ μέγ κα ὑπο[κύψ]ει τᾶι Ἰστίαι; an Arabian parallel in Eitrem (*supra* n. 34) 7 n. 1. Cf. the stamnos Munich 2412=*ARV*² 1036,5: the dithyrambic bull (*supra* n. 23) bowing to drink water poured by Nike; Italiote Calpis Altenburg, *CVA* pl. 84 (Germany 869): bull kneeling down to be adorned by a woman (the Phyle). A modern survival in Megas (*supra* n. 37) 18 (Lesbos): λένε ὅτι τότε γονατίζει τὸ ζῷο. . . .

46. "Dunkel" according to Meuli 265. Stengel concluded from the word προβάλοντο that the οὐλοχύται "originally" were thrown at the earth, *ergo* it was a gift to the earth-goddess (*Kultusaltertümer*³ 110); Ziehen used the term "cathartic," *Hermes* 37 (1902) 391 ff., *RE* XVIII (1939) 626 f.; Eitrem (*supra* n. 34) 262, saw the equivalence to the καταχύσματα but, following E. Samter, *Familienfeste der Griechen und Römer* (Berlin, 1901) 1 ff., he thought them to be a gift to ancestor-ghosts or demons. Χέρνιβά τ᾽ οὐλοχύτας τε κατάρχετο *Od.* 3.445, cf. E. *IA* 955, 1568 ff.; Ar. *Pax* 956 ff., *Av.* 850. That the knife is hidden (cf. Scandinavian customs of slaughter, E. Klein *ArchRW.* 28 [1930] 167) in the basket, is stated at Pl.Com. fr. 91 (*CAF* I.626), Ar. *Pax* 948 c. Schol., E. *El.* 810, *IA* 1565 f., Philostr. *VA* 1.1, Juv. 12.84. The barley is thrown at the victim, according to Schol. A *in Il.* 1.449, Schol. *in Od.* 3.441, Schol. *in* Ar. *Nu.* 260, D.H. 7.72.15; at the altar, according to E. *IA* 1112, *El.* 804, Schol. *in* Ap. Rh. 1.409, Eust. p. 132.25. Theophrastus thought the οὐλαί to be a relic of an "old way of life," Porph. *Abst.* 2.6, Schol. A *in Il.* 1.449, cf. Eust. (*supra*), Schol. *in Od.* 3.441; he seems to have taken as a real religious rite the φυλλοβολία *Od.* 12.357 f.: Eust. p. 132.39 f. In Pharasa the victim is pelted with χορτάρια καὶ λουλούδια, Megas (*supra* n. 37) 16. Ψηφῖδες instead of οὐλαί Paus. 1.41.9, at the sacrifice to Tereus in Megara, cf. Schol. *in* Ar. *Nu.* 260.

47. Eitrem (*supra* n. 34) 344 ff., takes it to be "eine selbständige Opfergabe," for the souls of the dead, of course (413). Meuli 265 f., who adduces a parallel from Mexico, refrains from giving an explanation. This ἀπάρχεσθαι is mentioned, e.g., *Od.* 3.446, 14.422; E. *Alc.* 74ff., *El.* 811. E. Hemingway, *For Whom the Bell Tolls*, describes the cutting of the hair as ἄρχεσθαι in another situation of violence.

48. Cf. Schol. *ad loc.*, A. *Ag.* 595, 1118; Hdt. 4.189. L. Deubner, *Ololyge und Verwandtes* (*AbhBerl.* 1941, 1). An inscription from Pergamon mentions αὐλητρίς and ὀλολύκτρια as belonging to the sanctuary, *SIG*³ 982.25.

49. The altars depicted on vase paintings clearly show the traces of the αἱμάσσειν τοὺς βωμούς; cf., e.g., B. 11.111, Poll. 1.27, Eust. p.1476,41; ἀμνίον *Il.* 3.4444; σφαγεῖον Poll. 10.65.

50. Cf. Meuli 218, 256 f., 262; D.H. 7.72.15 ff. That there was some rule how to place the pieces on the altar is implied in εὐθετίσας Hes. *Th.* 541. The flute-player is often seen on vase paintings (*supra* n. 37); cf. Hdt. 1.132; Apollod. 3.15.7.4; παιωνίζειν, Sokolowski, *Lois sacrées de l'Asie Mineure* no. 24 а.34 (Erythrai); the Paian of Iphigeneia, E. *IA* 1468 ff. Flutes play the Καστόρειον μέλος when the Spartans slaughter the σφάγια before battle, *Xen. Lac. pol.* 13.8, *HG* 4.2.20; Plut. *Lyc.* 22.2.

51. Cf. Meuli 246 f., 268 ff. That the σπλάγχνα were roasted on the altar is shown by the name σπλαγχνόπτης (Plin. *NH* 22.44, 34.81) together with the pictorial tradition (Rizza [*supra* n. 37]). On συσπλαγχνεύειν cf. Ar. *Pax* 1115, Eup. fr. 108 (*CAF* I.286), Ath. 9.410b; σπλάγχνων μετουσία D.H. 1.40.4; D.C. 37.30.3.

52. Cato *Agr.* 50: *ubi daps profanata comestaque erit;* καθαγισάντων δὲ ταῦτα . . . Ath. 149c; on the exception, οὐ φορά, *supra* n. 36.

53. Cf. Deubner (*supra* n. 24) 158 ff. I cannot discuss here his somewhat hypercritical treatment of Porph. *Abst.* 2.29 f.; Meuli 275 f.

54. *Das sogenannte Böse. Zur Naturgeschichte der Aggression* (Vienna, 1963).

55. Freud (*supra* n. 34) immediately saw the connection with tragedy, *Ges. Schr.* 10.187f. A. Winterstein, *Der Ursprung der Tragödie* (Leipzig, 1925) was too dependent on Freud on the one hand, on the philologists on the other, to bring progress. On man "aping" beasts of prey, R. Eisler, *Man into Wolf* (New York, 1951). A. E. Jensen (*supra* n. 34) tries to understand the rites of killing as an expression of a "mythical perception" (mythische Erkenntnis) of a fundamental law of life: man cannot exist without destroying other living beings for food. In this respect, however, a symbolic way of expression ought to be sufficient, and Jensen is forced to assume that actual bloodshed is a depravation of a more sublime form of religion.

56. Cf. Meuli 225 f., 250 f.

57. ἐπὶ δὲ τῷ τεθυμένῳ τόδε μέλος A. *Eu.* 328 f., τεθυμένος ἐτύγχανεν Xen. *HG.* 5.1.18.

58. Theophrastus (Porph. *Abst.* 2.27=fr. 13 Pötscher) already assumed, like some modern anthropologists (E. M. Loeb, *The Blood Sacrifice Complex* [*Mem. Anthropol. Assn.* 30, 1923]), that sacrifice arose out of cannibalism. Pythagoreans sacrificed animals ἀνθ᾽ ἑαυτῶν Porph. *Abst.* 2.28, cf. *FGrHist* 752 F 1. On Abraham sacrificing Isaac (Gen. 22.13, cf. Lev. 17.11), see Robertson Smith (*supra* n. 34) 309 ff. Munichia: Zen.Athous 1.8 p. 350 Miller, Eust. p. 331.25= Paus. *Gr.* ed. Erbse ε 35. Luc. *SyrD.* 58 tells how people sacrificed children in Bambyke, shouting "they are calves"; Athamas kills Learchos "as a deer," Apollod. 3.4.3. The rite described at Ael. *NA* 12.34 explains sufficiently why Palaimon of Tenedos could be called βρεφοκτόνος Lyc. 229. At Salamis (Cyprus), the human sacrifices were replaced by βουθυσία Porph. *Abst.* 2.54, as among the Carthaginians at least temporarily, G. Charles-Picard, *Les religions de l'Afrique antique* (Paris, 1954) 491. Cf. *infra* nn. 59 and 66.

59. D.C. 43.24.4, connected with the *equus-October*-sacrifice by G. Wissowa, *Religion und Kultus der Römer*² (Munich, 1912) 421 n. 2. Bacchides, general of Antiochus IV, is said to have "sacrificed" prisoners, ἔθυσεν εἰς φρέαρ LXX 1 Macc. 7.19. On the analogies of capital punishment and sacrifice, K. v. Amira, *Die germanischen Todesstrafen* (*AbhMünchen.* 1922).

60. Sallust *Cat.* 22; D.C. 37.30.3.

61. That Dionysus is killed as a goat is a theory advanced esp. by Cook and Nilsson (*supra* n. 2). Dionysus is called Ἔριφος in Sparta (Hsch. εἰραφιώτης); in myth he was transformed into an ἔριφος (Apollod. 3.4.3); but ἔριφος is not τράγος (*supra* n. 27). The theory of the Eniautos-Daimon was developed by J. Harrison in cooperation with F. M. Cornford and G. Murray, in *Themis*² (Cambridge, 1927) 331 ff., 341 ff. It is accepted, with modifications, by Webster (128 f.; *BullInstClassStud.* 5 [1958] 43 ff.); criticism in Pickard-Cambridge, *Dith.*¹ 185ff.; Else, *Origin* 27 f. The oriental texts are interpreted according to the "seasonal pattern" by Th. Gaster, *Thespis*² (New York, 1961). In fact, ἐνιαυτός is rather seldom personified and never called δαίμων (cf. *RE* V [1905] 2568 f.); what is more important, the "seasonal" festivals seem to be a secondary interpretation, indeed the most harmless designation of older ritual. The exceptional fires lit in times of emergency ("Notfeuer," Jahn [*supra* n. 42], 34 f.) are more primitive than the annual fires; and the fires as well as the combat rites can take place in any time of the year: the rites are independent of the seasons. Of course man has always been apt to project his feelings into surrounding nature, and the invention of agriculture and the establishment of an annual calendar of festivals were to stress this interpretation. Still, the main problem for man is not winter, but man.

62. *Uter musti plenus* Euanthius p. 13.10 Wessner; Serv. Auct. *in Georg.* 2.380; Diom. p. 488. Another possibility of mock resurrection would be that one of the participants dresses in the skin of the victim and begins to dance. There is abundant evidence for such customs elsewhere (Meuli 242 n. 2), and it would be tempting to see the interrelation goat-satyr in this way, but there is no Greek evidence to support it. Martial explicitly states that the he-goat was castrated in the moment of slaughter, 3.24; in a similar way, the *equus October* had   33

its tail torn off (cf. H. Wagenvoort, *Serta philologica Aenopontana* [Innsbruck, 1962] 273 ff.). Whether this rite was always connected with the Dionysiac goat-sacrifice, we do not know.

63. Hdt. 2.39 f., 42; Tib. 1.2.28; cf. Robertson Smith (*supra* n. 34) 299 ff., 430 ff. In Siebenbürgen (Rumania), there was, down to the nineteenth century, a ceremony of pig-slaughter called "pig-memorial" (Schweinegedenkmal: H. v. Wlislocki, *Aus dem Volksleben der Magyaren* [Munich, 1893] 30), in which "sich der jüngste Ehemann auf den Fussboden und zwar auf den Bauch gekehrt und ausgestreckt niederlegt. Er darf kein Glied rühren . . . während die Hausfrau auf einem grossen Teller den gesottenen oder gebratenen, mit Tannengezweig und Immergrün umwundenen Schweinskopf ihm auf das Hinterhaupt setzt, worauf die Gesellschaft ihn wild stampfend und jubelnd umtanzt. Fällt der Teller dabei von seinem Haupte, so gibt dem daliegenden Genossen jeder der Gäste einige Hiebe"; cf. Ἰκάριοι τόθι πρῶτα περὶ τράγον ὠρχήσαντο. On the kommos in tragedy, cf. esp. Nilsson, *Opuscula* I.75 ff.

64. H. Huchzermeyer, *Aulos und Kithara in der griechischen Musik* (diss., Münster, 1930) 54ff.

65. Meuli 228: "Die Jäger des Kreises Turudansk bemalen sich das Gesicht mit Russ, dann kennt sie der Bär nicht." In Württemberg (Germany), pigs are slaughtered on Shrove Tuesday, and mummers break into the house and fetch their share of the freshly killed meat: *Handwörterbuch des deutschen Aberglaubens* VII (1935–36) 1083.

66. E. *El.* 785 ff., 816, 838. Clytaemestra, too, arrives for sacrifice, 1125; 1132, 1142; afterward Orestes says: κατηρξάμαν (1222); cf. Murray in Harrison (*supra* n. 61) 356. Neoptolemus in Delphi is killed when sacrificing, E. *Andr.* 1112 ff.; Pi. *N.* 7.42, *Pae.* 6.116 ff. Polyphontes in E. *Kresphontes* is killed on occasion of a sacrifice (Hygin. *Fab.* 137). Cf. the saga of Titus Tatius, D.H. 2.52.3. Perhaps it is no coincidence that the Scholion on Harmodios and Aristogeiton expressly states that their deed occurred Ἀθηναίης ἐν θυσίαις (*Carm.Pop.* 895 Page).

67. Cf. E. *HF* 451 (with Wilamowitz *ad loc.*): Megara, returning toward the altar that failed to protect her, asks for the ἱερεύς, the σφαγεύς. Herakles himself is to accomplish the sacrifice (922 ff.; θῦμα 995), cf. *infra* n. 69. S. *El.* 1422 f.: φοινία δὲ χεὶρ στάζει θυηλῆς Ἄρεος . . . The metaphorical use of θύειν is found once in Pi., fr. 78, never in the earlier lyrics; it is common then in Timotheus (*Pers.* 29; cf. fr. 783 Page) and Philoxenus (fr. 823 Page), cf. Schol. A. *in Il.* 9.219. On βακχεύειν see A. *Septem* 498, E. *Hec.* 1077, *HF* 1119, *Or.* 1493. Orestes as *gravis sacerdos*, Accius *Erigone* fr. 55 Ribbeck.

68. This is completely overlooked by Else, who writes (*Origin* 63): "The regular source of tragic material is heroic epic, not religious cult." Of course the tragic poets drew on the epic, Stesichorus et al., but they saw them through the medium of their experience of Greek religious life, in which a hero was not a purely literary figure. It would lead too far, though it would not be impossible, to investigate the ritual of destruction in the case of Eteocles and Polyneices, of Aias, Antigone, or King Oedipus. It is significant, however, that even those plays of Euripides which seem to foreshadow Menander have as their climax a sacrifice: *Hel.* 1554 ff., *Ion* 1124 ff. R. Merkelbach drew my attention to the only surviving drama of the Maya: *Der Mann von Rabinal, oder Der Tod des Gefangenen, Tanzspiel der Maya-Quiché*, trans. and intr. by E. W. Palm (Frankfurt, 1961): here the whole play is an ἄρχεσθαι for the human sacrifice that forms its conclusion.

69. On the site of Mount Oeta, M. P. Nilsson *ArchRW.* 21 (1922) 310 ff.=*Opuscula* I (Lund, 1951) 348 ff.; Y. Béquignon, *La vallée du Spercheios* (Paris, 1937) 204 ff.; the main testimony: Schol. T *in Il.* 22.159 καὶ νῦν Οἰταῖοι Ἡρακλεῖ πεντετήριον ἀγῶνα ποιοῦντες βύρσας διδόασιν (to the victorious athletes); βύρσα usually is "oxhide" (the passage in Homer has βοείην), which presupposes βουθυσία. On Cape Cenaeum there was an altar of Zeus said to be founded by Herakles, S. *Tr.* 752 f., Apollod. 2.7.7.7. On earlier testimonies for

the myth, cf. S. G. Kapsomenos, *Sophokles' Trachinierinnen und ihr Vorbild* (Athens, 1963) 1 ff. Many vase paintings show Herakles as a θυτήρ, cf. Rizza (*supra* n. 37); sometimes he is represented in a "new garment," not in the lion-skin, holding a cantharus (e.g., Berlin 3232=*ARV*² 117,2), but the presence of a satyr makes it difficult to find here the event of Cape Cenaeum. In Sophocles, Hyllos is forced to sacrifice his father (1192); the Theban myth presents the reversal of the situation, Herakles burning his sons (Pherecydes, *FGrHist* 3 F 14, Apollod. 2.4.12). Pindar describes the pyre of the corresponding festival, "blazing up to the sky throughout the night" (*I.* 4.67 ff.).

70. Cf. sacrificial regulations as γυναικὶ οὐ θέμις, ξένῳ οὐ θέμις *SIG*³ 1024.9,27; Sokolowski, *Lois sacrées des cités grecques* nos. 63, 66; E. *IT* 1226 ff. Pohlenz (I.256, II.105) failed to understand the ritual language of Medea 1053 ff.; cf. the commentary of D. L. Page (Oxford, 1938) ad loc., who, however, thinks the words to be "simply a macabre metaphor." The three vase paintings (Paris Cab.d.Méd. 876; Louvre K 300; Munich 3296; see F. Brommer, *Vasenlisten zur griechischen Heldensage*² [Marburg, 1960] 349) are reproduced in L. Séchan, *Etudes sur la tragédie grecque dans ses rapports avec la céramique* (Paris, 1926) 403 f. and pl. 8.

71. On the Corinthian rite see M. P. Nilsson, *Griechische Feste* (Leipzig, 1906) 58, who, however, does not quote the most important sources: Phot. ed. Reitzenstein, *s.v.* αἰγὸς τρόπον, Zen.Athous 2.30 p. 361.12 ff. Miller (abridged in *App.Prov.* 4.16; by mistake, Zenobius and *Appendix Proverbiorum* have οἷς instead of αἴξ); Markellos in Eus. *Adv.Marc.* 1.3 (ed. Klostermann [Berlin, 1906] fr. 125). Markellos says: φασὶν γὰρ Μήδειαν ἐν Κορίνθῳ τὰ τέκνα ἀποκτείνασαν κατακρύψαι τὴν μάχαιραν αὐτόθι· τοὺς δὲ Κορινθίους κατὰ χρησμὸν αὐτοῖς δοθέντα αἶγα μέλαιναν ἐναγίζοντας ἀπορεῖν μαχαίρας· τὴν δὲ αἶγα σκάλλουσαν τῷ ποδὶ τὴν Μηδείας ἀνευρεῖν μάχαιραν. Zenobios has substantially the same but is more explicit on the rite: . . . οἱ δὲ Κορίνθιοι θύοντες ἀνὰ πᾶν ἔτος διὰ ζ' ἠιθέων καὶ παρθένων ὡσαύτως ζ' κρύπτουσι τὸ ξίφος ἐν τῷ ἱερῷ· τοῦ δὲ ἔτους περιελθόντος οἱ κληρωθέντες νέοι θύουσιν, ἡ δὲ οἷς . . . ἀνιχνεύει τὸ ξίφος. The "comedy of innocence" is particularly apparent in Photios: οἱ τὴν παροχὴν μεμισθωμένοι γῇ κρύψαντες τὴν μάχαιραν ἐσκήπτοντο ἐπιλελῆσθαι. . . . (=Paus. *Gr.* ed. Erbse η 2) . . . μετὰ τὸ ἐναγίσαι τὴν μάχαιραν ἀποκρύπτουσι, τῷ δὲ ἐξῆς ἔτει τὸ μέλλον πάλιν ἐναγίζεσθαι ἱερεῖον . . . (=Paus. *Gr.* ed. Erbse α 42; cf. Zen. *Par.* 1.27, Hsch. *s.v.* αἲξ αἴγα, Suda αι 235 etc.). It is not quite clear whether the knife was left in the soil for the whole year or removed and rehidden in secret, but this does not make any difference for the meaning of the rite. The fate of the goat was proverbial, Com.adesp. fr. 47 Demianczuk, Klearchos fr. 83a Wehrli; the anecdote was even transmitted to Arabs and Indians, S. Fraenkel, *ZDMG* 46 (1892) 737 ff.; R. Pischel, *ZDMG* 47 (1893) 86 ff. Besides the paroemiographers, the main testimony on the Corinthian rite is Parmeniskos in Schol. *in* E. *Med.* 264; black garments: Paus. 2.3.7. That Medea, though inadvertently, killed her own children in the temple of Hera Akraia was already in Eumelos (Paus. 2.3.11); as it seemed strange that the Corinthians should atone for Medea's crime, the myth was altered to make the Corinthians the murderers of the children. On the connection with initiation rites, A. Brelich, *Studi e materiali di storia delle religioni* 30 (1959) 227 ff. Cf. also G. Dobesch, *Wst.* 75 (1962) 83–89.

72. On θῦμα λεύσιμον see E. Fraenkel (Oxford, 1950) ad loc.; but he does not quote the decisive parallel from sacrificial ritual, the sacrifice to Dionysus in Tenedus, Ael. *NA* 12.34: ὅ γε μὴν πατάξας αὐτὸ (the calf) τῷ τελέκει λίθοις βάλλεται τῇ ὁσίᾳ καὶ ἔστε ἐπὶ τὴν θάλατταν φεύγει. Cf. the *aition* for the bull-sacrifice in Lindos, Philostr. *Im.* 2.24; the rite of mummification, D.S. 1.91; *infra* n. 74.

73. Aeschylus associates the net with fishing, 1382, 1432, but ἄγρευμα θηρός *Ch.* 998; the crater Boston 63.1246 (E. Vermeule, *AJA* 70 [1966] 1 ff., pl. 1–3) depicts it as a kind of Coan garment. On A. *Ag.* 1127 cf. Fraenkel's discussion.

74. On the cults performed in the Heraion, see Ch. Waldstein, *The Argive Heraeum* I (Boston, 1902) 1 ff.; Nilsson (*supra* n. 71) 42 ff. The myths were told at least in four different ways already in the old epics—Danais, Phoronis, Aigimios, Hesiodean Catalogues; cf. E. Meyer, *Forschungen zur alten Geschichte* I (Halle, 1892) 67 ff. The connection with Egypt may, however, be much older than Meyer argued, cf. Astour (*supra* n. 30) 80 ff., and T. T. Duke, *CJ* 61 (1965) 134. "Euboia," Paus. 2.17.1; sacred cowherds, Schol. *in* Pi. *N.* pp. 3 f. Drachmann; Argos and Io in the sanctuary, Apollod. 2.1.3; Zeus transformed into a bull, A. *Supp.* 301; Epaphos=Apis, Hdt. 2.153, Meyer (*supra*) 78;=Apopi "Bull," Duke (*supra*); Argos clad in oxskin, Apollod. 2.1.2, Schol. *in* E. *Ph.* 1116, vase paintings, e.g., *ABV* 148,2=Cook III.632, *ARV*² 579,84=Cook III.633, *ARV*² 1409,9=Cook I.460. Genealogists contrasted Argos the king to Argos Panoptes, though they differed considerably as to the relationship of the two Argoi (Hes. in Apollod. 2.1.3.3; Pherekydes, *FGrHist* 3 F 66/67 with Jacoby's commentary). Argos the king clearly is the secondary figure (cf. Meyer [*supra*] 90), the cult devoted to Argos (Varro in Aug. *Civ.* 18.6) must therefore originally have dealt with the Panoptes. Ζεὺς πανόπτης A. *Eu.* 1045, cf. Preller and Robert I (*supra* n. 36) 396 n. 1. Meyer thought there was no answer to the question "wie soll man es erklären, dass er (Argos), also ursprünglich Zeus, von Hermes erschlagen wird?" (*supra* 72 n. 1). On the death of the aboriginal king, cf. *Historia* 11 (1962) 365 ff. Hermes is called βουφόνος *Hymn.Merc.* 436. The symbolic lapidation of Hermes for slaying Argos: Xanthos, *FGrHist* 765 F 29, Antikleides, *FGrHist* 140 F 19, Eust. p. 1809.38 ff. Varro (Aug. *Civ.* 18.6, from *De gente populi Romani*; Varro, *RR* 2.5.4) mentions an Argive hero "Homogyros" (changed to "bomagiros" by Wilamowitz in the edition of Varro *RR* by G. Goetz [Leipzig, 1912], but he overlooked the parallel passage in Augustine), equivalent to the Athenian Buzyges, slain by the thunderbolt. Could his name mean "he who leads the bull round the altar" (cf. *supra*, nn. 37 and 44) in an Argive Buphonia-ritual?

2

THE LEGEND OF KEKROPS'S DAUGHTERS
AND THE ARRHEPHORIA: FROM INITIATION
RITUAL TO PANATHENAIC FESTIVAL

Anyone who ascends the zigzag path to the Athenian Acropolis and observes the unfolding play of shapes—the radiant marble structures, columns, and entablatures as they seem to glide together and apart—cannot fail to be moved by the mystery of the Classical period in Greece: a singular triumph that we can only accept and consider astounding. As soon as we try to delve into the details, however, to comprehend all that can still be comprehended and assimilate it, our pleasure suddenly turns into bewilderment. What a mass of primitive, dark, incomprehensible—or barely comprehensible—material confronts the modern observer! There is riddle after riddle: Sacred Pelasgian walls and the Erechtheion cult monument, the armed virgin and the snake, centaurs and triple-bodied monsters, autochthonous birth and birth from the head of Zeus. Yet both aspects, the primitive/alien as well as the Classical, must stand in a necessary relationship to one another, which does not mean that one simply followed the other as though by chance, but that the magnificent developments of later times were founded upon the vitality of the earlier period, as the blossom lives from the root. If one wishes to investigate these relationships, every bit of ancient evidence about the cults, rites, and myths of the Acropolis becomes meaningful. In this way, occasionally, significant links become apparent.

In his description of the Acropolis, directly following the account of the Erechtheion with its altar of Poseidon-Erechtheus, its *xoanon*, the archaic wooden statue, also the golden lamp of Athena, its precinct of Pandrosos and the sacred olive tree, Pausanias tells us:

> what I found most amazing is something not altogether comprehensible, but still I will describe how it works: two maidens live not far from the temple of Athena Polias; the Athenians call them Arrhephoroi. For a certain time they live their particular mode of

37

life together with the goddess. But when the festival comes round, they perform the following rites during the night. They put on their heads what Athena's priestess gives them to carry, and neither she who gives it nor they who carry it know what she gives them. Not far away in the city is the sacred precinct of "Aphrodite in the Gardens," with a natural entrance heading underground: this is where the virgin girls descend. They deposit there what they were carrying and take something else and bring it back covered up. They are then sent away, and other virgins are brought to the Acropolis instead. (1.27.3)[1]

The language of the text is clear, except for the question of whether the genitive τῆς καλουμένης ἐν Κήποις Ἀφροδίτης depends on περίβολος or οὐ πόρρω. This is connected with the topographical problem that the well-known sanctuary of "Aphrodite in the Gardens" is not located *en tēi polei,* but outside the city along the banks of the Ilissos. The decisive evidence in this regard was provided by the American excavations that were carried out on the northern slope of the Acropolis in the 1930s. Below the Erechtheion, and somewhat east, Oscar Broneer discovered a sanctuary of Eros and Aphrodite, securely identified through votive offerings and inscriptions. He at once made the connection with the *peribolos en tēi polei,* the enclosed precinct in the city mentioned by Pausanias. The precinct ends in a crevice. Since that time, archaeologists have also confidently identified the remains of a substantial building west of the Erechtheion along the northern wall of the Acropolis as the house of the Arrhephoroi. In the courtyard of this building is a shaft with stairs leading down at a steep angle. The technically very difficult excavation of this shaft in the year 1938 showed that a well had been tapped here in the thirteenth century B.C.—the survival of the Athenian polis presumably rested on this well in the crisis years when the Sea People and the Dorians invaded. The well was shut off in the twelfth century, but the stairs were renovated during this period, probably to accommodate the very cultic procedures described by Pausanias. The stairs end in a grotto below the house of the Arrhephoroi, commonly known as the Grotto of Aglauros. From there one can easily reach the precinct of Aphrodite. We can thus follow the path of the Arrhephoroi virtually step by step. Indeed, we can date the introduction of the rite with some probability to the twelfth century B.C. The old assessment that Pausanias's "description was deliberately obscure and at times much confused"[2] can no longer be accepted. The account is obscure only inasmuch as Pausanias offers no explanation of what he describes. His usual sources seem to have failed him in this instance; hence his statement, *ouk es hapanta gnōrima* (not altogether comprehensible). This is fortunate for us, however, since we are left with a straightforward description of the *drōmenon*, the "ritual," without the customary explanations in terms of myth or nature-allegory. The question of whether Pausanias himself or an earlier author witnessed the ritual is less important.

We are able to supplement Pausanias's account on certain points, even though our sources for the Arrhephoroi and their festival do not exactly flood us with information.[3] In Aristophanes' *Lysistrata* the women boast of their accomplishments on behalf of the city. At the top of the list (641), we find the following: "As soon as I was seven, I was *Arrhephoros*." This was thus an important duty for a girl to perform on behalf of the state. A client of Lysias (21.5) mentions among his public offices *architheōria kai Arrhēphoria kai alla toiauta* (chief of a sacred embassy, the procession of Arrhephoroi, and other such things). The title of one of Menander's comedies is *Arrhēphoros ē Aulētris* (The Arrhephoros or the Flute Girl). And Deinarchos, too, mentions *arrhēphorein* (serving as Arrhephoros) in a lost speech (fr. 6.4 B.-S.=Harpocr. *s.v.*). There were extended accounts in the Atthidographers and in Callimachus's *Hekale*; a few details survive in the literature of the Scholia and lexika: four girls from prominent families would be "chosen," presumably by the people—*echeirotonounto*; two of these were then selected, and they began the job of weaving the peplos that was bestowed on Athena at the Panathenaia.[4] The Suda preserves the technical expression: *ho basileus epiōpsato arrhēphorous* (the king selected the Arrhephoroi). By Classical times the word *epiopsasthai*, which appears in Homer in secular contexts (*Il.* 9.167, *Od.* 2.294), came to be used exclusively in Attic sacral terminology.[5] It refers to the supervision of sacred offices, a right of the king and hierophant, vested in them by divine authority. In Harpocration *ekrinonto* (they were selected), not *echeirotonounto*, corresponds to *epiopsasthai*, and the authoritative power of *epiopsasthai* suggests that the position was first created through this act: not "he selected among existing Arrhephoroi," but "he chose to serve as Arrhephoroi." One thinks of the *captio* of the *virgo vestalis*. The juxtaposition of *cheirotonein* and *epiopsasthai*, is understandable, even necessary so as to balance out democracy and sacral kingship. Two Arrhephoroi were appointed, then, not four as Deubner thought[6] (two, according to him, for the secret nocturnal rites, two to work on the peplos); and *epiopsasthai* does not mean merely assigning previously selected personnel to different jobs. Pausanias states explicitly that two maidens live on the Acropolis, "and the Athenians call them Arrhephoroi." It is hard to imagine that two other maidens worked on the peplos somewhere else in Athens, who also happened to be called Arrhephoroi. In what follows, the evidence shows that the work on the peplos and the secret rites are not unrelated, but that they cohere inseparably.

Further, the girls ranged in age from seven to eleven—the lexika supplement the details in Aristophanes. Their first task was to begin weaving the peplos. The solemn beginning of the weaving occurred at the festival of the Chalkeia on the thirtieth of the month Puanopsion, some nine months before the Panathenaia.[7] Many Athenian women probably took part in weaving the elaborate peplos, but the solemn beginning, the *diazesthai* (beginning the web) was the job of the priestess of Athena and the two Arrhephoroi. At the latest, then, they were appointed in autumn and so lived on the Acropolis for almost eight months. For according to the testimony of the Etymologica, the Arrhephoria festival occurred in Skirophorion, the last month of the Attic year.[8] Thereafter, or perhaps in connection with the rites described by Pausanias, the Arrhephoroi set aside their white robes and returned their gold jewelry to the goddess, for their duties had ended.

A further source of information, indeed a primary source, is provided by an extensive group of votive inscriptions from the Acropolis,[9] dating from the third century B.C. through the second century A.D. These appear on the bases of small statues, and the inscriptions tell us that parents dedicated an image of their daughter to Athena Polias, after she had been *errhēphoros*, θυγατέρα ἐρρηφορήσασαν ἀνέθεσαν. The spelling is regularly *errhēphorēsasan*—we are dealing with seventeen inscriptions of the same type, ten of which still have the initial letter epsilon. Besides these there are two inscriptions from Imperial times, in which we find *arrhēphorēsasan* or *arrhēphoron*. In addition, an Arrhephoros is attested at the festival of the Epidauria, while an inscription of Imperial date on a seat in the theater of Dionysos cites "two *ersēphoroi* of Chloē, daughter of Themis," ἐρσηφόροι β᾽ Χλόης Θέμιδος, and "two *ersēphoroi* of Eileithyia in Agrai," ἐρσηφόροι β᾽ Εἰλειθυίας ἐν Ἄγραις. Are *errhēphoroi* and *Arrhēphoroi* one and the same? One would surely answer yes, were it not that a scholar of the stature of Ludwig Deubner took great pains to keep them distinct. Yet his arguments do not hold water, indeed they are remarkably weak. There is a misinterpretation right at the outset, and after that come *argumenta ex silentio*.

Deubner claims, "First of all, the ancient grammarians separate the Arrhephoria from another festival, the Hersephoria" (13, "Zunächst

scheiden die alten Grammatiker von den Arrhephoria eine zweite Begeh-
ung, die Hersephoria"). But upon examining the testimony, the Etymologica and the Scholia to Aristophanes, one finds it clearly stated that the same
subject matter, the same festival, "is also called *Errhēphoria,*" that "some"
write the word with α, "others" with ε (see below, p. 55, n. 8). Corresponding to the two linguistic forms that designate the same thing are two "ety-
mologies": Arrhephoria from *arrhēta pherein,* and *Errhēphoria,* "in honor
of Herse, the daughter of Kekrops"—this latter explanation is attributed
to Istros. The two etiologies are by no means mutually exclusive; perhaps
there was cause to "carry secret objects" "in honor of Herse." Deubner's
additional arguments are even less conclusive, based as they are on the idea
that what is attested for Arrhephoria is not certain for Errhephoria, and
vice versa; our sources are meager enough as is. Deubner was unable to
convince Nilsson.[10] And we, too, may confidently view the statue bases on
the Acropolis as direct evidence for the life of those girls who, as Pausanias
describes them, lived for a time on the citadel, until their duties came to
so mysterious an end. We must exercise greater caution, however, in dealing with the suggestion that at least some of the archaic korai from the
Acropolis should be seen as statues of Arrhephoroi; likewise the old suggestion that the basket-, or *kistai*-bearing korai from the Karyatid-porch of
the Erechtheion may be Arrhephoroi is certainly most appealing but cannot
be directly proven.[11]

Any attempt to understand this custom necessarily means coming to
grips with Ludwig Deubner's basic study of the festivals of Athens (see
p. 55, n. 3). And if we cannot resist polemics, we must nonetheless empha-
size that our entire undertaking is only possible because generations of
scholars of the highest rank, including Ludwig Deubner, collected the evidence and presented it with the greatest care. Gratitude is thus the first
item on the agenda. Nor should we regard older interpretations as obsolete
simply because they are old. If we dare to refute Deubner's interpretations
and replace them with others, then we do so only because we can show that
Deubner's theory does not fully explain the evidence he himself collected,
indeed that it sometimes even does it violence, while another interpretation
thoroughly illuminates the source material both in its inner structure and
in the ramifications of seemingly secondary details. This will not require
less work, and scarcely the free play of imagination in place of attention to
detail; what we offer is, on the contrary, more precise.

Ludwig Deubner adopted an interpretation that Rutgers van der Loeff
had presented in 1916.[12] It was based on a Scholion to Lucian, which explains   41

the Thesmophoria and, in the process, describes the festival as analogous to (*echei ton auton logon* . . .) or identical with (*ta de auta* . . .) the Arrhetophoria [*sic*] and Skirophoria. The Scholion's source was evidently known to Clement of Alexandria, who likewise cites these three festivals in the same breath. The Scholion presents us, then, with a problem: Do the details it sets out all relate to the Thesmophoria, or do they also refer to rituals of the Skirophoria and Arrhe(to)phoria? But that problem cannot be dealt with here, since we would have to discuss the entire ritual of the Thesmophoria and Skirophoria along with it. Suffice it to say that if we take the Scholion to Lucian as our basis there will be an uncertainty right from the start. In any case it is clear that the bulk of the Scholion has to do with the Thesmophoria: it is keyed to the word *Thesmophoria* in Lucian, and the strange custom of *megarizein* is part of Thesmophoria festivals outside of Athens as well: female piglets, *choiroi,* are tossed into subterranean caves or chambers, *megara;* their remains are later brought back to the surface and mixed in together with the seed grain. Similarly, phalluses, pastry snakes, and also pinecones are thrown into the *megara.* The crude, unsavory aspect of what is evidently agrarian magic had long fascinated scholars of religion,[13] and they now extended this interpretation from the Thesmophoria to the supposedly analogous Arrhephoria. To be sure, the testimony of the Lexika located the Arrhephoria in the month of Skirophorion, which did not fit with the sowing—that came four months later in Puanopsion, the month of the Thesmophoria. Consequently, one had to posit two Arrhephorias, the one in Skirophorion, the other in Puanopsion— although two festivals of the same name was a most impractical novelty that could only lead to confusion. According to Deubner, secret objects were conveyed underground at the Arrhephoria in the month Skirophorion, while they would be brought back to the surface four months later at the Arrhephoria in Puanopsion. The only question was which of the two Arrhephoria festivals Pausanias referred to. Deubner decided it was the autumn festival because the process of bringing the objects to the surface, which Pausanias also discusses, "would have no apparent purpose" (11) in summer. Of course, according to Pausanias, the Arrhephoroi first and foremost carry something downward; Deubner explained this somewhat vaguely as a "substitute sacrifice." He said nothing more about Pausanias's clear emphasis on what is handed over and carried below at nighttime down the steep path, through the precinct of Aphrodite; nor did it bother him that Pausanias, just like the Etymologica, refers only to *one* festival, *hē*

hēortē. The texts were here made to fit the theory, rather than the other way around: the scholar liberated himself from the evidence. Two festivals sprang up out of one, transporting us from summer into fall: the *megara* of the Thesmophoria swallowed up the Arrhephoria in their insatiable maw; nothing remained but crude fertility magic. And what was the theory's foundation? The speculation of an ancient scholar who asserted the essential identity of three Attic cults on the basis of a *logos muthikos*, the myth of Demeter, which accompanies the Thesmophoria, and a *logos phusikos*, the fertility of earth and humankind.

It was obviously not the weight of the evidence that was decisive here, but the interpretive theory, which could thus find clear expression: What, the theory asks, ultimately underlies the celebration of festivals in the city of Athens? Its answer: Agrarian magic, the manipulation of beneficent powers and harmful powers, beneficent substances and harmful substances. During the summer, "one's efforts are doubtless aimed primarily at supplying new creative power to the exhausted earth by means of fertility symbols" (11), and in fall, "those things that had absorbed the earth's powers of fertility deep in the ground, must now be mixed with the seed grain and so guarantee a rich harvest" (10). Thus there was always a clear purpose, the harvest, which people strove toward in a reasonable and systematic manner; unfortunately of course the ancient Athenians were poorly informed about agricultural chemistry and fertilizers, so they tried to use "beneficent powers" instead of nitrogen and phosphates, and thus the office of the Arrhephoroi "was created for the performance of secret rituals" (12). We do not need to show in detail how disembodied and abstract, and thus how essentially modern this "concept of fertility" is: that which fructifies the exhausted earth is itself supposed to have absorbed the earth's powers of fertility, so that it can thereupon fructify the earth. . . . The ancient evidence is twisted in yet one further respect: according to the Scholion, the issue is the fertility of both earth and humankind, "the genesis of crops," *karpōn genesis*, and "procreation of men," *anthrōpōn spora;* for Deubner the only issue was the harvest.

Our purpose is not to ridicule and caricature, but quite simply to establish that the core of Deubner's interpretation—the duplication of the festival and thus its connection with the sowing—is completely unfounded, indeed that it contradicts the wording of the sources. And this despite the fact that Deubner only explains one isolated bit out of the entire complex, Arrhephoroi. Why use girls, aged seven to eleven? "Innocent children were favored for performing important rites, as their undefiled status seemed to guarantee the success of ceremonies deemed to be magical" (12). Could one, 43 therefore, just as well have chosen six-year-old boys? And what is meant by the "undefiled status" of children in ancient Greece? Why does Pausanias specify maidens, *parthenoi*? Further, why must they begin the work on the peplos? Here Deubner offers a historical explanation: the presentation of the peplos was first introduced when the Panathenaia were reformed in 566 (12; 30); the office of the Arrhephoroi was "originally" created for secret rites; later, however, "two other girls bearing the same title were designated for work on the peplos" because "the participation of innocent girls was pleasing to the goddess." It was thus a more or less serendipitous idea that the Arrhephoroi could do something else for a change—that, although there is no mention of "participation," only of a "beginning," *diazesthai* (beginning the web): here too Deubner is imprecise, quite apart from the fact, established above, that the same two Arrhephoroi who performed the secret rites also worked on the peplos. Finally, why did the Arrhephoroi live for at least seven months on the citadel? Are those beneficent powers for the exhausted earth to be found on the barren rocks of the Acropolis, of all places? There is nothing on this in Deubner.

Yet one passage in Deubner's account suggests something different, though it is almost illegitimate from the perspective of his theory, and in any case superfluous: "Out of the secret rites arose the story of the basket of Erichthonios, which the daughters of Kekrops were not supposed to open. In it we find a reflection of that implement which was carried by the Arrhephoroi" (11). We have a myth, then, that is intimately tied to the ritual. To be sure, Deubner tempered his suggestion as much as possible: the myth "arose from the rites," i.e., it was secondary—Jane Harrison brashly spoke of a "foolish myth."[14] Deubner referred in a note to Charles Picard's assumption that the myth of Erichthonios was an imitation of Eleusinian material, "made up for the sake of competition."[15] Once again there was a "clear purpose," in the myth as in the ritual. First, rituals were invented for the sake of fertility, then myths were made up in addition, as propaganda.

Now we cannot possibly address here the whole problem of the relationship of myth and cult. Yet matters of principle notwithstanding, we can assert from the outset that no matter how secondary it may be, even an etiological myth provides us with precious evidence, not just because it tells us what Greeks of historical times were actually thinking in connection with their cults, but above all because it can inform us—through the detour of a possibly fictitious etiology—about actual rituals performed in real life. In its narrative rhythm, myth—and etiological myth in particular—may

44

reflect the sequence of ritual, thereby revealing relationships where anti-quarian learning offers us only *disiecta membra*. Indeed, myth is the oldest form of talk about religion; scholarly/antiquarian accounts of cult come much later. We can state with Angelo Brelich[16] that no Greek festival can be understood without its accompanying myth.

And in fact, the myth of Kekrops's daughters[17] strikingly corresponds to the rites of the Arrhephoroi, down to the smallest details—except, it seems, for the numbers: Kekrops had *three* daughters: Aglauros, Herse, and Pandrosos. We are dealing here with myths of origin: Kekrops, sprung from the earth, half man, half snake, appears in all Attic genealogies as the very first king of Attica—he is in effect what existed before the first man.

The daughters of Kekrops grew up in their father's house, the royal palace on the Acropolis. The Athenians knew, of course, and archaeology has confirmed, that the "house of Erechtheus" (the Erechtheion) replaced the old royal palace, or rather continued it; the Arrhephoroi lived right next door. There were tales of how the daughters of Kekrops danced along the northern slope of the Acropolis (E. *Ion* 497); and we know from a chance reference (Plut. *Vit.* X or. 839c) that the Arrhephoroi had their own court for playing ball, *sphairistra*. In addition to play there was work: we read in Photius that Pandrosos "together with her sisters was the first to make clothes of wool for people"[18]—the Arrhephoroi, for their part, began the work on the sacred peplos; thus they repeated that primeval cultural begin-ning attributed to the daughters of Kekrops. Then came the turning point, the reason why the tale of Kekrops's daughters continued to be told: Athena gave the sisters a round basket, a *kistē*, with a strict warning never to open it. It is called "sacred basket," *hierē kistē*, in Euphorion (fr. 9 Powell, cf. Callim. fr. 260.29 Pf.); what the Arrhephoroi carry on their heads, and what the priestess of Athena gave them, is described as a *kistē* in the Scholia. Yet only Pandrosos obeyed the goddess. In the course of the night Aglauros and Herse opened the *kistē*. A fragment of Euphorion[19] shows that the lamp of Athena, which lit her temple with an eternal flame, was involved here: did it fall to the ground? Did something *from* the lamp—for instance, oil—spill on the ground? Did the light go out? In any case, as they opened the *kistē*, the sisters saw the child Erichthonios inside, and beside him a snake—occasionally two snakes are mentioned.[20] The virgins leaped away in ter-ror—a Late Archaic cup by the Brygos Painter in Frankfurt shows the horri-fied maidens pursued by an enormous snake (ca. 480 B.C.). They leaped to their deaths down the steep northern slope of the Acropolis.

The path of the Arrhephoroi was not quite as dramatic, but its meaning 45 was the same: they carried their *kistai* at night along the steep stairway down the northern slope of the Acropolis and then went underground like the dead: *kathodos hupogaios*—their duties thus were ended. Pandrosos remained forever on the citadel; that is where her precinct is, next to the sacred olive tree. Farther east on the slopes lay the sanctuary of Aglauros, where their death was commemorated; there also the ephebes took their oaths.[21] Scholars have searched in vain for a sanctuary of Herse. But the non-Attic form of her name shows that it is connected with literature, not with Attic cult. But the literary may be significant, too: according to Ovid (*Met.* 2.739), Herse lived between Pandrosos and Aglauros—just so the path of the Arrhephoroi (who were also etymologized as *ersēphoroi* [dew bearers]) stays between those of Pandrosos and Aglauros. Cult and myth illuminate each other reciprocally.[22] We saw that as an interpretive vehicle, fertility magic could only explain an isolated part of the Arrephoria. Here, however, the correspondence is complete: from living on the citadel, and working on the peplos, through the nocturnal crisis to the end.

At this point one cannot help thinking of another interpretive approach for the entire complex, one already proposed by Jeanmaire and Brelich:[23] that we are dealing with an initiation ritual, a passage from childhood to adulthood, or puberty rite. Initiation rituals have been studied in detail for a long time. Usually the focus has been on ceremonies for boys, and yet those for girls are no less important. Our purpose here, though, is not to pile up comparative evidence, but simply to acknowledge that there are rituals marking the passage from childhood to adulthood the world over, and to be aware of what they mean: wherever they occur, initiation rituals are a tribe's most important celebration, an individual's decisive experience. For by means of these the community regenerates itself—nothing less. Even quite simple social and cultural institutions can endure beyond the span of a single lifetime only if they succeed in transmitting themselves to the next generation. Only those social forms survive over the course of generations that leave a lasting impression on the rising generation, indeed that are burned into them like an indelible stamp—it is well-known how violent and gruesome primitive initiation rituals can be. Before literacy, before written contracts and laws, or a bureaucracy to administer communal life—and people lived together for hundreds of thousands of years before such things were invented some five thousand years ago—the necessary social order had to be stamped into the soul, even if it is the subconscious, instinctive aspect of the soul. Initiation rituals are the chief agents of this task. With the advent of literacy and urban culture, they recede and ultimately disappear—

though they have done so completely only in our present atomized society. The Greeks were still close to that primeval form of life that preceded literacy and urban culture.

Van Gennep established a threefold rhythm of initiation ritual, and indeed of *rites de passage* generally: separation from one's prior community, life in isolation (*en marge*), reintegration into the new community. A youth or maiden is torn away from its child's world, lives for a time in an abnormal state in isolation, in the bush or jungle or initiation house in the midst of the community, so as ultimately to be integrated into the community as a full adult member. In most places, the transition to a new status in life is shaped by means of extremely powerful symbolism: death and rebirth. The child dies, a new person emerges. In this context, a girl's initiation necessarily comprises two separate areas: on the one hand, she must learn to do women's work; spinning and weaving are the preeminent *erga gunaikōn.* On the other hand, she will take on the duties of wife and mother. In addition to child care, then, initiation involves an encounter with Eros, for which ethnologists are able to document everything from the crudest orgies to the most transcendent symbolism. This aspect of the ritual should neither receive excessive attention nor be prudishly set aside. It is equally important to carry on the work civilization has entrusted to humankind, and to bring new life to the world. If either is neglected, the society will die. The meaning of initiation rituals is thus self-evident both in their basic structure and in the individual forms they adopt. That is how they must have developed, and not otherwise, since primordial times according to the rhythm of life and the succession of generations. We are not chiefly concerned here with the beliefs or conceptions of a more or less primitive people; whether they believe in beneficient powers or dead souls, spirits or gods. What actually happens is the crucial thing. The rising generation must be molded in their elders' ways, and the elders must make room for the children. Otherwise, the social order dies out, as though it had never existed.

If one regards the rites of the Arrhephoroi, with their reflection in the myth of the daughters of Kekrops, as an initiation ritual for girls, then the whole thing becomes transparent, meaningful, and necessary from beginning to end. First came the separation from the house of their parents; the authoritative "selection," *epiopsasthai,* by the *basileus* tore the girls away from their child's world. To be sure, we may consider the years from seven to eleven to be a rather tender age. But the seventh year marks an important stage of life; Theseus is supposed to have abducted Helen when she was seven, and to have kept her at Aphidnai;[24] in Rome the age of betrothal was

47

seven, that of legal marriage twelve. The Arrhephoroi lived isolated on the citadel. Pausanias's use of the word *diaita*, "way of living," suggests special taboos in their lifestyle, rules about food and clothing, as are found in all initiations. A special regulation is usually needed so candidates for initiation can be supplied with food by official food carriers—in Athens there was a *deipnophoria*, a solemn procession with meat offerings for Aglauros, Herse, and Pandrosos (Ann. Bekk. I 239.7).[25] The Arrhephoroi began the work on the peplos, just as the daughters of Kekrops wove the first clothing: through their introduction to adult work, the candidates reenacted the beginnings of culture altogether; hence the designation *initia*, "initiation." After this came the *kistē* that was carried through the precinct of Aphrodite at night: no doubt this was the symbolic form given to that second aspect, the encounter with Eros. It is especially significant that the path of the Arrhephoroi originally led to a well.[26] In this encounter the virgin died and a young woman emerged. The myth tells us that the royal child Erichthonios was inside the *kistē*, together with the snake.

Since time immemorial the guardian snake, *oikouros ophis*, had gone together with Athena and the citadel. It is customary to speak of its "chthonic" significance, but this is too general. The snake is the quintessentially terrifying animal: all living beings are instinctively paralyzed with fear at the sight of it. It slithers up out of the dark depths of the earth; perhaps it may be identified with a dead ancestor, with his "soul" or force—snake symbols have been part of funerary cult since earliest times. At the same time, however, the snake with its slippery motion is a procreative power—thus, for instance, in the Latin concept of the *genius*, and in Greek, *ho ophis, ho drakōn*, can only be masculine. The snake and the phallus are symbolic equivalents in the Mysteries; snakes and phalluses of dough are thrown into the *megara* at the Thesmophoria.[27] Pausanias reports that Kekrops had dedicated in the temple of Polias a wooden Herm totally covered with myrtle branches. Frickenhaus suspected that this Herm was nothing more than a phallus.[28] In any case, Hermes was the lover of Herse and was also known as Erichthonios; and the myrtle belonged to Aphrodite—a symbol of marriage down to our own day. A cake called *anastatos*, "upstanding," was baked for the Arrhephoroi, and scholars of religion have had no doubt as to the meaning of this name.[29] These "virgins" were thus virtually surrounded by so-called fertility symbols—their path necessarily led to the precinct of Eros and Aphrodite. For this journey, of course, they had to remove their gold jewelry. In sum, then, the myth illuminates the ritual: Erichthonios and the snake embody the secret of procreation and mother-

hood that suddenly confronts the Athenian maidens, the daughters of Kekrops, during the night and brings to a close their status as girls.

In this connection we may recall the myth of Erichthonios's origins:
When Hephaistos tried to sexually assault Athena, his seed was absorbed
by the earth,[30] the goddess having used a swab of wool to wipe away the
"dew of Hephaistos"—*droson Hephaistoio*, in the words of Callimachus
(fr. 260.19, on which cf. Schol. A on *Il.* 2.547), "nuptual dew," *gamiēn
eersēn*, according to Nonnos (41.64). The myth here unites those features
that define the life of the Arrhephoroi. From this perspective the meaning
of the term Arrhe- or Errhephoroi becomes clear after all. A combination
with *hersē* (dew) is quite plausible from the standpoint of word formation;
while the development of this Indo-European stem may pose some riddles,
a formation into Attic *ἄρρη cannot be ruled out[31]—in colloquial speech
it was replaced by *drosos*. Since Indo-European times, the meaning of the
*ἄρρη-stem has evidently combined the notion of moistness and fertility:
in old Indic it formed the word for "rain" and "bull," while in Homer *hersai*
are the animals' young. *Arrhephoros* would thus be precisely the kind of
word we would expect in a mystery cult: seemingly innocuous—what could
be more innocent than dew—but able suddenly to assume an entirely different aspect, capable of striking terror.

One point remains to be explained: according to Pausanias the Arrhephoroi picked up "something else" in that grotto and brought it back "covered
up." In this instance the myth leaves us in the lurch: the daughters of
Kekrops are dead, there is no more to tell. In this case we have no choice
but to listen carefully to what Pausanias says. For the most part, scholars
all too willingly assume that basically the same sorts of "secret things,"
arrhēta, were carried below and then back up. Yet the text says, *labousai
de allo ti komizousin enkekalummenon* (they take something else and
bring it back covered up). There is nothing about *kistai*, no reference to
carrying on the head; "something else," "covered up," *enkekalummenon*:
in real terms that must mean something wrapped in a cloth. Now when a
Greek woman carries something wrapped in a cloth, there is normally just
one thing it is likely to be: a small child, a baby—though it may actually
turn out that she is hiding a bottle of wine (Ar. *Thesm.* 730 ff.) or a stone.
Thus once again the meaning of the ritual[32] stands revealed in the context
of initiation: life goes on in a new stage; after the virgin's death comes the
life of the woman and mother.

At this point it would be tempting to draw attention to parallels from
Greek myths and Greek cults, which virtually leap to mind. The ancient

scholar who compared the Thesmophoria and the myth of Demeter with the Arrhephoria was not so far from the mark: after all, Kore, the quintessential "maiden," was seized from her mother or—according to the "Orphic" version[33]—became the victim of the snake-shaped god as she sat at her weaving bench. Or again, there was the widespread custom of dedicating a maiden to service in the temple of the goddess—usually Athena or Artemis—"until she was ripe for marriage."[34] And the moment one looks at individual motifs, one is tempted to range farther afield, from the peplos of Penelope[35] to the vestal virgins, and on to the tale of Amor and Psyche, where the lamp plays a peculiar role at the sight of Eros. There is no lack of examples to show that ritual and myth elucidate each other.

If the most influential scholars of Greek religion take a dim view of the catchphrase "myth and ritual,"[36] they are right to the extent that we are not dealing with myths that perform a direct ritual function. In our case, nothing suggests that the myth of Kekrops's daughters was officially recited during the festival of the Arrhephoria, as the creation epic would have been at a given time and place during the Babylonian new year festival. At least from Homer on, Greek poetry had liberated itself from cult, and myths were handed over to the poets. But this observation does not preclude the possibility that myths originated in ritual, indeed that myths can inform us more directly about the meaning of rituals than can the hypotheses of modern scholars. What, after all, does the myth of Kekrops's daughters narrate? "The sufferings of Kekrops's daughters," *Kekropidōn pathē*, that is quite simply the fate of all female Athenians, for all Athenians are *Kekropidai*.

And yet in historical times only two of the thousands of Athenian girls were chosen to serve as Arrephoroi. Initiation came to be performed only in a symbolic, representative fashion.[37] As previously noted, we are now dealing with an urban culture, where initiation rituals in their original form were as impracticable as they were unnecessary. City dwellers could not live in the same way, or to the same rhythms, as those in a smaller (hence more tight-knit) village community. Private life—*idiai*—became separated from public life—*dēmosiai*; social order was upheld externally, through officials and laws; it no longer needed to be stamped in the soul. Symbolic rituals, where a few now stood in for the whole, sufficed to preserve the old social order. The other side of the coin is the recognition that even quasi-modern urban life was based on the old communal customs, and that these continued to influence the life of each individual, even if in a more moderate form. In Athens, every virgin about to be married had to be led on a certain day—*proteleia*, preliminary to the marriage rite—onto the Acropolis "to the goddess," *eis tēn theon*, i.e., presumably to Athena, in order to offer sacrifice.[38] Every virgin had to have been on the citadel, even if only two from noble families still had to stay there for the entire period of preparation. (Incidentally, there is social differentiation even in primitive initiation ritual; full initiation is the right and the duty of the highest social class.)[39]

Yet the matter did not end there. Immediately following the wedding, the priestess of Athena would come to the new wives bearing the "sacred" aegis.[40] Deubner knew about this: the priestess, he writes, "was no doubt characterized as representing the goddess herself." But what function did the aegis serve? According to Deubner, the goddess was supposed "to bless the marriage in this way, and in particular probably to ensure its fertility" (16). Beneficent powers, fertility—where could they possibly be out of place? But we need to examine the matter with greater precision, and allow Homer to tell us what it means when Athena appears with her aegis: "And now Athena waved the aegis, that blights humanity / from high aloft on the roof, and all their wits were bewildered; / and they stampeded about the hall, like a herd of cattle / set upon and driven wild by the darting horse-fly" (*Od.* 22.297 ff., trans. Lattimore). *tōn de phrenes eptoiēthen* (their wits were bewildered), that is her impact. In other words, after her wedding night every Athenian woman had to endure at least the semblance of that terror that drove the daughters of Kekrops to their deaths. Every woman experienced the fate of Aglauros. There was a breach along the way to her new status, a deadly crisis through which she must pass. After this, according to Athenian custom, when a child was born it was laid in a *kistē* and adorned with snake ornaments; and it seems that this happened in one of the caves along the northern slope of the Acropolis.[41] One can no doubt speak of a beneficent ritual here as well, and of the apotropaic power of the snake. But it is just as good—or better, more Greek—to say that through this ritual each child became the child Erichthonios and so participated directly in the mystery of the origin, in the fundamental order of life.

Did Athenians of historical times still see it this way? Euripides' *Ion* allows us to answer yes. Ion, the son of Apollo, was born in Athens— that is doubtless a relatively recent genealogical construct; but this recent construct goes far to conform to the ancient ritual patterns: Ion's conception and birth could occur nowhere but on the northern slope of the Acropolis with its mysterious caves; and it is no coincidence that the myth of the daughters of Kekrops comes up again and again in Euripides' *Ion*. Beside the tragedy there was a comedy: when the women of Athens decided to   51

follow Lysistrata's plan to abstain from sex with their husbands, they naturally took refuge on the Acropolis; the old men attacked bearing fire, just
as Hephaistos assaulted Athena; and when one of the women apparently,
or actually, wanted to break her oath of abstinence, then the only place she
could do it was again in the grottos of the northern slope of the Acropolis,
where the scene between Myrrhine and Kinesias is set.[42] Last, the antiquarians: ever since Klearchos of Soloi it had been said that Kekrops invented
marriage; this was justified by reference to the "double aspect" of Kekrops,
but that justification is so artificial that we may suspect that it was only
offered because Kekrops's daughters were here still viewed as the prototype
of Athenian brides.[43]

There is, however, one further aspect of the Arrhephoria and the myth
of Kekrops's daughters. Erichthonios, the mysterious child in the *kistē*, was
the second king of Athens; the genealogies are in surprising agreement on
that. Yet how did the child become king? About this the myth is silent. We
can only surmise that the child's exposure represented a crisis for him as
well, perhaps a death—or rather death and new life, initiation?[44] In any
case Erichthonios turns up again later as king. When one inquires what he
accomplished on behalf of the Athenians, the response of the antiquarians
is once again unanimous: Erichthonios was the first to harness horses to
the yoke and invent chariot racing; further, he founded the Panathenaic
festival. These two accomplishments go together, since two rituals were
central to the Panathenaia: first there was the agon, which included an especially old-fashioned type of chariot race, the *apobatēs*, or leap from the
chariot, with ensuing footrace; then the solemn presentation of the peplos.
Here again we see Erichthonios linked to the daughters of Kekrops, and
again in the context of etiological myth: Kekrops's daughters wove the first
robe, Erichthonios harnessed the first chariot; the peplos was now presented,[45] chariot driving was put to the test. As the chief festival of the
month Hekatombaion, the Panathenaia were, moreover, a new year's festival, marking the birthday of the city of Athens. As we learn from the
Marmor Parium,[46] its people came to be known as Athenians, starting with
Erichthonios's first Panathenaia, and it was in this month that the archon
and basileus assumed their offices.

At the start of the festival, new fire was brought by means of a torch
race from the Academy to the altar of Athena. In this way, the life of the
city began anew. This new foundation of the social order in the new year's
festival had to be preceded by the dissolution of the old order, as we see
most everywhere: carnival excess, the world run by fools and women. In

Athens the month of the Panathenaia was preceded by that of Skirophorion, the month of the Arrhephoria. With this ritual the social order that had been maintained on the Acropolis for almost a year was shattered, as reflected in the crisis in the lives of Kekrops's daughters, and in the emergence of the king of the Panathenaia from his place of concealment. But where was the old king? The only thing we know for sure about the Skira festival, after which the month is named, is that the priestess of Athena, the priest of Poseidon—i.e., of Erechtheus—and the priest of Helios were led out together beneath a canopy from the Acropolis to the city limits of Athens,[47] and that women would band together, (for instance) to plot the coup d'état of the *Ekklesiazousai*. Erechtheus and Erichthonios, who were at first probably identical, are characteristically differentiated in the myths that have come down to us: Erechtheus was the old king, Erichthonios the young one;[48] there were tales of the death of Erechtheus and of the birth of Erichthonios. Following the solstice, the king left the city together with the departing sun— that is the meaning of the procession. The men who were active in this *pompē*, a procession that was actually an "expulsion," an *apopompē*, made use of the *Dios kōidion*, the ram skin that could purify those tainted with murder—it almost looks like the ritual murder of a king. But following the dissolution of order came the establishment of the city's new order at the Panathenaia: Erechtheus is dead, long live Erichthonios! Woven into the fabric of Athena's peplos was a depiction of the battle of the gods against the giants, a further expression of the victory of order, of Athena's victory over rebellion and chaos. The work of the Arrhephoroi was thus fulfilled; the new king asserted his authority: he was the victor in the chariot race. We need do no more than mention the links between chariots and kings, from the grave steles of Mycenae to the *triumphator* and the *sella curulis*. The race with the leap from the chariot is meaningful: it marked the arrival of the king who takes possession of the land. When the Athenians of historical times had the chance to celebrate the arrival of an actual king, at the entry of Demetrios Poliorketes into Athens in 306, they dedicated the place where Demetrios leaped from his chariot to Zeus Kataibates (Plut. *Demetr.* 10). The leap from the chariot was of such great importance—it was the king's own leap.

Communal life is renewed through initiation rituals, and the polis order is renewed in the new year rituals that grew out of them. This was the case even in Greece of the Classical period. It was not a matter of giving the exhausted earth new powers of fertility in a more or less functional manner. The earth continued to function after a fashion, even if farmers always had reason to complain, food was always in short supply in Greece, and the deterioration of insufficiently fertilized farmland really was a problem. Yet the problems of the community and its social order were far more acute and immediate. Only that which was acknowledged as "sacred," transcending the realm of what might or might not be valued by an individual, could endure. The Greek polis-communities, including that of the Athenians, understood that their way of life was rooted in cult and festival rites—not because they thought in their primitive way they would thereby achieve the aims of agrarian magic, but because they felt that the inviolable sacredness of the rites, and the mythic narratives of the poets who illuminated them, maintained the social order that had come down to them from earliest times, indeed the fundamental order of human existence.

NOTES

This chapter is a revised version of a lecture held in Kassel, May 20, 1964, at the meeting of the Mommsen Gesellschaft. My thanks once more to all for the numerous suggestions made in the subsequent discussion. I wish, further, to thank the German Archaeological Institute in Athens for their cooperation and support during my visit to Athens in April 1964.

1. ἃ δέ μοι θαυμάσαι μάλιστα παρέσχεν, ἔστι μὲν οὐκ ἐς ἅπαντα γνώριμα, γράψω δὲ οἷα συμβαίνει. παρθένοι δύο τοῦ ναοῦ τῆς Πολιάδος οἰκοῦσιν οὐ πόρρω, καλοῦσι δὲ ᾿Αθηναῖοι σφᾶς ἀρρηφόρους· αὗται χρόνον μέν τινα δίαιταν ἔχουσι παρὰ τῇ θεῷ, παραγενομένης δὲ τῆς ἑορτῆς δρῶσιν ἐν νυκτὶ τοιάδε. ἀναθεῖσαί σφισιν ἐπὶ τὰς κεφαλὰς ἃ ἡ τῆς ᾿Αθηνᾶς ἱέρεια δίδωσι φέρειν, οὔτε ἡ διδοῦσα ὁποῖόν τι δίδωσιν εἰδυῖα οὔτε ταῖς φερούσαις ἐπισταμέναις—ἔστι δὲ περίβολος ἐν τῇ πόλει τῆς καλουμένης ἐν Κήποις ᾿Αφροδίτης οὐ πόρρω καὶ δι᾿ αὐτοῦ κάθοδος ὑπόγαιος αὐτομάτη—ταύτῃ κατίασιν αἱ παρθένοι. κάτω μὲν δὴ τὰ φερόμενα λείπουσιν, λαβοῦσαι δὲ ἄλλο τι κομίζουσιν ἐγκεκαλυμμένον· καὶ τὰς μὲν ἀφιᾶσιν ἤδη τὸ ἐντεῦθεν, ἑτέρας δὲ ἐς τὴν ἀκρόπολιν παρθένους ἄγουσιν ἀντ᾿ αὐτῶν. Some codices recentiores (fifteenth c.) change ἐς ἅπαντα into ἐς ἅπαντας, which has been adopted in all modern editions. What speaks against this is the fact that γνώριμος regularly takes a personal dative (e.g., Plato Soph. 218e ἆρ᾿ οὐ πᾶσί τε γνώριμον . . .) while the adverbial use of εἰς ἅπαντα is attested precisely with adjectives (S. Tr. 489 ἔρωτος εἰς ἅπανθ᾿ ἥσσων, cf. A. Prom. 736); moreover, γράψω δὲ is the logical antithesis to οὐκ ἐς ἅπαντα γνώριμα. On γνώριμος meaning "clear, understandable," cf. Philo De sobr. 35, De decal. 82, De Cher. 16, etc.; on γνώριμος ἐς, cf. Paus. 7.17.12.

2. Cf. J. Toepffer, Attische Genealogie (Berlin, 1889) 121; the edition of O. Jahn and A. Michaelis, Arx Athenarum a Pausania descripta (Bonn, 1901³) sets a † before δι᾿ αὐτοῦ. For the excavation reports by O. Broneer, see Hesperia 1 (1932) 31–55, 2 (1933) 329–417, 4 (1935) 1091–88; on the house of the Arrhephoroi, see G. P. Stevens, Hesperia 5 (1936) 489 ff.; on the well shaft, see O. Broneer, Hesperia 7 (1938) 168 ff., 8 (1939) 317–433; cf. the synthesis of I. T. Hill, The Ancient City of Athens (London, 1953) 12 f., 101 f.; S. E. Iakovidis, Ἡ Μυκηναϊκὴ ἀκρόπολις τῶν ᾿Αθηνῶν (Athens, 1962) 128 ff. On "Aphrodite in the Gardens" along the Ilissos, see Paus. 1.19.2; Plin. NH 36.16; E. Langlotz, SB Heidelberg (1953), 4/2.

3. Cf. J. E. Harrison and M. de G. Verrall, Mythology and the Monuments of Ancient Athens (London, 1890) xxvi ff.; Harrison, Prolegomena to the Study of Greek Religion (Cambridge, 1903; rept. 1957) 131 ff.; J. G. Frazer, Pausanias II (London, 1898) 344 f.; L. R. Farnell,

Cults of the Greek States III (Oxford, 1907) 89 ff.; A. B. Cook, *Zeus* (Cambridge, 1940) 165 ff.; L. Deubner, *Attische Feste* (Berlin, 1932) 9 ff.; F. Hiller v. Gaertringen, *RE* VI (1907) 549–51; M. P. Nilsson, *Geschichte der griechischen Religion* I² (Munich, 1955) 441 f.; F. R. Adrados, "Sobre los Arreforias o Erreforias," *Emerita* 19 (1951) 117–33; K. Kerenyi, *Die Jungfrau und Mutter der griechischen Religion* (Zurich, 1952) esp. 37 ff., 52 ff.

4. Cf. Harpocr. ἀρρηφορεῖν. . . . δ' μὲν ἐχειροτονοῦντο δι' εὐγένειαν ἀρρηφόροι, β' δὲ ἐκρίνοντο, αἵ τῆς ὑφῆς τοῦ πέπλου ἦρχον καὶ τῶν ἄλλων τῶν περὶ αὐτόν. λευκὴν δ' ἐσθῆτα ἐφόρουν. εἰ δὲ χρυσία περιέθεντο, ἱερὰ ταῦτα ἐγίνετο (abbreviated in the Suda 3848, An. Bekk. I 446.18); cf. *EM* 149.18: ἀρρηφορεῖν, τὸ χρυσῆν [sic] ἐσθῆτα φορεῖν καὶ χρυσία· τέσσαρες δὲ παῖδες ἐχειροτονοῦντο κατ' εὐγένειαν, ἀρρηφόροι, ἀπὸ ἐτῶν ἑπτὰ μέχρις ἕνδεκα. τούτων δὲ δύο διεκρίνοντο, αἵ διὰ τῆς ὑφῆς τοῦ ἱεροῦ πέπλου ἤρχοντο καὶ τῶν ἄλλων τῶν περὶ αὐτόν. λευκὴν δὲ ἐσθῆτα ἐφόρουν καὶ χρυσία. An. Bekk. I 202.3: ἀρρηφορεῖν· τὸ λευκὴν ἐσθῆτα φορεῖν καὶ χρυσία. ἦσαν δὲ τέσσαρες παῖδες χειροτονητοί κατ' εὐγένειαν, ἀρρηφόροι, ἀπὸ τῶν ἑπτὰ μέχρι ἕνδεκα.

5. Cf. Plato *Leg.* 947c; *IG* II/III² 1933 (330/20 B.C.): τούσδε ἐπιώψατο ὁ ἱεροφάντης τὴν κλίνην στρῶσαι τῷ Πλούτωνι καὶ τὴν τράπεζαν κοσμῆσαι κατὰ τὴν μαντείαν τοῦ θεοῦ; *IG* II/III² 1934; Hsch. ἐπιοψάμενος, ἐπιόψονται. Aristophanes of Byzantium (Schol. *Od.* 2.294) calls the word Ἀττικὸν λίαν.

6. Correctly already C. Robert, *GGA* (1899) 533; Adrados, "Sobre los Arreforias," 120; on the other hand, according to G. E. Schömann and J. H. Lipsius, *Griechische Altertümer* II⁴ (1902) 493.4, the wording of the passage in Harpocration "does not favor this view"; indeed, according to Deubner it is "utterly unambiguous" (*vollkommen eindeutig*), as though the text read δύο μὲν—δύο δέ; yet it is clear that two stages in the process of selection are set next to each other here (μὲν—δέ), and the duties of the ἀρρηφόροι are not all enumerated (καὶ τῶν ἄλλων). Although Deubner does not say where the peplos-weaving Arrhephoroi live, Frazer boldly explains (*Pausanias* 574.6) that Pausanias was mistaken; consequently, in modern scholarship four maidens are said to inhabit the house of the Arrhephoroi; (G. P. Stevens, *Hesperia* 5 (1936) 489 ff.; E. Kirsten and W. Kraiker, *Griechenlandkunde* (Heidelberg, 1962⁴) 71.

7. Cf. the Suda X35 Χαλκεῖα· ἑορτὴ ἀρχαία. . . . ἐν ᾗ καὶ ἱέρειαι μετὰ τῶν ἀρρηφόρων τὸν πέπλον διάζονται, cf. *Et. Gen.*/*EM* 805.43; Callim. fr. 520 Pf.; Deubner, *Attische Feste* 31.

8. *Et. Gen.* (cf. R. Reitzenstein, *Ind. Rostock* [1890/91] 15; *EM* 149.13; Callim. fr. 741 Pf.; cf. Hsch. *s.v.* ἀρρηφόρια): ἀρρηφόροι καὶ ἀρρηφόρια· ἑορτὴ ἐπιτελουμένη τῇ Ἀθηνᾷ ἐν Σκιροφοριῶνι μηνί. λέγεται δὲ καὶ διὰ τοῦ ε ἐρρηφόρια. παρὰ τὸ τὰ ἄρρητα καὶ μυστήρια φέρειν. ἢ ἐὰν διὰ τοῦ ε, παρὰ τὴν Ἔρσην τὴν Κέκροπος θυγατέρα ἐρσηφόρια· ταύτη γὰρ ἦγον τὴν ἑορτήν. οὕτω Σαλούστιος. Schol. Ar. *Lys.* 642: ἠρρηφόρουν· οἱ μὲν διὰ τοῦ α, ἀρρηφόρια, ἐπειδὴ τὰ ἄρρητα ἐν κίσταις ἔφερον τῇ θεῷ αἱ παρθένοι. οἱ δὲ διὰ τοῦ ε ἐρσηφόρια· τῇ γὰρ Ἔρσῃ πομπεύουσι τῇ Κέκροπος θυγατρί, ὡς ἱστορεῖ Ἴστρος [FGrHist 334 F 27; cf. Moeris: ἐρρηφόροι Ἀττικοί, αἱ τὴν δρόσον φέρουσαι τῇ Ἔρσῃ, ἥτις ἦν μία τῶν Κεκροπίδων); abbreviated in the Suda α 3863; A. Lentz, *Gramm. Gr.* III 2.479.3–5, traced a version back to Herodian, which he had reconstructed from *EM* and Hsch.—but this remains dubious; see H. Schultz, *RE* VIII 968 ff. The accent of the name of the festival is doubtless ἀρρηφόρια on the analogy of θεσμοφόρια, σκιροφόρια, ὡσχοφόρια, φαλλοφόρια, yet there also is an abstract noun ἡ ἀρρηφορία (Lys. 21.5). The festival calendar from the Attic deme of Erchiai, recently published by G. Daux (*BCH* 87 [1963] 603 ff.), provides evidence of sacrifices on the 3rd of Skirophorion ΕΜ ΠΟΛΕ ΕΡΧΙΑΣΙ for Kourotrophos, Athena Polias, Aglauros, Zeus Polieus, and Poseidon (i.e., Erechtheus?), which are doubtless connected with the rituals and myths of the Arrhephoria; the supposition that the Arrhephoria was consequently celebrated on the 3rd of Skirophorion, or more likely in the night from the 2nd to

55

the 3rd—the 3rd itself is Athena's birthday—is nonetheless quite uncertain: cults of a deme and those ἐν ἄστει need not correspond exactly. When we hear that the βουφόνια (Suda s.v.: 14 Skirophorion) come μετὰ τὰ μυστήρια, we cannot tell whether μυστήρια refers to the ἀρρηφόρια or the Skira. It is plausible that the Arrhephoria came before the Skira (cf. n. 47 below). It is no more than an arbitrary assumption that the Arrhephoria coincided with the Panathenaia (Adrados, "Sobre los Arreforias" 121) or came on the night before the Panathenaia (Kerenyi, *Jung frau* 53 f.; παραγενομένης—not παραγινομένης—τῆς ἑορτῆς δρῶσιν ἐν νυκτὶ . . . in Pausanias shows that the δρώμενα were the actual content of the nocturnal festival, rather than coming on the night before it).

9. Cf. *IG* II/III² 3461; 3465–66; 3470–73; 3482; 3486?; 3488; 3496–97; 3515–16; 3554– 56. Three times Ἀθηνᾷ (Πολιάδι) καὶ Πανδρόσῳ: 3472, 3488 (supplemented), 3515; different wording 3634 (epigram: ἐρρηφόρον); 3528 ἀρρηφόρον; 3960 ἀρρηφορήσασα. The Eleusinian votive inscriptions of the παῖδες ἀφ' ἑστίας μυηθέντες are comparable. From another context, *IG* II/III² 3729 ἐρρηφορήσασαν Δήμητρι καὶ Κόρῃ; 974.18 f. εἰς τὰ] Ἐπιδαύρια ἀρρηφοροῦσαν. For inscriptions on theater seats, see *IG* II/III² 5098–99. *IG* XII 2.255 from Mytilene (Imperial epoch): ἐρσοφόρον τῶν ἁγιωτάτων μυσταρίων. For a more general use of ἀρρηφόρος, see also D. H. *Ant.* 2.22; Philo *de ebr.* 129; Hsch. ἀρρηφόρος· μυσταγωγός.

10. Nilsson, *Geschichte* I² 441. Opposed to Deubner see also Adrados, "Sobre los Arreforias" 131 f.

11. For the archaic korai as Arrhephoroi, G. W. Elderkin, *Hesperia* 10 (1941) 120. For the korai of the Erechtheion as Arrhephoroi, C. E. Beulé, *L'Acropole d'Athènes*, vol. 2 (Paris, 1854) 254; G. W. Elderkin, *Problems in Periclean Buildings* (Princeton, 1912) 13 ff., *Hesperia* 10 (1941) 121; cf. G. P. Stevens and J. M. Paton, *The Erechtheum* (Cambridge, Mass., 1927) 235 n.

12. *Mnemosyne* 44 (1916) 331 ff. Cf. Schol. Luc. p. 275.23 ff. Rabe, and closely related, Clem. *Protr.* 2.17 with Schol.; cf. E. Rohde, *RhM.* 25 (1870) 548 ff.=*Kl. Schr.* II (1901) 355 ff.; E. Gjerstadt, *ARW* 27 (1929) 189–240; Deubner (*Attische Feste*) 10 f., 40 ff.; Nilsson, *Geschichte* I² 441 finds Deubner's analysis "impeccable." Against this, Gjerstadt—rightly, to my mind—argued that all the rituals described in the Scholion must refer to the Thesmophoria; Clement, after all (*supra*), clearly attributes the μεγαρίζειν to the Thesmophoria. The Lucian Scholia can easily be understood in this way: the subject of ἤγετο δὲ p. 275.24 is θεσμοφόρια. ἀναφέρονται δὲ καὶ ἐνταῦθα ἄρρητα ἱερά p. 276.15 f. in connection with the reference to the ἀρρητοφόρια [sic] means "here too" at the Thesmophoria there are ἄρρητα, which are carried up to the Thesmophorion, namely μιμήματα δρακόντων καὶ ἀνδρείων σχημάτων. The references to the Skirophoria and Arrhe(to)phoria are, however, not "interpolations" (thus Gjerstadt; against this, Deubner 40 f.), but simply parenthetic observations of an antiquarian who sought a unitary meaning in a variety of phenomena. On the Skira, see n. 47 below.

13. E.g., Nilsson, *Geschichte* I² 119: "This is as transparent and ancient a fertility ritual as possible." Yet agriculture is a quite "recent" invention in human history.

14. *Myth. and Mon.* xxxv; myth is "ritual misunderstood" (xxxiii); nevertheless, "a rite frequently throws light on the myth made to explain it" (Harrison, *Proleg.* 133). Nilsson, *Geschichte* I² 442 concluded that the Arrhephoria "actually belonged to the Dew-sisters (*Tauschwestern*)" and were "connected" with Athena after the fact. The link between the Arrhephoroi and Kekrops's daughters were already recognized by F. G. Welcker, *Griechische Götterlehre* III (Göttingen, 1862) 103 ff.

15. Deubner cites Ch. Picard, "Les luttes primitives d'Athènes et d'Eleusis," *Rev. hist.* 166 (1931) 1–76, inaccurately inasmuch as for Picard it is not the "story" but expressly the "rites" that he wishes to prove an imitation of the Eleusinian festival (40 f.).

16. *Le iniziazioni* II (Rome, 1961) 135.

17. The material is collected in L. Preller and C. Robert, *Griechische Mythologie* I⁴ (Berlin, 1894) 199 ff., II⁴ (Berlin, 1920) 137 ff.; B. Powell, *Erichthonius and the Three Daughters of Cecrops* (Ithaca, 1906); cf. Jacoby on *FGrHist* 328 F 105 (III b Suppl. 424 ff.); on depictions in vase painting, see F. Brommer, "Attische Könige," in *Charites* E. Langlotz (Bonn, 1957) 152–64; *Vasenlisten zur griechischen Heldensage* (Lahn, 1960²) 199. The manuscripts often read Ἄγραυλος; cf. also Porph. *Abst.* 2.54 on a cult in Salamis (Cyprus); Attic inscriptions read only Ἄγλαυρος.

18. προτόνιον· ἱματίδιον ὃ ἡ ἱέρεια ἀμφιέννυται. . . . προτόνιον δὲ ἐκλήθη ὅτι πρώτη Πάνδροσος μετὰ τῶν ἀδελφῶν κατεσκεύασε τοῖς ἀνθρώποις τὴν ἐκ τῶν ἐρίων ἐσθῆτα.

19. Euphorion fr. 9 Powell=*Berl. Kl. T.* V 1.58 (from a curse poem that calls down a variety of curses on an enemy):

]α φέροιτο
]θι κάππεσε λύχνου
]α κατὰ Γλαυκώπιον Ἔρση
[οὕνεκ᾽ Ἀθ]ηναίης ἱερὴν ἀνελύσατο κίστην
[δεσποίν]ης

On Γλαυκώπιον see Pfeiffer on Callim. fr. 238.11; on Athena's lamp see Paus. 1.26.6 f.; Strabo 9 p. 396; R. Pfeiffer, *Ausgew. Schr.* (Munich, 1960) 1–7. Following Euphorion, Nonnos links Athena's lamp and the κίστη of Erichthonios (13.172 ff.; 27.114 ff.; 320 ff. Cf. Wilamowitz, *Berl. Kl. T., supra*).

20. For one snake, Apollod. 3.14.6.5; Ovid *Met.* 2.561 (after Callim.?); a vase by the Brygos Painter, *Ann. d. Inst.* (1850) pl. G=*ARV²* p. 386; C. Robert, *Bild und Lied* (Berlin, 1881) 88; for two snakes, E. *Ion* 21 ff., 1427; a red-figure vase, London E 372, *Ann. d. Inst.* (1879) pl. F=*Roschers Mythologisches Lexikon* I 1307=*ARV²* p. 1218=*Greece and Rome* 10 (1963) suppl. pl. Ic; Amelesagoras *FGrHist* 330 F 1; cf. Hsch. *s.v.* οἰκουρὸς ὄφις. For Pandrosos's continued innocence, see Paus. 1.18.2; 27.2; Apollod. 3.14.6.4 (differently Amelesagoras, *supra*). There was also a tradition that Erichthonios and the snake were identical: Paus. 1.24.7; Hygin. *Astr.* 2.13; Philostr. *VA* 7.24; cf. below, n. 27.

21. The sanctuary of Aglauros was found at the eastern edge of the Acropolis (G. S. Dontas, *Hesperia* 52 [1983] 48–63; *SEG* 33, 115); on the ephebic oath, L. Robert, *Études épigraphiques et philologiques* (Paris, 1938) 296 ff.; M. N. Tod, *A Selection of Greek Historical Inscriptions* II (Oxford, 1948) 303 f.; the link between the Aglaureion and the ephebic oath is no coincidence (Hill, *Ancient City* 101: "later the sanctuary was devoted to other uses as well"); rather it rests on the necessary overlap between initiation rites for boys and girls. Later, of course, people no longer understood what the inquisitive virgin had to do with Attic soldiery and thus invented a heroic version of the death of Aglauros; see Philochoros *FGrHist* 328 F 105 (for Aglauros as bride of Ares, Hellanikos *FGrHist* 323a F 1). There was a priestess for Aglauros and for Pandrosos (*IG* II/III² 3459; *Hesperia* 7 [1938] 1 ff.); Aglauros (Harpocr., Suda *s.v.*) and Pandrosos (Schol. Ar. *Lys.* 439) were also epithets of Athena; Attic women swore by Aglauros and Pandrosos, but not by Herse (Schol. Ar. *Thesm.* 533). On the other hand, in the Kyrbantes cult at Erythrai there were orgies Ἔρσης [καὶ Φαναγ]όρης καὶ Φανίδος (J. Keil, *Österr. Jahresh.* 13 [1910] suppl. 29 f.). Alkman 43 D=57 Page may be a poetic invention. M. Ervin, *Archeion Pontou* 22 (1958) 129–66 wanted to identify a ΙΕΡΟΝ ΝΥΜΦΗΣ, attested on a boundary stone on the south slope of the Acropolis, with the Aglaureion; against this, W. Fuchs, *AM* 77 (1962) 244 n. 13.

22. Two other festivals that precede the Arrhephoria are connected with Aglauros: the

Kallynteria and the Plynteria. The Kallynteria (Phot. *s.v.*) are celebrated ὅτι πρώτη δοκεῖ ἡ Ἄγραυλος γενομένη ἱέρεια τοὺς θεοὺς κοσμῆσαι. Correspondingly in the ritual the statue of Athena must have been adorned (ignoring the mythical *aition*, Deubner, *Attische Feste* 20, asserts that "no evidence is transmitted" and so postulates that "it could only have to do with the purification of the temple"); we find references to the golden ornaments of the Arrhephoroi as well (n. 4 above). Shortly thereafter, during the Plynteria, the ornaments were removed from the statue, the statue covered up (Plut. *Alc.* 34), the sanctuaries roped off (Poll. 8.141)— on this day life went on without the gods. "Washing" was done, which had ceased for nearly a year after the death of Aglauros (Phot. [*supra*]); the fig-paste (ἡγητηρία) refers to the realm of the dead (e.g., Ath. 3.78c; according to Deubner, *Attische Feste* 20, it was a "small refreshment" for the goddess at her bath). When the golden ornaments of the Arrhephoroi "were consecrated," dedicated to the goddess (n. 4 above), they were presumably taken off the Arrhephoroi during a particular ceremony; thus adornment and removal of ornaments may have corresponded to the rhythm of the Kallynteria and Plynteria (cf. also the Pythagorean *akusma*, Iambl. V, p. 84: χρυσὸν ἐχούσῃ μὴ πλησιάζειν ἐπὶ τεκνοποιίᾳ. For removal of ornaments during incubation in the cult of Asklepios at Pergamon, see F. Sokolowski, *Lois sacrées de l'Asie Mineure* [Paris, 1955] 14). It is possible that the Plynteria and the Arrhephoria were separated by only four days. But the date of the Arrhephoria (n. 8, above) is as uncertain as the start of the Plynteria on the 29th of Thargelion (Phot., Kallynteria; evidence to the contrary in Deubner, *Attische Feste* 17 f.).

23. H. Jeanmaire, *Couroi et Courètes* (Lille, 1939) 264 ff.; Brelich, *Iniziazioni* 123 ff.; already Harrison spoke of the "unconscious initiation" of the Arrhephoroi (*Myth. and Mon.* xxxvi). For an overview of initiation rituals, see M. Eliade, *Das Mysterium der Wiedergeburt* (Zurich, 1961); among older studies, A. van Gennep, *Les rites de passage* (Paris, 1909); M. Zeller, *Die Knabenweihen* (diss. Bern, 1923); L. Weiser, *Altgermanische Jünglingsweihen und Männerbunde* (Bühl, 1927); A. E. Jensen, *Die Beschneidung und Reifezeremonien bei den Naturvölkern* (Stuttgart, 1933). Cf. also Brelich, "The Historical Development of the Institution of Initiation in the Classical Ages," *Acta Antiqua* 9 (1961) 267–83; G. Thomson, *Aeschylus and Athens* (London, 1941) 97–129; J. Gagé now gives an overview of the rituals of girls' and women's groups (*Frauenbünde*) at Rome in *Matronalia* (Brussels, 1963).

24. Cf. Hellanikos *FGrHist* 323a F 19 (ten years old, according to D.S. 4.63.2); on the Roman custom, M. Bang in L. Friedlaender, *Sittengeschichte Roms* IV (1921⁹/¹⁰) 133 ff.; M. Durry, *Gymnasium* 63 (1956) 187–90 (pointed out by Prof. E. Burck).

25. There were δειπνοφόροι at the Oschophoria as well; Harpocr. δειπνοφόρος· . . . αἱ τῶν κατακεκλειμένων παίδων μητέρες εἰσέπεμπον καθ' ἡμέραν αὐτοῖς τροφὴν εἰς τὸ τῆς Ἀθηνᾶς ἱερόν, ἐν ᾧ διῃτῶντο, καὶ αὐταὶ συν⟨εισ⟩ῄεσαν ἀσπασόμεναι τοὺς ἑαυτῶν; cf. Deubner, *Attische Feste* 144; *Hesperia* 7 (1938) 18 f.; *IG* II/III² 5151.

26. Demeter meets the king's daughters at the Parthenion well (=Kallichoron), cf. *Hymn to Dem.* 98 ff.; Amymone falls prey to Poseidon at the well of Lerna, A. fr. 13 ff. N.²=130 Mette (cf. G. M. A. Richter, *Red-figured Athenian Vases in the Metropolitan Museum* [New Haven, 1936] Pl. 122); Herakles fell upon Auge at a well in Tegea, Paus. 8.47.4; in connection with the festival of the Graces in Orchomenos, which was celebrated with nocturnal dancing, there was the legend that at the dance the Graces, daughters of king Eteokles, fell into a well, Geop. 11.4.

27. On the snake, E. Küster, *Die Schlange in der griechischen Kunst und Religion* (Giessen, 1913); W. Pötscher, *Gymnasium* 70 (1963) 408 ff.; Powell, *Erichthonius* 19 ff. The motif of "child and snake" comes in many forms, from equivalence (e.g., Paus. 6.20.41; Schol. *Od.* 5.272; in modern Greek an unbaptized child is called δράκος; see P. Kretschmer, *Der heutige lesbische Dialekt* [Vienna, 1905] 375), or useful helper (Pi. *O.* 6.45 ff.; Paus. 10.33.9 f.), to

causing the child's death (Archemoros in E. *Hyps.*) or being killed miraculously by the child himself (Herakles). For the δράκων διὰ τοῦ κόλπου in the mysteries of Sabazios, see Clem. *Protr.* 2.16.2; Arnob. 5.21; Firm. *Err.* 10, also Eduard Mörike, *Erstes Liebeslied eines Mädchens:* "Was im Netze? Schau einmal! Aber ich bin bange: Greif' ich einen süssen Aal? Greif' ich eine Schlange? . . . Schon schnellt mirs in Händen! Ach Jammer! O Lust! Mit Schmiegen und Wenden mir schlüpfts an die Brust . . ."

28. *Ath. Mitt.* 33 (1908) 171 f. on Paus. 1.27.1. For Hermes and Herse, Ovid *Met.* 2.708 ff., and on this passage see W. Wimmel, *Hermes* 90 (1962) 326–33: the story is modeled on the usual myth of Aglauros; Aglauros's discovery of Herse's passion corresponds here to the opening of the κίστη; Apollod. 3.14.3; Toepffer, *Att. Geneal.* 81 ff.; Jacoby on *FGrHist* 324 F 1, 323a F 24. Sophocles described the daughters of Kekrops as δράκαυλος (fr. 585 N.²=643 Pearson). Kerenyi is probably right to find a hint of the incest motif shining through. Kekrops is half snake, and Agraulos is also known as the wife of Kekrops and mother of his daughters. It is not all that outlandish when Athenagoras speaks of μυστήρια "for Agraulos and Pandrosos" (*Leg.* 1, Deubner 14.8) and Ann. Bekk. I 202 notes: ἀρρηφόρια· ἑορτὴ Διονύσου. For Ἑρμῆς Ἐριχθόνιος, see *EM* 371.49, *Et. Gud. s.v.* Ἐριχθόνιος, cf. "Epigonoi," Schol. S. *OC* 378.

29. Paus. *Attic.* ed. Erbse α 116: ἀνάστατοι· πλακοῦντος εἶδος, οὗτοι δὲ αὐταῖς ταῖς ἀρρηφόροις ἐγίνοντο. Cf. Deubner, *Attische Feste* 16 f.

30. *Danais* fr. 2 Kinkel=Harpocr. αὐτόχθονες, on which cf. the Tabula Borgiana, p. 4 Kinkel=*IG* XIV 1292; for the throne of Amyklai, Paus. 3.18.13; E. fr. 929 N.=Eratosth. *Catast.* 13; Amelesagoras *FGrHist* 330 F 1; Callim. fr. 260.19 Pf. etc.; cf. most exhaustively Cook, *Zeus* III 181 ff.; ἐρίῳ ἀπομάξασα τὸν γόνον εἰς γῆν ἔρριψε, Apollod. 3.14.6. M. Fowler, *CP* 38 (1943) 28–32 points to similar motifs in the Veda. The myth must belong to the Chalkeia festival; see Kerenyi, *Jungfrau* 54: according to S. fr. 760 N.²=844 Pearson, πᾶς ὁ χειρῶναξ λεώς approaches the goddess on this day στατοῖς λικνοῖσι. M. P. Nilsson, *The Dionysiac Mysteries of the Hellenistic Age* (Lund, 1957) 21 ff., argues that the λίκνον has only profane significance in pre-Hellenic times; nonetheless, it is used in weddings: cf. Paus. *Attic. s.v.* παῖς ἀμφιθαλής and the black-figure vase, London B 174; Nilsson (*supra*) 24.

31. Thus A. Fick, *KZ* 43 (1910) 132 f.; against this, but without support, H. Frisk, *Griechisches etymologisches Wörterbuch s.v.* ἀρρηφόρος. Side by side we find the forms ἐέρση—ἔρση, ἐερσήεις—ἐρσήεις (Homer), and further ἀέρσαν· τὴν δρόσον. Κρῆτες (Hsch.; ἀέρση in Poseidippos, Pap. Lit. Lond. 60, a slip of the pen?). If we reckon with an initial laryngial (J. Kurylowicz, *Études Indoeuropéennes* [1935] 31), we would expect the form ἀέρσα, from which Attic *ἄρση > *ἄρρη could be formed by contraction; from the standpoint of word formation, the zero grade *ursa > *ἄρσα > *ἄρση > *ἄρρη > (type: δίκη) would also be possible; this does not explain the differences in the initial sounds in the Greek, no more than it would if we assumed a prothetic vowel before F (Schwyzer, *Griechische Grammatik* [Munich, 1950–53] I 228; 411 f.). Since ἀρρη- and ἐρρηφόρος are both attested in the same dialect, it is natural to assume that one of the forms arose through folk-etymological reinterpretation—perhaps when Herse, who was originally not Athenian, was transferred to Athens by a poet or genealogical author? In the absence of inscriptional evidence, we cannot tell whether one ought to write ἐρρη- or ἐρρηφόρος in Attic Greek; on the Berlin cup mentioned below, n. 48, mixing Ionic and Attic orthography, we find ΕΡΣΕ beside ΓΕ and ΗΦΑΙΣΤΟΣ. For a votive inscription ΑΠΟΛΛΩΝΟΣ ΕΡΣΟ in the cave of the nymphs at Vari, cf. *IG* I² 783; cf. Ἔρρος· ὁ Ζεύς in Hsch.; also Kerenyi, *Jungfrau* 41. The derivation from ἀρρητοφόρος (n. 12 above; Deubner, *Attische Feste* 9 f.) breaks down if ἀρρηφόρος-ἐρρηφόρος. Adrados, "Sobre los Arreforias" 128 ff., derives ἀρρηφόρος from *ἀρρενο-φόρος, though this means that he must twice postulate secondary, analogous forms, rather than those one would expect 59

according to the laws of word formation, i.e., *ἀρρενοφόρος instead of *ἀρραφόρος, and then syncopated ἀρρηφόρος instead of *ἀρρεφόρος. Adrados, "Arrephorias" 132 f. openly acknowledges that a connection with ἔρση is possible according to the laws of phonetics.

32. Because this interpretation cannot be directly confirmed in the Greek sources, I am all the more pleased to find it has been proposed elsewhere: F. M. Hooker, *Greece and Rome* 10 (1963) suppl. p. 19: "originally it must have been an infant prince that was wrapped up and carried up to the Acropolis. . . ." With regard to ἐγκεκαλυμμένον, cf. the red-figure pelike in G. M. A. Richter, *Red-figured Athenian Vases* pl. 75, text p. 100, where Rhea presents Kronos with the wrapped-up stone.

33. For Kore sitting at the loom, see Kern, *Orphicorum Fragmenta* (Berlin, 1922) F 192 ff.; for Zeus in the shape of a snake, ibid. F 58, also D.S. 5.3.4.

34. Paus. 7.26.5: Artemis at Aigeira; Paus. 7.19.1: Artemis Triklaria at Patrai; Paus. 7.22.8 f.: Athena at Triteia; Paus. 2.33.3: Poseidon at Kalaureia; Paus. 6.20.2 f.: Eileithyia at Olympia; Strabo 17 p. 816: Ammon at Egyptian Thebes; Xen. *Eph.* 3.11.4: Isis.

35. The Arrhephoroi ritual was already compared with the peplos of Penelope by M. Delcourt, *Oedipe ou la légende du conquérant* (Paris, 1944) 169 f.; on this cf. Promathion *FGrHist* 817; on the weaving motif, R. Merkelbach, *Roman und Mysterium* (Munich, 1962) 46, 8, who (8 ff.) interprets the "fairy tale" of Amor and Psyche as a myth of Isis.

36. The phrase "myth and ritual" goes back to the book of S. H. Hooke (Oxford, 1933); cf. E. O. James, *Myth and Ritual in the Ancient Near East* (New York, 1958). Arguing against its application in the Greek realm, M. P. Nilsson, *Cults, Myths, Oracles and Politics in Ancient Greece* (Lund, 1951) 9 ff.; H. J. Rose, "Myth and Ritual in Classic Civilization," *Mnemosyne* IV S. 3 (1950) 281–87; N. A. Marlow, "Myth and Ritual in Early Greece," *Bull. of the J. Rylands Libr.* 43 (1960/1) 373–402. For the Babylonian creation epic in the context of the New Year's festival, J. B. Pritchard, *Ancient Near Eastern Texts* (Princeton, 1955²) 332. It is worth noting the depiction of an Attic festival of Dionysus in Philostr. *VA* 4.21: ὅτι αὐλοῦ ὑποσημήναντος λυγισμοὺς ὀρχοῦνται. καὶ μεταξὺ τῆς Ὀρφέως ἐποποιίας τε καὶ θεολογίας τὰ μὲν ὡς Ὧραι, τὰ δὲ ὡς Νύμφαι, τὰ δὲ ὡς Βάκχαι πράττουσιν.

37. On this see Brelich in the studies cited in nn. 16 and 23 above.

38. Suda π 2865 Προτέλεια· ἡμέραν οὕτως ὀνομάζουσιν, ἐν ᾗ εἰς τὴν ἀκρόπολιν τὴν γαμουμένην παρθένον ἄγουσιν οἱ γονεῖς εἰς τὴν θεὸν καὶ θυσίας ἐπιτελοῦσι. Deubner, *Attische Feste* 16 considers whether ἡ θεὸς here could mean Artemis of Brauron, to whom Athenian brides brought a κανηφορία (Schol. Theocr. 2.66 p. 284 Wendel). The ritual of Brauron, τὸ καθιερωθῆναι πρὸ γάμων τὰς παρθένους τῇ Ἀρτέμιδι (Krateros, *FGrHist* 342 F 9), provides a parallel to the Athenian Arrhephoria ritual. To what extent the two merged with each other after Peisistratos introduced the cult of Artemis of Brauron onto the Acropolis, cannot be determined given the meager evidence of our sources; yet the note in the Suda does not seem to square completely with the Theocritus Scholion. In the former we have a maiden in the company of her parents; in the latter a bride among brides—i.e., προτέλεια and κανηφορία presumably existed side by side.

39. On Samoa, for instance, M. Mead observed a remarkably smooth and unbroken transition between childhood and adulthood—only the most privileged girls, the *taupo*, underwent an intense initiation (*Coming of Age in Samoa* [New York, 1928; rpt. Mentor, 1949] 70).

40. Suda αι 60 αἰγίς· . . . ἡ δὲ ἱέρεια Ἀθήνησι τήν ἱερὰν αἰγίδα φέρουσα πρὸς τὰς νεογάμους εἰσήρχετο, *Paroem. Gr. Suppl.* I 65. Nilsson, *Geschichte* I² 443.4 is sceptical: "one of those ceremonies that arose in later times. . . ."

41. E. *Ion* 16 ff.: τεκοῦσ᾽ ἐν οἴκοις παῖδ᾽ ἀπήνεγκεν βρέφος ἐς ταὐτὸν ἄντρον οὗπερ ηὐνάσθη θεῷ Κρέουσα, κἀκτίθησιν ὡς θανούμενον κοίλης ἐν ἀντίπηγος εὐτρόχῳ κύκλῳ, προγόνων νόμον σῴζουσα τοῦ τε γηγενοῦς Ἐριχθονίου. κείνῳ γὰρ ἡ Διὸς κόρη φρουρὼ

παραζεύξασα φύλακε σώματος δισσὼ δράκοντε, παρθένοις Ἀγλαυρίσιν δίδωσι σῴζειν· ὅθεν Ἐρεχθείδαις ἐκεῖ νόμος τις ἔστιν ὄφεσιν ἐν χρυσηλάτοις τρέφειν τέκνα. . . . In his commentary (Berlin, 1926), Wilamowitz assumed a lacuna after v. 19; "if a verse is not missing here, then the νόμος προγόνων consists of her laying her child in the basket." That very interpretation becomes reasonable the moment we realize that ἀντίπηξ is no conventional basket, but corresponds to the ritual κίστη; see I. Bergson, *Eranos* 58 (1960) 11–19; we may thus dispense with the stopgap suggested by Owen (comm. [Oxford, 1939] ad loc.), of having νόμος refer only to what follows, the guardian snakes. On Ἐρεχθείδαις (cf. 1056; 1060), Wilamowitz: "the family, not all the Athenians"; but cf. *Supp.* 387, 681, 702; *Hipp.* 151; *HF* 1166; *Ph.* 852—Ἐρεχθεῖδαι always stands for the Athenians as a whole; the Kleisthenic *phylai* have nothing to do with such far older customs. What is meant, however, by ἐκεῖ in v. 24? Inasmuch as the speaker is Hermes in Delphi, it has been taken to mean "Athens" (Wilamowitz, Owen); yet those scholars who tried to remove ἐκεῖ by conjecture (ἔτι Barnes, ἀεὶ Elmsley) correctly sensed the trouble an Athenian audience in the Theater of Dionysus might experience displacing themselves imaginatively so as to make their actual location ἐκεῖ. The only indication of place immediately preceding, however, is ταὐτὸν ἄντρον (on the grotto of Apollo, W. Judeich, *Topographie von Athen* (Munich, 1905) 301 f.; it is linked with the familiar well, Klepsydra, on the Acropolis, just as the grotto of Aglauros is with the closed-up wellshaft, nn. 2 and 26 above). A quite similar ritual is attested in the Plato legend; Olympiod. *V. Pl.* 1 (cf. the parallels in A. S. Pease, *Cicero: De divinatione* (Urbana, 1920–23) ad 1.78): καὶ γεννηθέντα τὸν Πλάτωνα λαβόντες οἱ γονεῖς βρέφος ὄντα τεθείκασιν ἐν τῷ Ὑμηττῷ, βουλόμενοι ὑπὲρ αὐτοῦ τοῖς ἐκεῖ θεοῖς Πανὶ καὶ Νύμφαις καὶ Ἀπόλλωνι Νομίῳ θῦσαι, καὶ κειμένου αὐτοῦ μέλιτται προσελθοῦσαι πεπληρώκασιν αὐτοῦ τὸ στόμα κηρίων μέλιτος. J. H. Wright, *HSCP* 17 (1906) 131 ff., plausibly linked this story with the cave of Vari (on which see Cook, *Zeus* III 261 ff.) on the slope of Hymettos where Pan, Nymphs, and Apollo were worshipped; Wright also points out that the story could come from Speusippos's Πλάτωνος Ἐγκώμιον (the previous sentence in Olympiodoros corresponds with one by Speusippos in Diog. Laer. 3.2); Apollo fathering the child goes together with "depositing" it in Apollo's sanctuary, where it is given food (milk and honey; τρέφειν [E. *Ion*, v. 26, "to nurture children"]; for two vase paintings that depict Athena giving Erichthonios a drink from a cup, Brommer, *Charites E. Langlotz* [*supra*, n. 17] 157 f.); on rites of "depositing a thing in a temple" or (potentially) "exposing" it, cf. also the custom of the Gauls, *AP* 9.125; Delcourt, *Oedipe* 41 f.; A. Dieterich, *Mutter Erde* (Leipzig, 1905) 6 ff. In its basic meaning, the cult of Κουροτρόφος belongs in this same complex; she was worshipped in the sanctuary of Aglauros; *IG* II/III² 5152. Erichthonios was the first to offer sacrifice to Κουροτρόφος on the Acropolis; Suda *s.v.* κουροτρόφος. Cf. also the child in the κίστη on a votive tablet from Lokroi, *Ausonia* 3 (1908) 193. Ch. Picard, *Rev. hist.* 166 (1931) 47, first suggested that the Ion saga was modeled on the Erichthonios myth; one might interpret the apocryphal tradition that Apollo himself was the son of Athena and Hephaistos (i.e., Erichthonios) in a similar fashion; see Cic. *Nat. deor.* 3.55; 57; Clem. *Protr.* 2.28.

42. Cf. G. W. Elderkin, "Aphrodite and Athena in the *Lysistrata*," *CP* 35 (1940) 387–96. Perhaps Lysistrata herself stands for Lysimache, the priestess of Athena Polias; see D. M. Lewis, *ABSA* 50 (1955) 1 ff.

43. Cf. Klearchos fr. 73 Wehrli; Justin 2.6.7; Charax *FGrHist* 103 F 38; Schol. Ar. *Pl.* 773; Suda *s.v.* "Kekrops." Kekrops signifies the transition to the present order, the middle ground between beast and man, between promiscuity and marriage, between Kronos and Zeus. The tradition is therefore meaningful that Kekrops introduced the cult of Kronos; see Philochoros *FGrHist* 328 F 97.

44. Cf. the story of Demophon in the *Hymn to Dem.* 231 ff.; the Orphic version is explicit

about Demophon's death, *Berl. Kl. T.* V 1, p. 7=Kern, *Orph. Fragm.* 49, col. VI f.; similarly Apollod. 1.5.1.4; in legend, Demophon also appears as the son of Theseus and king of Athens.

45. It is often assumed that the two Arrhephoroi are depicted at the center of the Panathenaic frieze, next to the priest and the boy with the peplos; "they put on their heads what Athena's priestess gives them to carry," in this case two stools. A more precise interpretation is difficult: no information about the function of the Arrhephoroi at the Panathenaic festival has survived.

46. Marm. Par. *FGrHist* 239 A 10 Ἐριχ]θόνιος Παναθηναίοις τοῖς πρώτοις γενομένοις ἅρμα ἔζευξε καὶ τὸν ἀγῶνα ἐδείκνυε καὶ Ἀθηναίους [ὠν]όμ[ασε. . . . He is first to use a chariot according to Eratosth. *Catast.* 13; Ael. NA *Var. hist.* 3.38; Verg. *Georg.* 3.113; Varro in Serv. Auct. ad loc., etc. He also founded the Panathenaia, according to Hellanikos, *FGrHist* 323a F 2; Androtion, *FGrHist* 324 F 2; Philochoros, *FGrHist* 328 F 8; Harpocr., Phot., Suda s.v. "Panathenaia"; Schol. Plato *Parm.* 127a. Theseus, too, is called the founder of the Panathenaia; see Plut. *Thes.* 24, Paus. 8.2.1, cf. Jacoby on *FGrHist* 239 A 10. For the most detailed treatments of the Panathenaia, see A. Mommsen, *Feste der Stadt Athen* (Leipzig 1898) 41–159; Deubner, *Attische Feste* 22 ff.; L. Ziehen, *RE* XVIII 3 (1949) 457–93; on the ἀποβάτης ibid., 478 f.; Reisch, *RE* I 2814–17; D. H. *Ant.* 7.73.2 f.; Harpocr. ἀποβάτης; J. A. Davison, "Notes on the Panathenaia," *JHS* 78 (1958) 23–42; 82 (1962) 141 f. On the Panathenaia as a new year's festival, see Brelich, *Act. Antiqu.* (1961) 275, cf. already Wilamowitz, *SBBerlin.* (1929) 37 f. The formation of the penteteric festival occurred under the archon Hippokleides in the year 566/5 (Pherekydes, *FGrHist* 3 F 2, Arist. fr. 637, Euseb. *Chron.* on 566); the annual festival is attested earlier (*Il.* 2.550 f.); but the penteteric festival was not totally new: its meaning lay in initiation rituals (see Brelich, *Act. Antiqu.* [1961] 282 f.), and these do not have to happen every year. The indication of "seven to eleven years old" may point to an originally penteteric rhythm in the Arrhephoria (Robert, *GGA* (1899), Brelich, *Iniziazoni* 125), cf. Hes. *Erga* 698 ἡ δὲ γυνὴ τέτορ' ἥβωοι, πέμπτῳ δὲ γαμοῖτο; for five as the Pythagorean number for γάμος, v. Alex. *in Arist.* "*Met.*" p. 39.8; yet in the fifth century the duties of the ἀρρηφόροι scarcely lasted more than a year, per Ar. *Lys.* 641 f. The penteteric initiation festival was presumably transformed into an annual event in the context of the polis, while something of its older, popular character was restored in Peisistratean times (cf. the renewal of the cult of Dionysus and the development of the Eleusinian mysteries). Concerning agon and kingship, see F. M. Cornford in Harrison, *Themis* (Cambridge, 1912) 212 ff.; Hooker, *Greece and Rome* (1963) Suppl. p. 20; on agon and funerary cult, K. Meuli, *Antike* 17 (1941) 189 ff. And indeed, the two do coincide: "appeasement" (ἱλάσκεσθαι) of the dead and the testing of the king. The Panathenaic victor receives an olive wreath (Schol. Plato *Parm.* 127a)—an olive wreath surrounds the κίστη of Erichthonios on the London vase (n. 20 above), and a similar wreath is one of the tokens by which Ion is recognized (E. *Ion* 1433 ff.).

47. Cf. Lysimachides, *FGrHist* 366 F 3 in Harpocr. s.v. Σκίρον; Deubner, *Attische Feste* 46 ff.; Gjerstadt, *ARW* 27. Together with the Θεσμοφόρια, Πληροσία, Καλαμαία, the Σκίρα are one of the "days on which women band together according to ancestral custom" (συνέρχονται αἱ γυναῖκες κατὰ τὰ πάτρια), according to the testimony of the inscription from the Piraeus *IG* II/III² 1177.10; cf. Ar. *Eccl.* 59. In his *Laws* Plato makes the twelfth month into Pluton's month, a month of "dissolution" (διάλυσις 828d). The dispute as to whether the Skira were a festival of Athena or Demeter (Deubner 45 f.) is of no importance since the festival way led from the Acropolis to the precinct of Demeter. On the Διὸς κῴδιον, see Paus. *Attic.* ed. Erbse δ 18 . . . χρῶνται δ' αὐτοῖς οἵ τε Σκιροφορίων τὴν πομπὴν στέλλοντες καὶ ὁ δᾳδοῦχος ἐν Ἐλευσῖνι καὶ ἄλλοι τινὲς πρὸς τοὺς καθαρμοὺς ὑποστορνύντες αὐτὸ τοῖς ποσὶ τῶν ἐναγῶν. It is worth noting that we know of a festival cycle in Rome with the same meaning and at the same time of year: the Poplifugia (July 5) with its myth of the dismember-

ment of Romulus, followed by the women's festival of the Nonae Caprotinae (Burkert, *Historia* 11 [1962] 356 ff.; Brelich saw elements of a new year's festival in the rites, *SMSR* 31 [1960] 63 ff.).

48. On Erechtheus-Erichthonios, Preller and Robert, *Griechische Mythologie* I⁴ 198 ff.; Escher, *RE* VI 404 ff., 439 ff.; Kerenyi, *Jungfrau* 48, 52. The general assumption that the two were originally identical is entirely justified. It is supported above all by *Il.* 2.547 ff., in which the birth legend of Erechtheus is attested in a form corresponding to the story of Erichthonios current in later times, and also Erechtheus's funerary cult (ἰλάσκονται); cf. Schol. *ad loc.* and Hdt. 8.44, where Erechtheus is successor to Kekrops. See also E. Ermatinger, *Die attische Autochthonensage bis auf Euripides* (diss. Zurich, 1897). The differentiation young king—old king is especially clear on the Berlin cup with captions F 2537=*ARV*² 1268 f.; see Brommer, *Charites E. Langlotz* 152 f., pl. 21: Erichthonios as youth, Erechtheus bearded, although in the usual genealogies Erichthonios is placed before Erechtheus since the mystery of the origins must stand at the start, i.e., Kekrops-Erichthonios. This is not the place to deal with the various accounts of the death of Erechtheus; it is worth noting, however, that war with Eleusis often plays a role in it, just as the Skira procession heads toward Eleusis.

3

JASON, HYPSIPYLE, AND NEW FIRE
AT LEMNOS: A STUDY IN MYTH AND RITUAL

History of religion, in its beginnings, had to struggle to emancipate itself from classical mythology as well as from theology and philosophy; when ritual was finally found to be the basic fact in religious tradition, the result was a divorce between classicists, treating mythology as a literary device, on the one hand, and specialists in festivals and rituals and their obscure affiliations and origins on the other.[1] The function of myth in society was studied by anthropologists,[2] the interrelation of myth and ritual was stressed by orientalists,[3] but the classicists' response has been mainly negative.[4] It cannot be denied that Greeks often spoke of correspondence of *legomena* and *drōmena*,[5] that rituals are usually said to have been instituted "on account of" some mythical event; but it is held that these myths are either "etiological" inventions and therefore of little interest, or that "well-known types of story" have been superimposed on "simple magical rites and spells," as Joseph Fontenrose concluded from his study of Python: "The rituals did not enact the myth; the myth did not receive its plot from the rituals."[6]

Still, a formula such as "simple magical rites" should give rise to further thinking. Life is complex beyond imagination, and so is living ritual. Our information about ancient ritual is, for the most part, desperately scanty, but to call it simple may bar understanding from the start; the simplicity may be just due to our perception and description. It is true that we do not usually find Greek myths as a liturgically fixed part of ritual; but this does not preclude the possibility of a ritual origin of myth; and if, in certain cases, there is secondary superimposition of myth on ritual, even the adopted child may have a real father—some distant rite of somehow similar pattern. Only detailed interpretation may turn such possibilities into probability or even certainty. But it is advisable to remember that those combinations and superimpositions and etiological explanations were made by people with firsthand experience of ancient religion; before discarding them, one should try to understand them.

One of the best-known Greek myths, from Homer's time (*Od.* 12.70) throughout antiquity, is the story of the Argonauts; one incident, the "Lemnian crime," followed by the romance of Jason and Hypsipyle, enjoyed proverbial fame. That it has anything to do with ritual, we learn only through sheer coincidence: the family of the Philostrati were natives of Lemnos, and one of them included details of Lemnian tradition in his dialogue *Heroikos*, written about A.D. 215.[7] The Trojan vine-dresser who is conversant with the ghost of Protesilaus describes the semidivine honors allegedly paid to Achilles by the Thessalians long before the Persian war, and he illustrates them by reference to certain Corinthian rites and to a festival of Lemnos; the common characteristic is the combination of propitiation of the dead, *enagismata*, with mystery rites, *telestikon:*

ἐπὶ δὲ τῷ ἔργῳ τῷ περὶ τοὺς ἄνδρας ὑπὸ τῶν ἐν Λήμνῳ γυναικῶν ἐξ Ἀφροδίτης ποτὲ πραχθέντι καθαίρεται μὲν ἡ Λῆμνος †καὶ καθ᾽ ἕνα τοῦ ἔτους† καὶ σβέννυται τὸ ἐν αὐτῇ πῦρ ἐς ἡμέρας ἐννέα· θεωρὶς δὲ ναῦς ἐκ Δήλου πυρφορεῖ, κἂν ἀφίκηται πρὸ τῶν ἐναγισμάτων, οὐδαμοῦ τῆς Λήμνου καθορμίζεται, μετέωρος δὲ ἐπισαλεύει τοῖς ἀκρωτηρίοις, ἔς τε ὅσιον τὸ ἐσπλεῦσαι γένηται. θεοὺς γὰρ χθονίους καὶ ἀπορρήτους καλοῦντες τότε καθαρόν, οἶμαι, τὸ πῦρ τὸ ἐν τῇ θαλάττῃ φυλάττουσιν. ἐπειδὰν δὲ ἡ θεωρὶς ἐσπλεύσῃ καὶ νείμωνται τὸ πῦρ ἔς τε τὴν ἄλλην δίαιταν ἔς τε τὰς ἐμπύρους τῶν τεχνῶν, καινοῦ τὸ ἐντεῦθεν βίου φασὶν ἄρχεσθαι.[8]

(In response to the deed once wrought on account of Aphrodite by the Lemnian women against their husbands, Lemnos is purified [each year? text uncertain] and the fire there is quenched for nine days. A festal ship brings fire from Delos, and if it arrives before the dead are propitiated it does not put in anywhere in Lemnos, but rides out in the open water by the promontories until the hallowed time for its arrival. That is because, I suppose, they keep that fire out at sea and pure while they call upon secret gods from under the earth. When the vessel sails in and they distribute the fire where their lives require it, particularly to the craftsmen who have to do with fire, at that point they say they are starting a new life.)

It is frustrating that one important detail, the time of the festival, is obscured by corruption. The reading of the majority of the manuscripts, *kath' hekaston etos* (every year), is too obvious a correction to be plausible. 65

But the ingenious suggestion of Adolf Wilhelm[9] to read *kath' henatou etous* (every ninth year) has to be rejected, too: it introduces an erroneous orthography of old inscriptions into a literary text of the Imperial age, it gives an unattested meaning to *kata* with genitive,[10] and it fails to account for the *kai;* it is as difficult to assume two unrelated corruptions in the same passage as to imagine how the misreading of *henatou* should have brought forth the superfluous *kai.* Looking for other remedies, one could surmise that a masculine substantive, required by *kath' hena,* is missing, hiding in that very *kai: kairon kath' hena tou etous* (at one given moment of the year)— an unusual word order, modeled on Herodotus's frequent *chronon epi pollon* (through much time) and similar expressions and thus combining archaism with peculiarities of later Greek.[11] Of course it is possible that more serious corruption has occurred; still the traditional emendation *kath' hekaston etos* (every year) may not be far off the mark as to the content: Achilles received his honors which the Lemnian custom is meant to illustrate, *ana pan etos* (each year) too (ii. 207, 2, Teubner ed.).

Nilsson, in *Griechische Feste* (470), has Philostratus's account under the heading "festivals of unknown divinities." This is an excess of self-restraint. There is one obvious guess as to which god must have played a prominent role in the fire festival: Lemnos is the island of Hephaistos,[12] the main city is called Hephaistia throughout antiquity, it has the head of Hephaistos on its coins. Incidentally, one Lucius Flavius Philostratus was *hiereus tou epōnumou tēs poleōs Hēphaistou* (priest of Hephaistos, after whom the city is named) in the third century A.D. (*IG* XII. 8, 27). But Hephaistos is the god of fire, even fire himself (*Il.* 2.426): the purification of the island of Hephaistos, brought about by new fire, was a festival of Hephaistos. Philostratus indeed alludes to this: the new fire, he says, is distributed especially "to the craftsmen who have to do with fire," i.e., to potters and blacksmiths. The island must have been famous for its craftsmen at an early date: the Sinties of Lemnos, Hellanicus said (*GFrHist* 4 F 71), invented fire and the forging of weapons. The "invention," the advent of fire, is repeated in the festival. It is true that Philostratus mentions Aphrodite as the agent behind the original crime: she ought to have a place in the atonement, too.[13] But the question: to which god does the festival "belong," seems to be rather a misunderstanding of polytheism: as the ritual mirrors the complexity of life, various aspects of reality, i.e., different deities, are concerned.[14] The "beginning of a new life" at Lemnos would affect all the gods who played their part in the life of the community, above all the Great Goddess who was called Lemnos herself.[15]

To get farther, it is tempting to embark on ethnological comparison. Festivals of new fire are among the most common folk customs all over the world; striking parallels have been adduced from the Red Indians as well as from East Indian Burma;[16] and one could refer to the Incas as well as to the Japanese. Nilsson, wisely, confines himself to Greek parallels, not without adding the remark (GF 173): "Daß das Feuer durch den täglichen Gebrauch . . . seine Reinheit verliert, ist ein überall verbreiteter Glauben." (It is a ubiquitous belief that fire loses its purity through daily use). "Ubiquitous belief" is meant to explain the ritual. Where, however, one ought to ask, do such ubiquitous beliefs come from? The obvious answer is, from the rituals.[17] People, living with their festivals from childhood, are taught their beliefs by these very rituals, which remain constant as against the unlimited possibilities of primitive associations. Thus the comparative method does not, by itself, lead to an explanation, to an understanding of what is going on—if one does not take it for granted that whatever Greeks or Romans told about their religion is wrong, but what any savage told to a merchant or missionary is a revelation. At the same time, by mere accumulation of comparative material, the outlines of the picture become more and more blurred, until nothing is left but vague generalities.

In sharp contrast to the method of accumulation, there is the method of historical criticism; instead of expanding the evidence, it tries to cut it down, to isolate elements and to distribute them neatly to different times and places. The *purphoria* (carrying of fire) described by Philostratus connects Delos and Lemnos. This, we are told, is an innovation that betrays Attic influence. The suggestion cannot be disproved, though it is remarkable that Philostratus wrote at a time when Lemnos had just become independent from Athens, that the Athenians got their new fire not from Delos, but from Delphi (Plut. *Num.* 9), and that the role of Delos as a religious center of the islands antedates not only Attic, but plainly Greek influence.[18] Still, the critical separation of Lemnian and Delian worship has its consequences: if the Lemnians originally did not sail to Delos, where did their new fire come from? Obviously from an indigenous source: the miraculous fire of Mount Mosychlos.[19] This fire has a curious history. The commentators on Homer and Sophocles and the Roman poets clearly speak of a volcano on Lemnos;[20] this volcano was active in literature down to the end of the nineteenth century, with some scattered eruptions even in later commentaries on Sophocles' *Philoctetes*,[21] though geographical survey had revealed that there never was a volcano on Lemnos at any time since this planet has been inhabited by *homo sapiens*.[22] Thus the volcano disappeared, but its fire 67 remained: scholars confidently speak of an "earth fire," a perpetual flame nourished by earth gas on Mount Mosychlos. As earth gas may be found nearly everywhere and fires of this kind do not leave permanent traces, this hypothesis cannot be disproved. Nothing has been adduced to prove it either. The analogy with the fires of Baku ought not to be pressed; no reservoir of oil has been found at Lemnos.

There is no denying that "Lemnian fire" was something famous and uncanny. Philoctetes, in his distress, invokes it:

ὦ Λημνία χθὼν καὶ τὸ παγκρατὲς σέλας ἡφαιστότευκτον (986).

[O land of Lemnos and all-conquering flash wrought by Hephaistos.]

Antimachus mentions it in comparison (fr. 46 Wyss):

Ἡφαίστου φλογὶ εἴκελον, ἥν ῥα τιτύσκει
δαίμων ἀκροτάτης ὄρεος κορυφαῖσι Μοσύχλου.

[Like to the flame of Hephaistos, which the god creates
on the highest peaks of the mountain Mosychlos.]

This fire on the summit of the mountain is in some way miraculous, *daimonion*—but *tituskei* (creates) (after *Il.* 21.342) is hardly suggestive of a perpetual flame. There is, however, another invocation of Lemnian fire in the *Philoctetes*: τῷ Λημνίῳ τῷδ᾽ ἀνακαλουμένῳ πυρὶ ἔμπρησον (800 f.; burn me with that Lemnian fire, for which men plead), the hero cries. *anakaloumenōi* (object of invocation) has proved to be a stumbling-block for believers either in the volcano or the earth fire.[23] *anakalein, anakaleisthai* is a verb of ritual, used especially for "imploring" chthonic deities: Deianeira implores her *daimōn* (S. *Tr.* 910), Oedipus at Colonus his *arai* (S. *OC* 1376). Thus *anakaloumenōi* seems to imply a certain ceremony to produce this demoniac fire; it is not always here. Understood in this way, the verse turns out to be the earliest testimony to the fire festival of Lemnos; it confirms the guess that the fire was not brought from Delos at that time. How the fire was kindled in the ritual may have been a secret. Considering the importance of Lemnian craftsmen, the most miraculous method for *chalkeis* (smiths) would be to use a *chalkeion*, a bronze burning-mirror to light a new fire from the sun.[24] Hephaistos fell on Lemnos from heaven, the *Iliad* says (1.593), on Mount Mosychlos, native tradition held,[25] he was very feeble, but the Sinties at once took care of him. In the tiny flame rising from the tinder in the focus, the god has arrived—alas, this is just a guess. But it seems advisable to send the earth fire of Mosychlos together with the volcano after the volcanic vapors of Delphi, which, too, vanished completely under the spade of the excavators; the miracles of ritual do not need the miracles of nature; the miracles of nature do not necessarily produce mythology.

To get beyond guesses, there is one clue left in the text of Philostratus: the purification is performed "on account of the deed wrought by the Lemnian women against their husbands." It is by myth that ancient tradition explains the ritual. Modern scholarship has revolted against this. As early as 1824, Friedrich Gottlob Welcker found a "glaring contrast" between the "deeper" meaning of the festival and the "extrinsic occasion" said to be its cause.[26] George Dumézil,[27] however, was able to show that the connection of myth and ritual, in this case, is by no means "extrinsic": there is almost complete correspondence in outline and in detail.

The myth is well known:[28] the wrath of Aphrodite had smitten the women of Lemnos; they developed a "foul smell" (*dusōdia*) so awful that their husbands, understandably, sought refuge in the arms of Thracian slave-girls. This, in turn, enraged the women so much that, in one terrible night, they slew their husbands and, for the sake of completeness, all the male population of the island. Thereafter Lemnos was a community of women without men, ruled by the virgin queen Hypsipyle, until the day when the ship arrived, the Argo with Jason. This was the end of Lemnian celibacy. With a rather licentious festival the island returned to bisexual life. The story, in some form, is already known to the *Iliad:* the son of Jason and Hypsipyle is dwelling on Lemnos, Euneos, the man of the fine ship.

With this myth, the fire ritual is connected not in a casual or arbitrary manner, but by an identity of rhythm, marked by two *peripeteiai* (peripeties): first, there begins a period of abnormal, barren, uncanny life, until, second, the advent of the ship brings about a new, joyous life—which is in fact the return to normal life.

Correspondences go even farther. The mythological *aition* compels us to combine with the text of Philostratus another testimony about Lemnian ritual, which, too, is said to be a remnant of the Argonauts' visit. Myrsilos of Lesbos is quoted for a different explanation of the infamous *dusōdia:* not Aphrodite, but Medeia caused it; in accordance with the older version ousted by Apollonius,[29] Myrsilos made the Argonauts come to Lemnos on their return from Kolchis, though the presence of Medeia brought some complications for Jason and Hypsipyle. The jealous sorceress took her revenge: καὶ δυσοσμίαν γενέσθαι ταῖς γυναιξίν· εἶναί τε μέχρι τοῦ νῦν κατ᾽ ἐνιαυτὸν ἡμέραν τινά, ἐν ᾗ διὰ τὴν δυσωδίαν ἀπέχειν τὰς γυναῖκας ἄνδρα τε καὶ   69 υεῖς(And an evil odor descended on the women. And even down to our time there is a certain day of the year on which, because of the evil odor, women stay away from their husbands and sons).[30]

Thus one of the most curious features of the myth reappears in ritual, at least down to Hellenistic times: the foul smell of the women, which isolates them from men. Evidently this fits very well into that abnormal period of the purification ceremony. Extinguishing all fires on the island—this in itself means a dissolution of all normal life. There is no cult of the gods, which requires incense and fire on the altars, there is no regular meal in the houses of men during this period, no meat, no bread, no porridge; some special vegetarian diet must have been provided. The *hestia* (hearth), the center of the community, the center of every house is dead. What is even more, the families themselves are broken apart, as it were by a curse: men cannot meet their wives, sons cannot see their mothers. The active part in this separation of sexes is, according to the text of Myrsilos, played by the women; they are the subject of *apechein* (stay away from). They act together, by some sort of organization; probably they meet in the streets or the sanctuaries, whereas the male population is scared away. Thus the situation in the city closely reflects the situation described in the myth: disagreeable women rule the town, the men have disappeared.

Dumézil already went one step farther and used the myth to supplement our information about the ritual. There is the famous fate of King Thoas, son of Dionysus, father of Hypsipyle: he is not killed like the other men; Hypsipyle hides him in a coffin, and he is tossed into the sea.[31] Valerius Flaccus (*Arg.* 2. 242 ff.) gives curious details: Thoas is led to the temple of Dionysus on the night of the murder; on the next day, he is dressed up as Dionysus, with wig, wreath, garments of the god, and Hypsipyle, acting as Bacchant, escorts the god through the town down to the seashore to see him disappear. It is difficult to tell how much of this Valerius Flaccus took from older tradition;[32] the general pattern, the *apopompē* (sending away) of the semidivine king, the way to the sea, the tossing of the *larnax* (box) into the water surely goes back to very old strata.[33] It is fitting that the new life, too, should arrive from the sea—*apopompē* and *adventus* correspond.

One step farther, beyond Dumézil's observations, is to realize that the bloodshed wrought by the women, the killing of the men, must have had its counterpart in ritual, too: in sacrifices, involving rather cruel spectacles of bloodshed.[34] It would be impossible to "call secret gods from under the earth" (Philostr. loc. cit.) without the blood of victims, flowing into a pit, possibly at night; the absence of fire would make these acts all the more dreary. Women may have played an active part in these affairs; at Hermione, in a festival called Chthonia, four old women had to cut the throats of the sacrificial cows with sickle swords (Paus. 2.35). In Lemnos a ram-sacrifice must have been prominent; a ram is often represented on the coins of Hephaistia.[35] The fleece of a ram, *Dios kōidion,* was needed in many purification ceremonies;[36] incidentally, the Argonauts' voyage had the purpose of providing a ram's fleece.

Most clearly the concluding traits of the myth reflect ritual: the arrival of the Argonauts is celebrated with an *agon;* the prize is a garment.[37] This is as characteristic a prize as the Athenian oil at the Panathenaia, the Olympian olive-wreath in Olympia; the Lemnian festival must have ended with an *agon,* though it never attained Panhellenic importance. The garment, made by women, *aglaa erga iduiai* (who are knowledgeable in glorious crafts), is a fitting gift to end the war of the sexes; if Jason receives the garment of Thoas (Ap. Rh. 4.423–34), continuity bridges the gap of the catastrophe. There is one more curious detail in Pindar's account of the Lemnian *agon:* the victor was not Jason, but a certain Erginos, who was conspicuous by his untimely grey hair; the others had laughed at him.[38] Erginos "the workman," grey-haired and surrounded by laughter, but victorious at Lemnos after the ship had arrived—this seems to be just a transformation, a translation of Hephaistos the grey-haired workman, who constantly arouses Homeric laughter.[39] Thus the myth itself takes us back to the fire festival: this is the triumph of Hephaistos, the reappearing fire that brings new life, especially to the workmen in the service of their god. It is possible that laughter was required in the ritual as an expression of the new life—as in Easter ceremonies, both the new fire and laughter, even in churches, are attested in the Middle Ages.[40] Another peculiarity seems to have been more decidedly "pagan": surely neither Aeschylus nor Pindar invented the unabashed sexual coloring of the meeting of Lemniads and Argonauts; in Aeschylus, the Lemniads force the Argonauts by oath to make love to them.[41] Behind this, there must be ritual *aischrologia* (shameful words) or even *aischropoiia* (shameful acts) at the festival of licence which forms the concluding act of the abnormal period.

Many details are bound to escape us. Hephaistos, at Lemnos, was connected with the Kabeiroi. The Kabeirion, not far from Hephaistia, has been excavated; it offers a neat example of continuity of cult from pre-Greek to Greek population, but it did not yield much information about the mysteries, except that wine-drinking played an important role.[42] Myth connects the Kabeiroi of Lemnos with the Lemnian crime: they left the accursed island.[43] Since their cult continued at Lemnos, they evidently came back, when the curse had come to an end. In Aeschylus's *Kabeiroi*, they somehow somewhere meet the Argonauts; they invade the houses and mockingly threaten to drink everything down to the last drop of vinegar.[44] Such impudent begging is characteristic of mummery;[45] these Kabeiroi, grandchildren of Hephaistos, reflect some masked club, originally a guild of smiths, probably, who play a leading role at the purification ceremony anyhow. It is tempting to suppose that the ship of the Argonauts arriving at Lemnos really means the ship of the Kabeiroi; since they are associated with seafaring everywhere, it fits them to arrive by ship. The herald of the Argonauts who rises to prominence only in the negotiations of Argonauts and Lemniads is called Aithalides, "man of soot";[46] this binds him to the blacksmiths of Lemnos; the island itself was called Aithalia.[47] These Kabeiroi-blacksmiths would, after a night of revel, ascend Mount Mosychlos with their magic cauldron and light the fire, which was then, by a torch-race, brought to the city and distributed to sanctuaries, houses, and workshops—seductive possibilities.

Equally uncertain is the connection of the purification ceremonies with the digging of "Lemnian earth." *Lēmnia gē* (red-colored clay), described by Dioskurides and Galen, formed an ingredient of every oriental drugstore down to this century;[48] superstition can even outlive religion. Travelers observed how the clay was dug under the supervision of the priest at the hill which, by this, is identified as Mount Mosychlos; in the time of Galen, it was the priestess of Artemis[49] who collected it, throwing wheat and barley on the ground, formed it into small disks, sealed it with the seal of a goat, and sold it for medical purposes. The priestess of the goddess operating at the mount of Hephaistos—it is possible to connect this with the fire festival. Indeed it is all the more tempting because, owing to the continuity of ritual, this would give a clue as to the date of the festival: Lemnian earth was collected on 6 August; this corresponds with the time of Galen's visit.[50] Late summer is a common time for new-year festivals in the ancient world; incidentally, the *mustai* (initiates) of the Kabeiroi at Lemnos held conventions in Skirophorion,[51] i.e., roughly in August. Still, these combinations do not amount to proof.

One question has been left unsolved: what about the recurrent *dusōdia*? Can this be more than legend or slander?[52] The simple and drastic answer is given by a parallel from Athens: the authority of Philochoros[53] (*FGrHist* 328 F 89) is quoted for the fact that the women ἐν (δὲ) τοῖς Σκίροις τῇ ἑορτῇ ἤσθιον σκόροδα ἕνεκα τοῦ ἀπέχεσθαι ἀφροδισίων, ὡς ἂν μὴ μύρων ἀποπνέοιεν (in the festival of the Skira [the women] eat garlic so as to abstain from sexual relations, as they would not smell of perfume). Thus we have an unmistakable smell going together with disruption of marital order, separation of the sexes, at the Skira. The women flock together at this festival according to ancient custom,[54] and Aristophanes' fancy has them plan their coup d'état on this occasion (*Eccl.* 59). But there is even more similarity: the main event of the Skira is a procession that starts from the old temple of the Akropolis and leads toward Eleusis to the old borderline of Attica, to a place called Skiron. The priest of Poseidon–Erechtheus, the priestess of Athena, and the priest of Helios are led together under a sunshade by the Eteobutadai:[55] Erechtheus is the primordial king of Athens; he left his residence, the myth tells us, to fight the Eleusinians *epi Skireōi* (at Skiron) and disappeared mysteriously in the battle; his widow became the first priestess of Athena.[56] Thus we find in Athens, on unimpeachable evidence, the ritual *apopompē* of the king which was inferred from myth for the corresponding Lemnian festival. At Athens the concluding *agon* has been moved farther away: the "beginning of new life" is the Panathenaia in the following month Hekatombaion, the first of the year. If the perennial fire in the sanctuary of Athena and Erechtheus, the lamp of Athena, is refilled and rekindled only once a year,[57] this will have happened at the Panathenaia when the new oil was available and used as a prize for the victors. The month Skirophorion coincides approximately with August, the time of the digging of Lemnian earth. The name *Skira* is enigmatic, but most of the ancient explanations concentrate on some stem *skir- (skur-)*, meaning "white earth," "white clay," "white rock." At the place Skiron there was some kind of white earth, and Theseus is said to have made an image of Athena out of white earth and to have carried it in procession when he was about to leave Athens.[58] Were the *skira* some kind of amulets "carried" at the *skirophoria*, though less successful in superstitious medicine than their Lemnian counterparts?

There was another festival at Athens where the women ate garlic in considerable quantities:[59] the Thesmophoria. This festival was among the most widespread all over Greece, the there must have been many local variants; but there are features strikingly reminiscent of the pattern treated so far: the disruption of normal life, the separation of sexes; the women gather (cf. n. 59 below) for three or four days, they live at the Thesmophorion in huts or tents; in Eretria they did not even use fire (Plut. *Q. Gr.* 31). They performed uncanny sacrifices to chthonian deities; subterranean caves, *megara*, were opened, pigs thrown down into the depths; probably there

73

was a bigger, secret sacrifice toward the end of the festival. In mythological fantasy, the separation of the sexes was escalated into outright war.
The lamentable situation of the *kēdestēs* (father-in-law) in Aristophanes'
Thesmophoriazusai is not the only example. The Laconian women are said
to have overpowered the famous Aristomenes or Messene, when he dared
to approach them at the time of the Thesmophoria; they fought, by divine
instigation, with sacrificial knives and spits and torches—the scenery implies a nocturnal *aporrhētos thusia* (secret sacrifice) (Paus. 4.17.1). The
women of Kyrene, at their Thesmophoria, smeared their hands and faces
with the blood of the victims and emasculated King Battos, who had tried
to spy out their secrets.[60] The most famous myth in this connection concerns
those women whom Euripides already compared with the Lemniads (*Hec.*
887): the Danaids. They slew their husbands all together at night, too, with
one notable exception, as at Lemnos: Lynkeus was led to a secret escape by
Hypermestra the virgin. As the Argives kept the rule of extinguishing the
fire in a house where somebody had died,[61] the night of murder must have
entailed much extinguishing of fires. Lynkeus, however, when he was in
safety, lit a torch in Lyrkeia, Hypermestra answered by lighting a torch at
the Larisa, ἐπὶ τούτῳ δὲ Ἀργεῖοι κατὰ ἔτος ἕκαστον πυρσῶν ἑορτὴν
ἄγουσι (for this reason the Argives celebrate an annual festival of torches,
Paus. 2.25.4). It is questionable whether this ritual originally belongs to the
Danaid myth;[62] the word-play Lyrkeia-Lynkeus does not inspire confidence.
The myth at any rate has much to tell about the concluding *agon,* in which
the Danaids were finally given to husbands.[63] After the outrage against nature, a new life must begin, which happens to be just ordinary life. But it
is Herodotus who tells us that it was the Danaids who brought to Greece
the *teletē* (rite) of Demeter Thesmophoros, i.e., introduced the festival
Thesmophoria.[64] Thus the similarity of the myths of the Danaids and Lemniads and the similarity of the rituals of Thesmophoria and the Lemnian
fire festival is finally confirmed by Herodotus, who connects myth and
ritual.

One glance at the Romans: their *megistos tōn katharmōn* (greatest of
purifications) (Plut. *Q. R.* 86) concerns the *virgines Vestales* and the fire of
Vesta, and it covers a whole month. It begins with a strange *apopompē:*
twenty-seven puppets are collected in sanctuaries all over town, brought to
the *pons sublicius* and, under the leadership of the *virgo,* thrown into the
Tiber. They are called Argei, which possibly just means "grey men."[65] There
follows a period of Lent and abstinences: no marriage is performed in this
period,[66] the *flaminica,* wife of the *flamen Dialis,* is not allowed to have

intercourse with her husband. From 7 to 15 June, the temple of Vesta is opened for nine days; the *matronae* gather, barefoot, to bring offerings and prayers. Especially strange is the rule of the Matralia on 11 June: the *matronae*, worshiping Mater Matuta, are not allowed to mention their sons; so they pray for their nephews. Finally on 15 June the temple of Vesta is cleaned; *quando stercus delatum fas*, ordinary life may start again. The correspondence with the Lemnian *purphoria* is striking: the *apopompē* and tossing into the water, the separation of the sexes, of man and wife, even of mother and son, while the fire is "purified" on which the *salus publica* is thought to depend.

Enough of comparisons;[67] the danger that the outlines of the picture become blurred as the material accumulates can scarcely be evaded. Whether it will be possible to account for the similarity of pattern which emerged, by some historical hypothesis, is a formidable problem. There seems to be a common Near Eastern background; the pattern of the Near Eastern new-year festival has been summed up in the steps of mortification, purgation, invigoration, and jubilation,[68] closely corresponding, in our case, to *apopompē, aporrhētos thusia*, abstinences on the one hand, *agon* and marriage on the other. There appear to be Egyptian influences; more specifically, there are the traditions about the pre-Greek "Pelasgians" in Argos, Athens, Lemnos (according to Athenian tradition), and even in Italy.[69] But there is not much hope of disentangling the complex interrelations of Bronze Age tribes, as tradition has been furthermore complicated by contamination of legends. It may only be stated that similarities of ritual ought to be taken into account in such questions as much as certain names of tribes or of gods or certain species of pottery.

Still there are some definite conclusions, concerning the problem of myth and ritual: there is correspondence that goes beyond casual touches or secondary superimposition. But for the isolated testimonies of Myrsilus and Philostratus, we would have no clue at all to trace the myth back to Lemnian ritual, as we know nothing about the Thesmophoria of Argos. But the more we learn about the ritual, the closer the correspondence with myth turns out to be. The uprising of the women, the disappearance of the men, the unnatural life without love, the blood flowing—all this people will experience in the festival, as well as the advent of the ship that brings the joyous start of a new life. So far Jane Harrison's formula proves to be correct: "the myth is the plot of the dromenon";[70] its *peripeteiai* (sudden vicissitudes) reflect ritual actions. The much-vexed question, whether, in this interdependence, myth or ritual is primary, transcends philology,[71] since both myth and ritual were established well before the invention of writing. Myths are more familiar to the classicist; but it is important to realize that ritual, in its function and transmission, is not dependent on words. Even today children will get their decisive impressions of religion not so much from words and surely not from dogmatic teaching, but through the behavior of their elders: that special facial expression, that special tone of voice, that poise and gesture mark the sphere of the sacred; the seriousness and confidence displayed invite imitation, while at the same time relentless sanctions are added against any violation: thus religious ritual has been transmitted in the unbroken sequence of human society. By its prominence in social life, it not only provided stimulation for storytelling, but at the same time some kind of "mental container"[72] which accounts for the stability, the unchanging patterns of mythical tradition. Thus for understanding myth, ritual is not a negligible factor.

Still one can look at flowers without caring much for roots: myth can become independent from ritual; ritual origin does not imply ritual function—nor does the absence of ritual function exclude ritual origin. Ritual, if we happen to know about it, will be illustrative especially of strange features in a myth; but as these tend to be eliminated, myth can live on by its own charm. Apollonios did not bother about Lemnian festivals, and he dropped the *dusōdia*. The first and decisive step in this direction was, of course, Homer; or to be more exact, Greek myth found its final form in the oral tradition of skilled singers which is behind the *Iliad*, the *Odyssey*, and the other early epics. As a consequence of this successful activity of *aoidoi* (singers) and *rhapsōidoi* (rhapsodes) there took place, of course, all kinds of conflation, exchange, and superimposition of myths, as local traditions were adapted to "Homeric" tales. Thus myths are often attached to rituals by secondary construction; in this case, the details rarely fit. Poets and antiquarians are free to choose between various traditions, even to develop new and striking combinations. One myth may illustrate or even replace another, the motifs overlap, as the underlying patterns are similar or nearly identical.

Still more clear than the importance of ritual for the understanding of myth is the importance of myth for the history of religion, for the reconstruction and interpretation of ritual. Myth, being the "plot," may indicate connections between rites that are isolated in our tradition; it may provide supplements for the desperate lacunae in our knowledge; it may give decisive hints for chronology. In our case, Philostratus's testimony comes from the third century A.D., Myrsilus's from the third century B.C., Sophocles' allusion takes us back to the fifth; but as the Hypsipyle story is known to the *Iliad*, both myth and ritual must antedate 700 B.C. This means that not even Greeks are concerned, but the pre-Greek inhabitants of Lemnos, whom Homer calls *Sinties*, the later Greeks *Turrhēnoi*.[73] Excavations have given some picture of this pre-Greek civilization and its continuity into the Greek settlement; in spite of continuous fighting and bloodshed, there seems to have been a surprising permeability in religion, in ritual, and even in myths, between different languages and civilizations, and an equally surprising stability of traditions bound to a certain place.

If myth reflects ritual, it is impossible to draw inferences from the plot of the myth as to historical facts, or even to reduce myth to historical events. From Wilamowitz down to the *Lexikon der Alten Welt*,[74] we read that the Lemnian crime reflects certain adventures of the colonization period, neatly registered in *IG* XII. 8, p. 2: "Gracci ± 800—post 700" inhabiting Lemnos— as if the Lemniads had been slain by the Argonauts or the Argonauts by the Lemniads. To be cautious: it is possible that the crisis of society enacted in a festival breaks out into actual murder or revolution, which is henceforth remembered in the same festival;[75] but actual atrocities by themselves produce neither myth nor ritual—or else our century would be full of both. Another historical interpretation of the myth, given by Bachofen but envisaged already by Welcker, has, through Engels, endeared itself to Marxist historians:[76] the Lemnian crime as memory of prehistoric matriarchal society. The progress of research in prehistory, however, has left less and less space for matriarchal society in any pre-Greek Mediterranean or Near Eastern civilization. Indeed Hypsipyle did not reign over men—which *would* be matriarchy—the men have simply disappeared; and this is not a matriarchal organization of society, but a disorganization of patriarchal society, a transitional stage, a sort of carnival—this is the reason why the Lemniads were an appropriate subject for comedy.[77] Social order is turned upside down just to provoke a new reversal, which means the re-establishment of normal life.

If ritual is not dependent on myth, it cannot be explained by "beliefs" or "concepts"—which would be to substitute another myth for the original one. Ritual seems rather to be a necessary means of communication and solidarization in human communities, necessary for mutual understanding and cooperation, necessary to deal with the intrahuman problems of attraction and, above all, aggression. There are the never-dying tensions between young and old, and also between the sexes; they necessitate periodically some sort of "cathartic" discharge; it may be possible to play off one

77

conflict to minimize the other. This is what the myth is about: love, hatred, and their conflict, murderous instincts and piety, solidarity of women and family bonds, hateful separation and lustful reunion—this is the story of Hypsipyle, this is the essence of the ritual, too; only the myth carries, in fantasy, to the extreme what, by ritual, is conducted into more innocent channels: animals are slain instead of men, and the date is fixed when the revolution has to come to an end. Thus it is ritual that avoids the catastrophe of society. In fact only the last decades have abolished nearly all comparable rites in our world; so it is left to our generation to experience the truth that men cannot stand the uninterrupted steadiness even of the most prosperous life; it is an open question whether the resulting convulsions will lead to *katharsis* (purification) or catastrophe.

NOTES

This chapter originally appeared in *Classical Quarterly* 20, no. 1 (1970): 1–16. Reprinted by permission of Oxford University Press.

1. This paper was read at the Joint Triennial Classical Conference in Oxford, September 1968. The notes cannot aim at completeness of bibliography. The preponderance of ritual as against myth was vigorously stated by W. Robertson Smith, *Lectures on the Religion of the Semites* (1889; 1927³), ch. 1, pressed further by Jane Harrison: myth "nothing but ritual misunderstood" (*Mythology and Monuments of Ancient Athens* [1890] xxxiii). In Germany, it was the school of Albrecht Dieterich who concentrated on the study of ritual. Thus mythology is conspicuously absent from the indispensable handbooks of M. P. Nilsson (*Griechische Feste von religioser Bedeutung* [1906; hereafter: Nilsson, *GF*] and *Geschichte der griechischen Religion* [1, 1940; 1³, 1967; hereafter: Nilsson, *GGR*]) and L. Deubner (*Attische Feste* [1932; hereafter: Deubner]), whereas Wilamowitz stated that mythology was the creation of poets: "Der Mythos . . . entsteht in der Phantasie des Dichters" (*Der Glaube der Hellenen* 1 [1931] 42). Mythology tried to re-establish itself in the trend of phenomenology and C. G. Jung's psychology, largely ignoring ritual: see the surveys of J. de Vries, *Forschungsgeschichte der Mythologie* (1961); K. Kerényi, *Die Eröfnung des Zugangs zum Mythos* (1967); "die Religionswissenschaft ist vornehmlich Wissenschaft der Mythen" (K. Kerényi, *Umgang mit Göttlichem* [1955] 25).

2. B. Malinowski, *Myth in Primitive Psychology* (1926); D. Kluckhohn, "Myths and Rituals: A General Theory," *HThR.* 35 (1942) 45–79.

3. S. H. Hooke, ed., *Myth and Ritual* (1933), defining myth as "the spoken part of the ritual," "the story which the ritual enacts" (3); *Myth, Ritual, and Kingship* (1958); Th. H. Gaster, *Thespis* (1961²). Independently, W. F. Otto, in his *Dionysos* (1934), spoke of "Zusammenfall von Kultus und Mythos" (43 and *passim*). In fact connections between myth and ritual had been recognized by F. G. Welcker and, in an intuitive and unsystematic manner, by Wilamowitz ("Der mythische Thiasos aber ist ein Abbild des im festen Kultus gegebenen," *Euripides Herakles* 1 [1889] 85, cf. "Hephaistos" [*GGN*, 1895, 234 f.; hereafter: Wilamowitz; =*Kl. Schr.* v. 2, 5–35], on the binding of Hera). In interpretation of Greek tragedy, due attention has been paid to ritual; e.g., E. R. Dodds, *Euripides Bacchae* (1960²) xxv–xxviii.

4. Nilsson, *GGR* 14 n. with reference to Malinowski: "für die griechischen Mythen trifft diese Lehre nicht zu"; cf. *Cults, Myths, Oracles, and Politics in Ancient Greece* (1951) 10;

H. J. Rose, *Mnemosyne* iv. s. 3 (1950) 281–87; N. A. Marlow, *BRL* xliii (1960–61) 373–402; J. Fontenrose, *The Ritual Theory of Myth* (1966). As a consequence, historians of religion turn away from the Greek; see M. Eliade, *Antaios* ix (1968) 329, stating "daß wir nicht einen einzigen griechischen Mythos in seinem rituellen Zusammenhang kennen."

5. With regard to mysteries, as Nilsson (cf. n. 4 above) remarks (Gal. *UP* 6, 14 [iii. 576 K.]; Paus. 1.43.2; 2.37.2; 2.38.2; 9.30.12, cf. Hdt. 2.81; 2.47; 2.51; M.N.H. van den Burg, ΑΠΟΡ–ΡΗΤΑ ΔΡΩΜΕΝΑ ΟΡΓΙΑ [diss., Amsterdam, 1939]), not because there was nothing similar in nonsecret cults, but because only the secrecy required the use of general passive expressions as λεγόμενα, δρώμενα. Ritual as μίμησις of myth, e.g., D.S. 4.3.3; Steph. Byz. *s.v.*῎Αγρα. Cf. Ach. Tat. 2. 2 τῆς ἑορτῆς πατέρα διηγοῦνται μῦθον.

6. *Python* (1959) 461–62, against Hooke (above, n. 3) and J. E. Harrison, who wrote "the myth is the plot of the δρώμενον" (*Themis* [1927²] 331).

7. On the problem of the Philostrati and the author of the *Heroikos*, K. Münscher, *Die Philostrate* (1907) 469 ff.; F. Solmsen, *RE* 20 (1941) 154–59; on the date of the *Heroikos*, Münscher, 474, 497–98, 505; Solmsen 154.

8. Ch. 19 § 20 in the edition of G. Olearius (1709; followed by Kayser)=ch. 20 § 24 in the edition of A. Westermann (1849; followed by Nilsson, *GF* 470)=II.207 of the Teubner edition (C. L. Kayser, 1871); critical editions: J. F. Boissonade (Paris, 1806) 232; Kayser (Zurich, 1844, 1853²) 325. καὶ καθ᾽ ἕνα τοῦ ἔτους is found in three codices (γ, φ, ψ) and apparently in a fourth (p) before correction; the printed editions, from the Aldina (1503), dropped the καί at the beginning; Boissonade and Westermann adopted καθ᾽ ἕκαστον ἔτος found in the other manuscripts. Kayser lists 32 codices altogether.

9. *AAWW* (1939) 41–46, followed by M. Delcourt, *Héphaistos ou la légende du magicien* (1957; hereafter: Delcourt) 172—73; Nilsson, *GGR* 97, 6. S. Eitrem *SO* 9 (1930) 60 tried καθαίρονται ἡ Λῆμνος καὶ ⟨οἱ Λήμνιοι⟩ καθ᾽ ἕνα κατ᾽ ἔτος.

10. κατά c. gen., "down to a certain deadline" in the instances adduced by Wilhelm: a contract κατ᾽ εἴκοσι ἐτῶν, κατὰ βίου, κατὰ τοῦ παντὸς χρόνου. Cf. W. Schmid, *Der Attizismus* 4 (1898) 456.

11. Moer.: ὥρα ἔτους Ἀττικοί, καιρὸς ἔτους ῞Ελληνες; see Schmid, *Attizismus*, 361. For inversion of word order, cf. *Heroikos* 12.2 κρατῆρας τοὺς ἐκεῖθεν.

12. *Il.* 1.593, *Od.* 8.283–84 with Schol. and Eust. 157.28; Ap. Rh. 1.851–52 with Schol.; Nic. *Ther.* 458 with Schol., etc.; cf. Wilamowitz; C. Fredrich, "Lemnos" *MDAI(A)* 31 (1906) 60–86, 241–56 (hereafter: Fredrich); L. Malten, "Hephaistos," *JDAI* 27 (1912) 232–64 and *RE* VIII. 315–16. Combination with the fire festival: F. G. Welcker, *Die aeschyleische Trilogie Prometheus und die Kabirenweihe zu Lemnos* (1824; hereafter: Welcker) 155–304, esp. 247 ff.; J. J. Bachofen, *Das Mutterrecht* (1861), 90=*Ges. Werke*, 2. 276; Fredrich, 74–75; Delcourt 171–90, whereas L. R. Farnell, *Cults of the Greek States*, 5 (1909) 394 concluded from the silence of Philostratus that the festival was not connected with Hephaistos. The importance of the craftsmen was stressed by Welcker 248, Delcourt 177. That the festival belongs to Hephaistia, not Myrina, is shown by the coins already used by Welcker, cf. n.35 below.

13. Cf. Ap. Rh. 1. 850–52, 858–60; a dedication Ἀ]φροδίτει Θρα[ικίαι from the Kabeirion of Lemnos, *ASAA* 3/5 (1941/43) 91 no. 12; a temple of Aphrodite at Lemnos, Schol. Stat. *Theb.* 5.59; the κρατίστη δαίμων in Ar. *Lemniai* (fr. 365) may be the same "Thracian Aphrodite."

14. The sacrificial calendars regularly combine different deities in the same ceremonies; as the most extensive example, the calendar of Erchiai, G. Daux, *BCH* 87 (1963) 603 ff., S. Dow, *BCH* 89 (1965) 180–213.

15. Phot., Hsch. *s.v.* μεγάλη θεός=Ar. fr. 368; Steph. Byz. *s.v.* Λῆμνος. Pre-Greek representations: Fredrich 60 ff. with pl. viii/ix; A. Della Seta, *AE* (1937) 644, pl. 2/3; Greek coins in B.V. Head, *Historia Numorum* (1911²) 263.

16. Fredrich 75; J. G. Frazer, *The Golden Bough* (hereafter: Frazer, *GB*; 1911³) 8.72–75, 10.136; generally on fire festivals: 2.195–265, 10.106–11.44.

17. Usually "beliefs" are traced back to emotional experience; but see C. Lévi-Strauss, *Le Totémisme aujourd'hui* (1962) 102 f.: "Ce ne sont pas des émotions actuelles . . . ressenties à l'occasion des réunions et des cérémonies qui engendrent ou perpétuent les rites, mais l'activité rituelle qui suscite les émotions."

18. F. Cassola, "La leggenda di Anio e la preistoria Delia," *PP* 60 (1954) 345–67; there is an old sanctuary of the Kabeiroi on Delos, B. Hemberg, *Die Kabiren* (1950; hereafter: Hemberg) 140–53; the Orion myth combines Delos and Lemnos, below, n. 24.

19. Fredrich 75; with reference to a custom in Burma, Frazer, *GB* 10.136; Malten, "Hephaistos," 248 f.; Fredrich, however, thinks that the earth fire came to be extinguished at an early date.

20. κρατῆρες: Eust. 158.3, 1598.44; Schol. S. *Phil.* 800, 986; Val. Flacc. 2.332–39; Stat. *Theb.* 5.50, 87; *Silv.* 3.1.131–33. Less explicit: Heraclit. *All.* 26.15 (echoed by Eust. 157.37, Schol. *Od.* 8.284) ἀνίενται γηγενοῦς πυρὸς αὐτόματοι φλόγες (F. Buffière, *CB* 1962 keeps the manuscript reading ἐγγυγηγενοῦς, "un feu qu'on croirait presque sorti de terre," but this is hardly Greek); Acc. Trag. 532 "nemus exspirante vapore vides . . ." is incompatible with the volcano-, though not with the earth-fire-hypothesis.

21. L. Preller and C. Robert, *Griechische Mythologie* I⁴ (1894) 175, 178; R. C. Jebb, Sophocles, *Philoctetes* (1890) 243–45; P. Mazon, Sophocles, *Philoctète* (*CB* 1960), note on v. 800.

22. K. Neumann and J. Partsch, *Physikalische Geographie von Griechenland* (1885) 314–18, who immediately thought of the earth fire, cf. Fredrich 253–54, Malten, "Hephaistos," 233, *RE* VIII. 316, Nilsson, *GGR* 528–29; R. Hennig, "Altgriechische Sagengestalten als Personifikation von Erdfeuern," *JDAI* 54 (1939) 230–46. Earth fires are well attested at Olympos in Lycia (Malten, *RE* VIII. 317–19), where the Hephaistos cult was prominent, and at Trapezus in Arcadia (Arist. *Mir.* 127, Paus. 8.29.1) and at Apollonia in Epirus (Theopompus, *FGrHist* 115 F 316) without the Hephaistos cult.

23. Meineke and Pearson changed the text to ἀνακαλούμενον, Mazon translates "que tu évoqueras pour cela," though keeping ἀνακαλουμέμῳ; Jebb translates "famed as," with reference to S. *El.* 693, where, however, ἀνακαλούμενος is "being solemnly proclaimed" as victor.

24. Ancient burning-mirrors were always made of bronze; the testimonies in J. Morgan, "De ignis eliciendi modis," *HSCP* 1 (1890) 50–64; earliest mention: Thphr. *Ign.* 73, Eucl. *Opt.* 30 (burning-glass: Ar. *Nu.* 767); used in rituals of new fire: Plut. *Num.* 9 (Delphi and Athens, first cent. B.C.); Heraclit. *All.* 26.13 κατ᾽ ἀρχὰς οὐδέπω τῆς τοῦ πυρὸς χρήσεως ἐπιπολαζούσης ἄνθρωποι χρονικῶς χαλκοῖς τισιν ὀργάνοις ἐφειλκύσαντο τοὺς ἀπὸ τῶν μετεώρων φερομένους σπινθῆρας, κατὰ τὰς μεσημβρίας ἐναντία τῷ ἡλίῳ τὰ ὄργανα τιθέντες.

Parallels from the Incas, Siam, China: Frazer, *GB* 2.243, 245; 10.132, 137. Fredrich 75.3 thought of the burning-mirror in connection with the myth of Orion, who recovers his eyesight from the sun with the help of the Lemnian Kedalion (Hes. fr. 148 M.–W.). "Fire from the sky" lit the altar at Rhodes, the famous center of metallurgy (Pi. *O.* 7.48). The practice may have influenced the myth of Helios's cup as well as the theories of Xenophanes and Heraclitus about the sun (21 A 32, 40; 22 A 12, B 6 DK).

25. Galen 12.173 K., cf. Acc. Trag. 529–31.

26. *Trilogie Prometheus* 249–50.

27. *Le Crime des Lemniennes* (1924; hereafter: Dumézil).

28. Survey of sources: Roscher, *Myth. Lex.* 1. 2853–56 (Klügmann), 2.73–74 (Seeliger), 5. 808–14 (Immisch); Preller and Robert, *Griech. Mythologie* II⁴ (1921), 849–59; cf. Wilamowitz,

Hellenistische Dichtung 2 (1924), 232–48. Jason, Hysipyle, Thoas, Euncos in Homer: *Il.* 7.468–69, 14.230, 15.40, 21.41, 23.747; cf. Hes. fr. 157, 253–56 M.-W.

29. Pi. *P.* 4.252–57.

30. *FGrHist* 477 F 1a=schol. Ap. Rh. 1.609/19e; F 1b=Antig. *Hist. mir.* 118 is less detailed and therefore likely to be less accurate: κατὰ δή τινα χρόνον καὶ μάλιστα ἐν ταύταις ταῖς ἡμέραις, ἐν αἷς ἱστοροῦσιν τὴν Μήδειαν παραγενέσθαι, δυσώδεις αὐτὰς οὕτως γίνεσθαι ὥστε μηδένα προσιέναι. Delcourt, 173, 2 holds that only the information about Medeia goes back to Myrsilos; but the Scholiast had no reason to add a reference to "contemporary" events, whereas Myrsilos was interested in contemporary *mirabilia* (F 2; 4–6). Welcker, 250, already combined Myrsilos's with Philostratos's account.

31. Ap. Rh. 1. 620–26; Theolytos, *FGrHist* 478 F 3, Xenagoras, *FGrHist* 240 F 31, and Kleon of Kurion in Schol. Ap. Rh. 1. 623/6a; cf. E. *Hyps.* fr. 64, 74 ff.; 105 ff. Bond; Hypoth. Pi. *N.* b, iii. 2, 8–13 Drachmann; Kylix Berlin 2300=*ARV*² 409,43=G.M.A. Richter, *The Furniture of the Greeks, Etruscans and Romans* (1966) 385.

32. Cf. Immisch, *Roschers Myth. Lex.* 5. 806. Domitian had made a very similar escape from the troops of Vitellius in A.D. 68: *Isiaco celatus habitu interque sacrificulos* (Suet. *Dom.* 1.2, cf. Tac. *Hist.* 3:74; Jos. *Bell. Iud.* 4.11.4; another similar case in the civil war, App. *BC* 4.47; Val. Max. 7.3.8).

33. This is the manner of death of Osiris, Plut. *Is.* 13.356c. Parallels from folk custom: W. Mannhardt, *Wald- und Feldkulte,* 1 (1875) 311 ff.; Frazer, *GB* 2. 75, 4. 206–12; Dumézil 42 ff. Hypsipyle is a telling name; "vermutlich war Hypsipyle einst eine Parallelfigur zu Medea: die 'hohe Pforte' in ihrem Namen war die Pforte der Hölle" (Wilamowitz, *Griechische Tragoedien* 3⁷ [1926], 169,1)—or rather, more generally, the "high gate" of the Great Goddess. The same name may have been given independently to the nurse of the dying child—another aspect of the Great Goddess (*Hymn. Cer.* 184 ff.)—at Nemea.

34. See chapter 1 in this volume, §§II–III.

35. Cf. *Königliche Museen zu Berlin, Beschreibung der antiken Münzen* (1888) 279–83; Head *Historia*² 262–63; A. B. Cook, *Zeus,* III (1940) 233–34; Hemberg 161. A similar ram-sacrifice has been inferred for Samothrace (Hemberg 102, 284). Instead of the ram, the coins of Hephaistia sometimes have torches, πῖλοι (of Kabeiroi Dioskouroi), and kerykeion, also vines and grapes; all these symbols have some connection with the context of the festival treated here.

36. Nilsson, *GGR* 110–13; Paus. *Attic.* δ 18 Erbse.

37. Simonides, 547 Page; Pi. *P.* 4.253 with Schol.; cf. Ap. Rh. 2.30–32; 3.1204–6; 4.423–34.

38. Pi. *O.* 4.23–31; cf. Schol. 32 c; Callim. fr. 668. Here Erginos is son of Klymenos of Orchomenos, father of Trophonios and Agamedes (another pair of divine craftsmen, with a fratricide-myth, as the Kabeiroi), whereas Ap. Rh. 1.185, after Herodorus, *FGrHist* 31 F 45/55, makes him son of Poseidon, from Miletus, cf. Wilamowitz, *Hellenistische Dichtung,* 2. 238.

39. The constellation Erginos–Jason–Hypsipyle is akin to the constellation Hephaistos–Ares–Aphrodite in the famous Demodocus hymn (*Od.* 8.266–366): another triumph of Hephaistos amid unextinguishable laughter. A special relation to Lemnos is suggested by a pre-Greek vase fragment, found in a sanctuary in Hephaistia (A. Della Seta, *AE* [1937] 650; Ch. Picard, *RA* XX [1942–43] 97–124; to be dated about 550 B.C., as B. B. Shefton kindly informs me; cf. Delcourt 80–82: a naked goddess vis-à-vis an armed warrior, both apparently fettered. This is strikingly reminiscent of Demodocus's song, as Picard and Delcourt saw, though hardly a direct illustration of Homer's text, rather of "local legend" (cf. K. Friis Johansen, *The Iliad In Early Greek Art* [1967] 38, 59), i.e., a native Lemnian version. The crouching position of

the couple reminded Picard of Bronze Age burial customs; anthropology provides examples of human sacrifice in the production of new fire: a couple forced to mate and killed on the spot (see E. Pechuel-Loesche, *Die Loango-Expedition* 3.2 [1907] 171 ff.). Surely Homer's song is more enjoyable without thinking of such a gloomy background.

40. Mannhardt 502–8, Frazer, *GB* 10. 121 ff.; on "risus Paschalis," P. Sartori, *Sitte und Brauch* (1914) 3. 167.

41. Fr. 40 Mette, cf. Pi. *P.* 4.254; Herodorus, *FGrHist* 31 F 6.

42. Preliminary report *ASAA* 1/2 (1939/40) 223–24; inscriptions: *ASAA* 3/5 (1941/43), 75–105; 14/16 (1952/54), 317–40; D. Levi, "Il Cabirio di Lemno," *Charisterion A. K. Orlandos* 3 (Athens, 1966) 110–32; Hemberg 160–70. Wine-vessels bore the inscription Καβείρων. Kabeiroi and Hephaistos: Akousilaos, *FGrHist* 2 F 20, Pherekydes, *FGrHist* 3 F 48 with Jacoby *ad loc.*; O. Kern, *RE* X. 1423 ff.; this is not the tradition of Samothrace nor of Thebes (where there is one old Κάβιρος, Nilsson, *GGR*, pl. 48, 1) and thus points toward Lemnos. In the puzzling lyric fragment, adesp. 985 Page, Kabeiros son of Lemnos is the first man.

43. Photios *s.v.* Κάβειροι· δαίμονες ἐκ Λήμνου διὰ τὸ τόλμημα τῶν γυναικῶν μετενε-χθέντες· εἰσὶ δὲ ἤτοι Ἥφαιστοι ἢ Τιτᾶνες.

44. Fr. 45 Mette; that the Kabeiroi are speaking is clear from Plutarch's quotation (*Q. conv.* 633a): αὐτοὶ παίζοντες ἠπείλησαν.

45. K. Meuli, "Bettelumzüge im Totenkult, Opferritual und Volksbrauch," *Schweizer Archiv für Volkskunde*, 28 (1927/8) 1–38.

46. Ap. Rh. 1.641–51, cf. Pherekydes *FGrHist* 3 F 109.

47. Polyb. 34.11.4, Steph. Byz. Αἰθάλη.

48. Fredrich, 72–74; F. W. Hasluck, *ABSA* 16 (1909/10) 220–30; F.L.W. Sealey, *ABSA* 22 (1918/19) 164–65; Cook, III. 228 ff.; Diosc. 5.113; Galen, 12. 169–75 K. (on the date of his visit to Lemnos, Fredrich, 73.1; 76.1: late summer A.D. 166). According to Dioskurides, the blood of a goat was mixed with the earth, but Galen's informants scornfully denied this. The "priests of Hephaistos" used the earth to heal Philoktetes: Schol. AB B 722, Philostr. *Her.* 6.2, Plin. *NH* 35.33. Philoktetes' sanctuary, however, was in Myrina (Galen, 12. 171).

49. Possibly the "great Goddess"; cf. above, n. 15.

50. Cf. n. 48 above.

51. *ASAA* 3/5 (1941/43) 75 ff. no. 2; no. 6; but no. 4 Hekatombaion.

52. General remarks in Dumézil 35–39. Welcker 249 thought of some kind of fumigation. Cf. Frazer, *GB* 8. 73 for the use of purgatives in a New Fire festival. A marginal gloss in Antig. *Hist. mir.* 118 (cf. above, n.30) mentions πήγανον, cf. Jacoby, *FGrHist* 3. Comm. 437, n. 223.

53. E. Gjerstad, *ARW* XXVII (1929/30) 201–3 thinks Philochoros misunderstood the sense of the ritual, which was rather "aphrodisiac"; though he recognizes himself that short absti-nence enhances fertility.

54. *IG* II/III² 1177. 8–12 ὅταν ἡ ἑορτὴ τῶν Θεσμοφορίων καὶ Πληροσίαι καὶ Καλα-μαίοις καὶ τὰ Σκίρα καὶ εἴ τινα ἡμέραν συνέρχονται αἱ γυναῖκες κατὰ τὰ πάτρια.

55. Lysimachides, *FGrHist* 366 F 3; Schol. Ar. *Eccl.* 18; fullest account: E. Gjerstad, *ARW* XXVII (1929/30) 189–240. Deubner's treatment (40–50) is led astray by Schol. Luk. p. 275. 23 ff. Rabe, cf. Burkert, *Hermes* XCIV (1966) 23–24, 7–8.

56. E. *Erechtheus* fr. 65 Austin; death and tomb of Skiros: Paus. 1.36.4.

57. Paus. 1.26.6–7.

58. An. Bekk. 304.8 Σκειρὰς Ἀθηνᾶ· εἶδος ἀγάλματος Ἀθηνᾶς ὀνομασθέντος οὕτως ἤτοι ἀπὸ τόπου τινὸς οὕτως ὠνομασμένου, ἐν ᾧ γῆ ὑπάρχει λευκὴ . . . (shorter *EM* 720, 24); Schol. Paus. p. 218 Spiro σκιροφόρια παρὰ τὸ φέρειν σκίρα ἐν αὐτῇ τὸν Θησέα ἢ γύψον· ὁ γὰρ Θησεὺς ἀπερχόμενος κατὰ τοῦ Μινωταύρου τὴν Ἀθηνᾶν ποιήσας ἀπὸ γύψου ἐβάστασεν (see Wilamowitz, *Hermes* XXIX [1894] 243; slightly corrupt *Et. Gen.* p. 267

Miller=*EM* p. 718, 16, more corrupt Phot., Suda *s.v.* Σκίρα, who speak of Theseus's return); Schol. Ar. *Vesp.* 926 'Αθηνᾶ Σκιρράς, ὅτι γῇ (τῇ codd.) λευκῇ χρίεται. R. van der Loeff, *Mnemosyne* 44 (1916) 102–3; Gjerstad 222–26; Deubner 46–47 tried to distinguish Σκίρα and 'Αθηνᾶ Σκιράς, Deubner 46, 11, even Σκίρα and the place Σκῖρον (Σκίρον? Herodian, *Gramm. Gr.* 3. 1, 385. 1–4; 3. 2, 581. 22–31 [cf. Steph. Byz. Σκίρος] seems to prescribe Σκῖρον; Σκίρα Ar. *Thesm.* 834, *Eccl.* 18); *contra*, Jacoby, *FGrHist* 3B Suppl., nn. 117–18. The changing quantity (cf. οἶρός) is less strange than the connection σκιρ-, σκυρ- (cf. LSJ *s.v.* σκῖρον, σκῖρος, σκίρρος, σκῦρος), which points to a non-Greek word. On Σκῦρος (see Oros. *EM* 720, 24) Theseus was thrown down the white rock (Plut. *Thes.* 35).

59. *IG* II/III². 1184 διδόναι . . . εἰς τὴν ἑορτὴν . . . καὶ σκόρδων δύο στατῆρας. On Thesmophoria, Nilsson, *GF*, 313–25, *GGR*, 461–66, Deubner 50–60.

60. Ael., fr. 44=Suda *s.v.* σφάκτριαι and θεσμοφόρος. Nilsson, *GF*, 324–25.

61. Plut. *Q. Gr.* 24.296 F.

62. Cf. Nilsson, *GF* 470, 5; Apollod. 2.22, Zenob. 4.86, etc. point to a connection of Danaid myth and Lerna (new fire for Lerna: Paus. 8.15.9).

63. Pi. *P.* 9.111 ff., Paus. 3.12.3, Apollod. 2.22. Dumézil, 48 ff. discussed the similarities between the Argive and the Lemnian myth, without taking notice of the Thesmophoria.

64. Hdt. 2.171 τῆς Δήμητρος τελετῆς πέρι, τὴν οἱ Ἕλληνες θεσμοφόρια καλέουσι . . . αἱ Δαναοῦ θυγατέρες ἦσαν αἱ τὴν τελετὴν ταύτην ἐξ Αἰγύπτου ἐξαγαγοῦσαι καὶ διδάξασαι τὰς Πελασγιώτιδας γυναῖκας. The connection of Danaoi and Egypt is taken seriously by modern historians (G. Huxley, *Crete and the Luwians* [1961] 36–37; F. H. Stubbings, *CAH* XVIII [1963] 11 ff.; P. Walcot, *Hesiod and the Near East* [1966] 71); Epaphos may be a Hyksos name. Now Mycenean representations mainly from the Argolid show "Demons" (Nilsson, *GGR*, 296–97) in ritual functions—processions, sacrifice—whose type goes back to the Egyptian hippopotamus-Goddess Taurt, "the Great One" (Roeder, *Roschers Myth. Lex.* 5 878–908). S. Marinatos, *Proc. of the Cambridge Colloquium on Mycenean Studies* (1966) 265–74, suggests identifying them with the Δίψιοι of Linear B texts. If these "Demons" were represented by masks in ritual (E. Heckenrath, *AJA* 41 [1937] 420–21) it is tempting to see in this ritual of the "Great Goddess," influenced from Egypt, the Thesmophoria of the Danaids. Cf. also n. 33 above.

65. G. Wissowa, *Religion und Kultus der Römer* (1912²) 420; K. Latte, *Römische Religionsgeschichte* (1960) 412–14; on Vestalia: Wissowa 159–60, Latte 109–10; on Matralia: Wissowa 111, Latte 97–98, G. Radke, *Die Götter Altitaliens* (1965) 206–9, J. Gagé, *Matronalia* (1963) 228–35. The flogging of a slave-girl at the Matralia has its analogy in the role of the Thracian concubines at Lemnos and the hair-sacrifice of the Thracian slave-girls in Erythrai (below, n. 67). With the "tutulum" (=*pilleum lanatum*, Suet. apud Serv. Auct. *Aen.* 2.683) of the Argei, cf. the πῖλοι of Hephaistos and Kabeiroi (above, n. 35).

66. Plut. *Qu. R.* 86, 284 F: no marriage in May; Ov. *Fast.* 6.219–34: no marriage until 15 June, the *flaminica* abstains from combing, nail-cutting, and intercourse.

67. There is connection between the Lemnian festival and the Chian myth of Orion (above, n.24); a cult legend of Erythrai implies another comparable ritual: "Herakles" arrived on a raft, and Thracian slave-girls sacrificed their hair to pull him ashore (Paus. 7.8.5–8).

68. Th. Gaster, *Thespis* (1961²); for necessary qualification of the pattern, C. J. Bleeker, *Egyptian Festivals, Enactment of Religious Renewal* (1967) 37–38.

69. The evidence is collected by F. Lochner-Hättenbach, *Die Pelasger* (1960). The Athenians used the legends about the Pelasgians, whom they identified with the Τυρρηνοί (Thuc. 4.109.4), to justify their conquest of Lemnos under Miltiades (Hdt. 6.137 ff.). There was a family of Εὐνεῖδαι at Athens, acting as heralds and worshiping Dionysos Melpomenos; J. Toepffer, *Attische Genealogie* (1889) 181–206; Preller and Robert, *Griechische Mythologie* 2. 83

852–53. On Pelasgians in Italy, Hellanikos, *FGrHist* 4 F 4, Myrsilos, *FGrHist* 477 F 8 apud Dion. Hal. Ant. 1.17 ff., Varro apud Macr. *Sat.* 1.7.28 f.; on Camillus-Καδμῖλος, A. Ernout and A. Meillet, *Dict. étym. de la langue latine* (1959⁴) *s.v. Camillus.*

70. *Themis* (1927²) 331.

71. Cf. above, n. 3. In Egypt, there were clearly rituals without myths; Bleeker, 19; E. Otto, *Das Verhältnis von Rite und Mythus im Ägyptischen, SBHeidelberg.* 1958, 1. Biologists have recognized rituals in animal behavior; K. Lorenz, *On Aggression* (1966) 54–80.

72. An expression coined by W. F. Jackson Knight, *Cumaean Gates* (1936) 91 for the function of the mythical pattern relevant to historical facts.

73. Identification of Sinties and Tyrrhenians: Philochoros, *FGrHist* 328 F 100/1 with Jacoby *ad loc.* Main report on the excavations (interrupted before completion by the war): *ASAA* XV/XVI (1932–33); cf. D. Mustilli, *Enc. dell'arte antica,* III (1960) 230–31, L. Bernabo-Brea, ibid., IV (1961) 542–45. It is remarkable that there are only cremation burials in the pre-Greek necropolis (*ASAA,* supra 267–72). Wilamowitz 231 had wrongly assumed that the pre-Greek "barbarians" would have neither city nor Hephaistos-cult.

74. Wilamowitz, 231; *LAW, s.v.* "Lemnos."

75. In several towns of Switzerland, there are traditions about a "night of murder" allegedly commemorated in carnival-like customs; a few of them are based on historical facts; see L. Tobler, "Die Mordnächte und ihre Gedenktage," *Kleine Schriften* (1897) 79–105.

76. Welcker 585 ff.; Bachofen, cf. above, n. 12; F. Engels, *Der Ursprung der Familie, des Privateigentums und des Staats* (1884), Marx–Engels, *Werke* 21. 47 ff.; G. Thomson, *Studies in Ancient Greek Society* (1949) 175 (more circumspect: *Aeschylus and Athens* [1941; 1966³] 287). For a cautious re-evaluation of the theory of matriarchy, see K. Meuli in Bachofen, *Ges. Werke,* 3. 1107–15; on the Lycians, S. Pembroke, "Last of the matriarchs," *Journ. of the Econ. and Soc. Hist. of the Orient* 8 (1965) 217–47.

77. Λήμνιαι were written by Aristophanes (fr. 356–375), Nikochares (fr. 11–14), and Antiphanes (fr. 144–45); cf. Alexis (fr. 134), Diphilos (fr. 54), and Turpilius (90–99).

4

BUZYGES AND PALLADION: VIOLENCE AND
THE COURTS IN ANCIENT GREEK RITUAL

These days the word *ritual* appears mainly in contexts that suggest our emancipation from it, to denounce traditional order and behavior as irrational and primitive and thus sweep it away. And in fact, received models of behavior[1] clearly no longer suffice to regulate the world. At the same time, however, our necessarily increased awareness compels us to explain and understand those things in human society that previously functioned without examination. If rituals played such an important role, and if they were largely considered absolute and "sacred," they must have a particular meaning, an essential purpose. Thus to discard them thoughtlessly would be dangerous indeed.

The religion of ancient Greece in the pre-Christian era is particularly interesting in this regard, since here primeval ritual persisted amid an extraordinarily developed and variegated spirituality. To be sure, the interpretation of religion through myth had already collapsed with the beginnings of philosophy. The withering critique to which Xenophanes had subjected myths about the gods went unrefuted. Indeed, Plato stripped cult of a naive belief in its "magical" purpose by proving that an absolutely good god could not possibly be influenced by "sacrifice and prayer."[2] Nevertheless, the cults of the gods persisted with their problematic rituals, as did the festivals of the polis, for at least seven hundred years beyond the time of Xenophanes. The majority of citizens remained convinced that the city's morality and survival depended on the piety that was shaped in cult. Organizing the festivals had thus always been one of the chief tasks of the magistrates. And the year of military service required of the ephebes served to introduce them to the cults, through which the city marked the high points of its year, and which the ephebes helped prepare and carry out so that "from their earliest youth they would fulfill their obligation by diligently tending to the sacrifices and processions, acquiring the honors connected with these things, and thus learning to function within the customs of their city."³ In this way they were trained to become "good men and heirs of the city."⁴ Religion and tradition were virtually identical. The question of precisely how "diligently tending to the sacrifices and processions" would have such an effect, initially seems puzzling to an outsider. Yet it might become clear, if we could picture in our minds such a traditional ritual, both in its dramatic details and in its overall rhythm. We attempt to do just that in one particular instance.

Among the festivals performed by the ephebes between the Eleusinian mysteries in fall and the Greater Dionysia in spring, there is a ritual for Pallas Athena cited in three inscriptions: "they also helped lead Pallas out to Phaleron, and from there back in again, by torchlight, with all necessary discipline."⁵ At the bay of Phaleron Athens had its closest access to the sea. Thus the path of Pallas evidently leads "out" from her sanctuary in or near the city, and back "in" to her sacred precinct. The torches indicate a nighttime procession. While these inscriptions come from the years 123–106 B.C., a fragmentary notice in the local author Philochoros takes us back as far as the end of the fourth century B.C. Here we learn that the "guardians of the laws" must regulate the procession of Pallas "when the cult statue is taken to the sea."⁶ A far later inscription, around A.D. 265, which lists all officers of the ephebic organization, mentions in a prominent passage a "charioteer of Pallus."⁷ Pallas evidently rode in a war chariot, as gods regularly do in the Greek pictorial tradition, but a practice now used only in horse races. This introduces a vivid detail into the otherwise sketchy picture of the torch-lit nighttime procession of the ephebes down to the sea and back.

At first sight, a link with the Plynteria, the "washing festival" of Athena, appears to fill out the picture further.⁸ As now confirmed through an inscription, this festival took place in the summer, on the 29th of the month Thargelion. Xenophon (*Hell.* 1.4.12) and Plutarch (*Alc.* 34.1) relate how Alcibiades entered Athens in the year 408 on precisely this day, and that this already suggested the bad outcome that was in store for him. For this was a day of pollution: priests and priestesses of the Praxiergidai family performed eerie rites upon the wooden statue of Athena Polias, which stood in the Erechtheion on the Acropolis; they "remove[d] its adornments and cover[ed] up the statue." Since the festival's name indicates washing, and Greek women ever since Nausikää took their wash to the sea, and since a procession during the Plynteria is explicitly attested, it seemed reasonable to equate it with Pallas's procession to the sea at Phaleron and back. There is clearly something plausible in the idea of a great festival of purification, in which the functional necessity of cleaning the temple and cult-statue extends to removing demonic forces of harm, or harmful substances. In any case, a linkage between Pallas's procession and the Plynteria is found in almost every handbook or specialized study.[9] But don't the descriptions in Xenophon and Plutarch imply rather that the cult image remains in the temple under wraps, hidden in a shroud like the statues in St. Peter's during Passiontide? The name Plynteria points only to washing the clothes, not bathing the goddess.[10] Moreover, the "four villages," among which Phaleron is grouped, have their own cult tradition, separate from that of the Athenian Acropolis.[11] The goddess in the Erechtheion, to whom the Panathenaic peplos is brought, is officially named Athena Polias and is called Athena precisely in connection with the Plynteria entry in the festival calendar (n. 8 above); the ephebic inscriptions on the other hand consistently speak of "Pallas," as does Philochoros.[12] Above all, however, there are problems with the festival calendar: the Plynteria come in midsummer, while the procession of Pallas is always mentioned between the Mysteries in fall and the Dionysia in spring.[13] In all likelihood, then, Pallas's procession occurred around the beginning of winter, between the Proerosia, the festival before plowing, and the Lesser Dionysia in the Piraeus,[14] which were celebrated in winter, before the Greater Dionysia.[15] That would presumably bring us to the month of Maimakterion, which is far indeed from the month of the Plynteria.

What we find particularly confusing in the alien polytheistic system is the juxtaposition of similar cults that are nonetheless distinct—probably a reflection of an already pluralistic society in early urban cultures. The old carved image of Athena on the Athenian citadel was not the only Athena worshiped in Athens. There was at least one other extremely sacred wooden statue of the goddess, one especially linked with the name Pallas: the Palladion. Every Greek would have known about the Palladion from the Trojan cycle of myth: Troy could be conquered only once Diomedes and Odysseus had stolen the diminutive, portable statue of Pallas from Troy in a daring nighttime raid. Where it ended up was a matter of dispute: Argos, home of Diomedes, had a Palladion on display, but so did Athens, and likewise New Ilion on the site of ancient Troy. Local historians fought about the authenticity or inauthenticity of these Palladions by means of bold legendary-historical constructs until the partisans of the Romans ultimately won with their claim that the Palladion was in the temple of Vesta in Rome, in that inner sanctum that no one was allowed to enter.[16]

But Trojan or not, a primitive wooden statue of an armed Pallas stood in Athens, too, in its own sanctuary, where one of the highest ranking priests of Athens officiated, the "priest of Zeus at the Palladion and Buzyges."[17] It was his job to accomplish a "sacred plowing" with a team of oxen—whence the name "Buzyges" (ox-yoker)—and the curse of the Buzyges upon those who transgressed certain fundamental moral precepts was proverbial. The fact that the goddess is present in the form of her old carved image, while the god is represented only by his priest—linked with altar and sacrifice—may well be a pairing that goes back to remotest antiquity.[18] One of the most important Athenian courts, moreover, second only to that on the Areopagus, was located "at the Palladion." Its purview included illicit killings, incitement to murder, and unlawful acts of violence against slaves and foreigners.[19] What this motley array of offenses share is the punishment that followed upon a guilty verdict: not the death penalty, but banishment. Those convicted had to leave the land by a "fixed route" and could return only if the victim's family waived its right to vengeance, and following certain purificatory ceremonies.[20] This system of punishment—the path into banishment and the return—remained at least until the time of Demosthenes primarily a ritual, not an administrative act. As to the site "at the Palladion," it has not been precisely located: scholars have looked for it in the southeast, toward the Stadium and Ardettos hill, or toward Phaleron. The question has hardly come up as to whether the *disiecta membra* of the tradition—the old image of the armed goddess, the sacred plowing and the curse of Buzyges, and finally the court itself—could share more than merely their locale.

As early as the nineteenth century, it was occasionally suggested that the ephebes escorted this very Palladion in a procession to the sea and back.[21] Topography suggested this conclusion, the name "Pallas" even more so, not to mention an analogous procession to a "bath" held in connection with the Argive Palladion.[22] But most of all, the festival calendar supports it: the "sacred plowing" of the Buzyges belongs in the month Maimakterion,[23] the very month to which the information in the ephebic inscriptions had pointed, and the same one—as we can infer from the orator Antiphon and a Scholion to Aristophanes—in which the court "at the Palladion" opened its session.[24] The fact that three independent witnesses agree in this point of chronology surely indicates that the plowing, the procession of Pallas, and the court stand in some as yet obscure relationship to one another.

The etiological myth takes us a step farther. It tells of a presumed past, in which the foundations were laid for ongoing customs, especially for festivals and rituals, which are of course themselves reflected in the tale. After the poets, local historians—in Athens above all the "Atthidographers" of the fourth century—took on the task of elucidating the tradition by means of plausible tales of its origins, and so of handing it on. Historians of religion have paid scant attention to the apparently arbitrary and contradictory information that they present. Yet if one looks carefully at what they have to say about the Palladion in Athens, one not only confirms beyond all doubt the connection between the procession to Phaleron and the Palladion but also glimpses the way in which the cults concerned with the ancient statue, the "ox-yoking" priest of Zeus, and the court for bloodguilt fit together.

The patriotic Atthidographers do not doubt that the Athenian Palladion is genuine, that is, that it comes from Troy. Just how it got from Diomedes to Athens remained to be explained. The epic of Troy's sack[25] mentioned two sons of Theseus, Demophon and Akamas, who took part in the fighting at Troy. One might expect that they would somehow have received the wondrous statue from Diomedes. What we generally hear instead is the tale of bloody strife in Attica: Some Argives carrying the Palladion home with them from Troy landed in Phaleron at night; the Athenians took them for robbers and killed the strangers on the spot. Akamas then recognized the dead men as Argives and found the Palladion. They buried them, honored them with an altar dedicated to those who were "unknown"—evidently the famous altar of the "unknown gods" in Phaleron, which gave the apostle Paul his cue for the speech on the Areopagus—and built a sanctuary for the Palladion at the site of the bloody deed, where the court would henceforth punish illicit killing and the murder of foreigners.[26] The sequence of events from the bloody battle in which the Palladion is acquired to the establishment of the court is confirmed in variants of the tale, which, however, intensify the narrative even further: In the nighttime tumult King Demophon himself seized the Palladion, "abducted" it,[27] and killed many men in so doing; indeed he fled with the statue on his royal chariot, crushing beneath his wheels some of the enemy in the process[28] or even an Athenian.[29] On this scenario Demophon was not so much the court's founder as its first accused, and thus, as the exemplar, he was the first to undergo the ritual to which those found guilty "at the Palladion" had to submit. One version of the etiological myth states explicitly that when Demophon snatched away the Palladion "he took it down to the sea and after purifying it on account of the killings he set it up in this place."[30]

What other versions had merely hinted at, this one makes quite explicit: 89

The etiological legends about the capture of the Palladion and the founding of the court reflect a ritual, i.e., Pallas's journey in the chariot to the sea at Phaleron. Every detail that is known to us about the procession may be found in the legends: the locale, its nocturnal setting, the image of the goddess on the chariot, the purification in the sea, and the return to the sanctuary. That the ephebic procession accompanied the Palladion—and not the Plynteria of Athena Polias—is thus assured, and its function becomes clear: the renewed dedication of the cult-statue each year, and opening of the court.

There is still the question of what ritual act in the festival corresponds to the bloody deed that lies at the heart of the myth. Here we must make a detour to a non-Attic cult in which a cursing "ox-yoker" likewise plays a part. At Lindos on Rhodes, where Athena Lindia held sway atop the picturesque and craggy citadel, a peculiar ox sacrifice was performed below the fortress, which made Lindos proverbial. The priest, in sharpest contrast to the solemn silence normally maintained during sacrifice, was expected to rail and curse with all his might, and the people evidently found this amusing. By way of explanation, the myth told of how Herakles, the gluttonous globe-trotter, came to Lindos one evening, encountered a farmer plowing with two oxen, and demanded food. When the farmer hesitated, Herakles promptly unyoked one of the oxen, slaughtered, roasted, and ate it, the aggrieved farmer's bitter curses only whetting his appetite. For that reason, right then and there he proclaimed the farmer his priest, and since that time the sacrifice is conducted in this unusual way in Lindos.[31]

The similarity to the Attic proceedings is more than just coincidence: here as there the "ox-yoker" and his curse function within Athena's sphere of power. The fact that Herakles figures in the story at Lindos scarcely matters if one asks who in reality would have stood in for Herakles at the sacrifice and devoured the ox: it was usually the ephebes who identified with the daring son of Zeus, and cattle sacrifice was among their favorite accomplishments, an opportunity to prove their strength and appetite. Thus it was presumably the job of ephebic groups to unyoke the Buzyges' plowox and to sacrifice it; they were the ones, moreover, who would roast the ox and eat it at the foot of the Lindian acropolis as evening fell, to the accompaniment of laughter prompted by the ritual barrage of curses and raillery.

There was no comparable burlesque at Athens. Nonetheless, the Athenian Buzyges' raging curse became proverbial—one could say, "Why are you screaming like a Buzyges?"[32] suggesting that the curse must have had its place and occasion at a public festival. One of the curses applied to the person who killed the plow-ox, an action resembling murder.[33] The Lindian parallel leads us to conclude that killing the plow-ox was not an eventuality to be prevented, but rather a *fait accompli*. There was no question of Athenian farmers letting their plow-oxen die of a happy old age;[34] they slaughtered them after they had tilled their fields, despite the fact that the cattle were their collaborators, their servants, their housemates—a conflict that cannot be avoided, just resolved inasmuch as expiation follows the "holy" sacrifice, as does the appointment of a court.

"These are no longer sacred rites, but sacrilege! Here they call 'holy' what elsewhere is punished in the most severe fashion." Thus the Christian author Lactantius in response to the Lindian rite (*Inst.* 1.21.37), and he cuts straight to the heart of the matter. In every animal sacrifice, life is affirmed through the act of killing;[35] this fact is frequently covered up through deadening routine, but it often breaks terrifyingly into the open, notably in some of the great bull-sacrifices. There was just such a "bovicide," Bouphonia, at year's end in late summer on the Acropolis. The priest who struck the fatal blow had to flee; a court was subsequently convened, which (veering toward the burlesque) sentenced the knife, whereupon that implement was thrown into the sea.[36] There were "unspeakable," "forbidden/secret" sacrifices elsewhere as well, conducted mainly at night. The sacred is the extraordinary, the overturning of the everyday; this is where boundaries are burst and we are forced to look into the abyss. The route back from terror to order is then marked by rituals of flight, by purificatory ceremonies, by consecrating the remains—for example, bull's horns—and constructing a monument or statue, by staging a combat or agon, a special instance of which may be the trial before a court. From a historical perspective, blood sacrifice is probably a continuation of paleolithic hunting customs adapted by farming and urban cultures for the sake of their sociological/psychological function. In a secure and hallowed space our destructive instincts and murderous desires are given free rein so as to build a renewed and sanctified order out of fear and guilt. The experience of violence shapes the bounds of the law.

Thus the ritual of "yoking the oxen," the procession of the ephebes in honor of Pallas, and the opening of the court come together in the dramatic arc of a festival: the "sacred plowing" ends the tilling of the fields in autumn; in the evening the plow-ox is unhitched from the plow and dies, felled by the blow of an axe in the sanctuary of Zeus and Pallas. As elsewhere, the ephebes presumably performed the sacrifice. The bloody act of violence provokes a curse, yet the ritual shows the way to avoid its effects: the image of Pallas is seized, set on a wagon, and taken in a procession to the sea, which after all "washes away all human ills" (E. *IT.* 1193). The procession returns by torchlight, while it is still night; and flames presumably flare up now upon the altars as well, and the remains of the slaughter dissolve amid incense and the smells of sacrifice. At daybreak the court can convene in the holy sanctuary of the newly installed goddess. This completes the transition from an act of violence to the community of law, a community still possible despite that act. The curse of the Buzyges is included in this change: his three preeminent curses target the man who refuses to give water to another, to allow fire to be kindled from his own, and to show the way to one who is lost.[37] These precepts, which have to do especially with foreigners, are proclaimed from within the sanctuary of Zeus and Pallas, where the murder of foreigners and slaves is likewise punished, and they are fundamental indeed. The ritual marks the way in which the community can come to terms with bloodguilt. After all, the "fixed path" of the guilty man into banishment is set by the court "at the Palladion," as are the "purifications" of those permitted to return. According to the myth, it was Demophon who first drove down this path with the Palladion. The festival repeats the constitutive act, the capture and installation of the Palladion. And inasmuch as it mirrors the primeval act in myth, it defines for the real world the shape of the everyday order.

For more than one thousand years, a polis like Athens survived with a certain structural identity, with—and in a certain sense through—its religious organization. This evidently penetrated deeper than did Xenophanes' critique. It was only in the period of general social, economic, and military collapse at the end of antiquity that the cities and the old religion vanished almost simultaneously. What survived was the problem of aggression and violence. Even those who forecast the future should not disdain, perhaps, to look with care at the evidence of the past when they try to distinguish between possible and impossible forms of human society.

NOTES

This chapter is a revised version of an inaugural lecture delivered at the University of Zurich on June 23, 1969. Footnotes were limited to the essential. I cite the following frequently, and only by the name of the author: F. F. Chavannes, *De Palladii raptu* (diss., Berlin, 1891); A. B. Cook, *Zeus* I–III (Cambridge, 1914–40); L. R. Farnell, *The Cults of the Greek States* I–V (Cambridge, 1896–1909); L. Deubner, *Attische Feste* (Berlin, 1932); F. Imhof-Blumer and P. Gardner, *Numismatic Commentary on Pausanias* (London, 1885–87); J. H. Lipsius, *Das attische Recht und Rechtsverfahren* (Berlin, 1905–14); A. Mommsen, *Feste der Stadt Athen im*

BUZYGES AND PALLADION

Altertum (Leipzig, 1898); M. P. Nilsson, *Geschichte der griechische Religion* I³ (Munich, 1967); E. Pfuhl, *De Atheniensium pompis sacris* (Berlin, 1900); J. Toepffer, *Attische Genealogie* (Berlin, 1889).

1. Since Sir Julian Huxley, the term *ritual* has been usurped by the behavioral sciences and used in the sense of a behavioral pattern that has lost its practical function and is used for communication instead; see K. Lorenz, *Das sogenannte Böse* (Vienna, 1963, 1970²⁵=Aggression, 1966) ch. 5—in my view a productive point of departure toward understanding this topic, even if there is nothing analogous to "the sacred" in zoology. see also P. Weidkuhn, *Aggressivität, Ritus, Säkularisierung* (Basel, 1965).

2. Plato *Leg.* 885b, 716d ff., 905d ff., *Rep.* 364b ff. What remained as the meaning of cult was the "approximation to the divine." Xenokrates' solution for the traditional rituals was to claim that they were directed toward lesser Demons (fr. 23-25 Heinze).

3. *IG* II/III² 1039.26–28: ὅπως ἀπὸ τῆς πρώτης ἡλικίας ἐν τεῖ [τ]ε [περὶ τὰς θυ]σία[ς καὶ τὰς πομπὰ]ς ἐπιμελείᾳ τὸ τ[εταγμένον ποιού]μενοι καὶ τυγχάνοντες τῆς περὶ ταῦτα τιμ[ῆς ἐν] τοῖς τ[ῆς πόλεως] ἐθισμοῖς ἀναστρ[αφῶσιν. . . . Cf. Livy 27.8.5 (with A. D. Nock, *RAC* II 111) on the *cura sacrorum et caerimoniarum*.

4. *IG* II/III² 1006.52–54: ὁ δῆμος . . . βουλόμενος το[ὺ]ς ἐκ τῶν πα[ί]δων μεταβαίνοντας εἰς τοὺς ἄνδρας ἀγαθοὺς γίνεσθαι τῆς πατρίδος διαδόχους. . . .

5. *IG* II/III² 1006.11: συνεξήγαγον δὲ καὶ τήν Παλλάδα Φαληροῖ κἀκεῖθεν πάλιν συνεισήγαγον μετὰ φωτὸς μετὰ πάσης εὐκοσμίας, cf. 75 f. (123/2 B.C.); 1008.9f. (119/8 B.C.); 1011.10 f.: συνεξήγαγον δὲ καὶ τ[ὴ]ν Παλλάδα μετὰ τῶν γεννητῶν καὶ πάλιν εἰ[σήγαγ]ον μετὰ πάσης εὐκοσμίας (107/6 B.C.).

6. *FGrHist* 328 F 64b (cf. Jacoby *ad loc.*): (οἱ νομοφύλακες) καὶ τῇ Παλλάδι τὴν πομπὴν ἐκόσμουν, ὅτε κομίζοιτο τὸ ξόανον ἐπὶ τὴν θάλασσαν.

7. *IG* II/III² 2245.299 (A.D. 262/3 or 266/7). The ἡνίοχος τῆς Παλλάδος stands in between σωφρονισταί, γυμνασίαρχοι, and συνστρεμματάρχαι. Thus it can hardly just be a position created ad hoc for a one-time consecration of a statue (thus Kirchner *IG ad loc.*). For Attic coins from the Roman Empire with Pallas Athena on her chariot, see Imhof-Blumer 136, pl. AA 22/23; J. N. Svoronos, *Les monnaies d'Athènes* (Munich, 1923) pl. 88, #8-22 (galloping away over a recumbent figure: #8/9).

8. See Deubner 17–22, Nilsson 120. The beginning on the 29th of Thargelion was confirmed—against Deubner 18—by a fragment of the official calendar of Nikomachos for the state of Attica: [δευτέραι] φθίνοντος [᾿Αθηνά]αι φᾶρος (*Hesperia* 4 [1935] 321, 517; F. Sokolowski, *Lois sacrées des cités grecques* [Paris, 1962] #10).

9. W. Rinck, *Die Religion der Hellenen* (Zurich, 1854) II 178; Mommsen 7 f., 10 f., 496.3, 499–504 (similarly *Heortologie* [Leipzig, 1864] 429 ff.); Toepffer 135; L. Preller and C. Robert, *Griechische Mythologie* I⁴ (Berlin, 1894) 209.3; Pfuhl 90; P. Stengel, *Die griechischen Kultusaltertümer* (Munich, 1920³) 247; J. Harrison, *Prolegomena to the Study of Greek Religion* (Cambridge, 1922³) 115; Deubner 18 f.; Cook III 749; L. Ziehen, *RE s.v.*"Plynteria" XXI 1060–62; Nilsson 102; Chr. Pelekidis, *Histoire de l'éphébie attique* (1962) 251; E. R. Walton, *Lexikon der Alten Welt* (Zurich, 1965) *s.v.* "Plynteria." Cf. n. 21 below.

10. The distinction between λούειν, "bathe" and πλύνειν, "wash" was emphasized by Farnell I 262a and Pfuhl 91.21. Thus the two names in Phot. *s.v.* λουτρίδες· δύο κόραι περὶ τὸ ἕδος τῆς ᾿Αθηνᾶς· ἐκαλοῦντο δὲ αὗται καὶ πλυντρίδες· οὕτως ᾿Αριστοφάνης (fr. 841): the statue λούεται, the robe πλύνεται. The Athenian festival was called Plynteria, not Λουτρά, presumably because "washing" alone belonged to the public procession.

11. The procession of the Skirophoria, which starts at the Erechtheion, heads toward Eleusis, not Phaleron (Lysimachides, *FGrHist* 366 F 3; Deubner 46). On the *tetrakomoi*, see Poll. 4.99; 105; Hsch. Τετράκωμος; Steph. Byz. ᾿Εχελίδαι.

93

12. Emphasized by O. Jahn, *De antiquissimis Minervae simulacris Atticis* (Bonn, 1866) 21; Farnell I 261.

13. Mommsen 496.3 tries to get around this by assuming that the ephebic inscriptions did not enumerate the cults in chronological order. But the procession of Pallas cannot be assigned to any particular subject category, and the basic chronological framework is clear: the Dionysia, for instance, are never mentioned before the Mysteries.

14. *IG* II/III² 1006.10; Deubner 68.

15. *IG* II/III² 1008.13; 1011.12; Deubner 137.

16. See Chavannes *passim*; Wörner, *Roschers Myth Lex.* III 1301–24, 3413–50; J. Sieveking, *Roschers* III. 1325–33; L. Ziehen, *RE* XVIII, 3 171–89; G. Lippold, *RE* XVIII, 3 189–201; C. Koch, *RE* VIII A 1731.

17. ἱερεὺς τοῦ Διὸς τοῦ ἐπὶ Παλλαδίου καὶ βουζύγης *IG* II/III² 3177, cf. 1906 on the occasion of the consecration of a new statue with approval of the Delphic oracle (#457 H. W. Parke and D. E. W. Wormell, *The Delphic Oracle* [Oxford, 1956] 2 vols.) in Augustan times. For a theater seat Βουζύγου ἱερέως Διὸς ἐν Παλλαδίωι cf. *IG* II/III² 5055; for funds Ἀθε-ναίας ἐπὶ Παλλαδίοι Δεριον[εί]οι in a financial document, cf. *IG* I² 324.78; 95 (426/2 B.C.; cf. *SEG* 22, 47). Δεριονείοι is obscure; Ziehen, *RE* XVIII, 3 179, deduces a Derioneus as founder; Derione appears as the name of an amazon at Quintus of Smyrna 1.42, 230, 258. On the Buzyges, see Toepffer 136–49; *RE* III 1094–97; Cook III 606–10. The legend in Polyainos 1.5 (n. 25 below) assumes that the Buzyges has the Palladion in safe keeping.

18. It may hark back to paleolithic statuettes of women; see *Technikgeschichte* 34 (1967) 289–92.

19. See Th. Lenschau, *RE s.v.* ἐπὶ Παλλαδίῳ XVIII, 3, 168–71 with bibliography; Lipsius 20 assumes that the court is older than that of the Areopagus. On its location see W. Judeich, *Topographie von Athen* (Munich, 1931²) 421: the only evidence is Kleidemos's statement (*FGrHist* 323 F 18) that the Amazons attacked "starting from the Palladion, from Ardettos and Lykeion." The altar of the "unknown" ones was in Phaleron (Paus. 1.1.4). The excerpts of Phanodemos imply that the Palladion was consecrated "at that very place," but according to the ephebic inscriptions the place where it was normally kept was specifically not Phaleron. The excerpts presumably confused the beginning and the end of the τακτὴ ὁδός (below, n. 20). Despite Akamas's role in the etiological legend, there seems to be no possible place in the phyle Akamantis for the sanctuary ἐπὶ Παλλαδίῳ. See the map in E. Kristen, *Atti del III. Congresso internazionale di epigrafia greca e latina* (Rome, 1959) pl. 26.

20. Demosthenes 23.72: τὸν ἁλόντα ἐπ᾽ ἀκουσίῳ φόνῳ ἔν τισιν εἰρημένοις χρόνοις ἀπελθεῖν τακτὴν ὁδὸν καὶ φεύγειν, ἕως ἂν αἰδέσηταί τινα (τις eds.,) τῶν ἐν γένει τοῦ πεπον-θότος· τηνικαῦτα δ᾽ ἥκειν δέδωκεν (ὁ νόμος) ἔστιν ὃν τρόπον, οὐχ ὃν ἂν τύχῃ, ἀλλὰ καὶ θῦσαι καὶ καθαρθῆναι καὶ ἄλλ᾽ ἄττα διείρηκεν ἃ χρὴ ποιῆσαι.

21. Chr. Petersen, *Die Feste der Pallas Athene in Athen* (1855) 12; O. Jahn (n. 12 above); Chavannes 36; Farnell I 261 f. Chavannes and Farnell already referred to the etiological legends. W. Dittenberger, *De ephebis Atticis* (diss., Göttingen, 1863) 63 and D. Dumont, *Essai sur l'ephébie Attique* (1875–76) I 283 considered whether the procession could be at the Oscho-phoria.

22. See Callim. Λουτρὰ Παλλάδος, and L. Ziehen, *Hermes* 76 (1941) 426–29. Callim. vv. 35–42 (cf. the Schol. to v. 37) likewise refers to an etiological legend: the priest Eumedes, having been condemned to death as a traitor, seized the Palladion together with the shield of Diomedes and fled into the mountains. His return evidently coincided with the Heraklids' takeover of power, and their authority was consolidated by the newly "installed" Palladion. On hearing of the priest of Pallas in Argos riding in the chariot with the shield of Diomedes and the statue of the goddess, one cannot help thinking of the thrilling scene in *Il.* 5, where

Pallas Athena herself leaps onto Diomedes' chariot and guides his spear to wound Ares. To what extent could the Iliadic scene already reflect the Argive rite?

23. We conclude this on the basis of the Athenian calendar frieze, Deubner 250 on pl. 36 #8.

24. Scholia V on Ar. *Av.* 1047 criticizes the summons of Peisthetairos "during Munichion," ὡς ἐν τούτῳ τῶν ἐναγομένων ξένων ἀπὸ τῶν πόλεων καλουμένων. οὐκ ἦν δέ, ἀλλ᾽ ὁ Μαιμακτηριών, for which Philetairos fr. 12 Kock is cited as proof. According to Antiphon 6.42, 44 the basileus is not allowed to pass on to his successor a charge of murder. Thus the earliest it can be filed is in Hekatombaion. After this there are τρεῖς προδικασίαι ἐν τρισὶ μησὶ, before the main hearing can take place—that is, in the fifth month, Maimakterion.

25. *Iliupersis* fr. 3 Allen-Bethe=Lysimachos *FGrHist* 382 F 14. The cup by Makron, Leningrad 649 (*ARV*[2] 460, 13; Wiener Vorlegeblätter A 8), depicts ΑΚΑΜΑΣ and ΔΕΜΟΦΟΝ fighting with ΔΙΟΜΕΔΕΣ and ΟΛΥΤΤΕΥΣ, each of whom hold a Palladion; ΑΓΑΜΕΣΜΟΝ is in the middle. One of the Palladions that will come to Athens is evidently authentic, the other inauthentic; see Polyainos 1.5; Ptolemaios Chennos in Phot. *Bibl.* 148a 29; cf. also Dionysios *FGrHist* 15 F 3=Clem. *Protr.* 4.47.6; Chavannes 1–3; 33.

26. Phanodemos *FGrHist* 325 F 16=Paus. *Attic.* ε 53 Erbse. For a more detailed account, though largely corresponding word for word, cf. Poll. 8.118 and Schol. to Aeschin. 2.87; much abridged, Schol. Patm. Dem. 23.71 and Hsch. ἀγνῶτες θεοί. On the altar of the "unknown gods," see Paus. 1.1.4; Tert. *Ad nat.* 2.9; *Adv. Marc.* 1.9; Philostr. *VA* 6.3; Hieronymus *PL* 26, 607B. E. Norden, *Agnostos Theos* (Leipzig, 1913) esp. 55, 115; O. Weinreich, *De Dis Ignotis* (Halle, 1914) esp. 25 ff.=*Ausgew. Schriften* (Amsterdam, 1969) 273 ff.

27. Cf. Kleidemos *FGrHist* 323 F 20=Paus. *Attic.* ε 53 Erbse, and quite similarly Harpocr. *s.v.* ἐπὶ Παλλαδίῳ; Schol. Patm. *Dem.* 23.37 contaminates the Phanodemos tradition with that of Kleidemos, already juxtaposed by Paus. *Attic.*

28. An. Bekk. 311.3: Δημοφῶντα ἁρπάσαντα Διομήδους τὸ Παλλάδιον φεύγειν ἐφ᾽ ἅρματος, πολλοὺς δὲ ἐν τῇ φυγῇ ἀνελεῖν συμπατήσαντα τοῖς ἵπποις. The description very closely approximates that of Kleidemos, except that he refers to Agamemnon rather than Diomedes. Diomedes, on the other hand, appeared in this context in Lys., fr. 220 B.-S.=Schol. Arist. III 320 Dind.

29. Cf. Paus. 1.28.8 f.: Δημοφῶντα . . . τὸ Παλλάδιον ἁρπάσαντα οἴχεσθαι. Ἀθηναῖόν τε ἄνδρα οὐ προιδόμενον ὑπὸ τοῦ ἵππου τοῦ Δημοφῶντος ἀνατραπῆναι καὶ συμπατηθέντα ἀποθανεῖν· ἐπὶ τούτῳ Δημοφῶντα ὑποσχεῖν δίκας. Cf. the saga in Paus. 5.1.8: Aitolos ran over Apis with the wagon and was punished with banishment ἐφ᾽ αἵματι ἀκουσίῳ. Cf. also Tullia and Servius Tullius; J. Grimm, *Deutsche Rechtsaltertümer* II (Göttingen, 1899[4]) 266, 273; n. 7 above.

30. Cf. Schol, Patm. *Dem.* 23.71: τὸ Παλλάδιον τὸ ἐκ Τροίας κεκομισμένον ὑπὸ τῶν Ἀργείων τῶν περὶ Διομήδην λαβὼν ὁ Δημοφῶν καὶ καταγαγὼν ἐπὶ θάλατταν καὶ ἁγνίσας διὰ τοὺς φόνους ἱδρύσατο ἐν τούτῳ τῷ τόπῳ.

31. Callim. fr. 22/3, Lactantius *Inst.* 1.21.31 etc., cf. Nilsson, *Griechische Feste* (Leipzig, 1906) 450 f.; Höfer in *Roschers Myth. Lex.* V 556–66; R. Pfeiffer, *Kallimachosstudien* (Munich, 1922) 78–102; likewise, on the quite parallel myth of Herakles, the Dryopes and Theiodamas, which evidently came up already in Hesiod's tale of the Keukos Gamos (R. Merkelbach and M. West, *RhM* 108 [1965] 304–5). Note the detail in Schol. Ap. Rh. 1.1212–19a that in his battle with the Dryopes, which followed upon the sacrifice of an ox, Herakles armed Deianeira, who was then wounded in the breast: the Amazon beside Herakles (on a chariot?) as the counterpart to Pallas beside Diomedes or Demophon. Asine, the city of the Dryopes, was destroyed by Argos already in the eighth century B.C. (W. S. Barrett, *Hermes* 82 [1954] 425–29), so that no ritual survived, only the myth. For a corresponding ritual without myth, see 95

Paus. 9.12 concerning the altar of Apollo Spodios in Thebes, where they sacrificed a βοῦς ἐργάτας "from a wagon that just happened to come by." There was no blood sacrifice for Athena Lindia herself, but there is ample testimony to the Βοκόπια below the citadel, beside or alternating with Θεοδαίσια: see Chr. Blinkenberg, *Lindos II 2: Inscriptions* (Berlin, 1941), 896–946, #580–619; against the view of Hiller von Gaertringen, *RE* III 1017, and Pfeiffer (*supra*) 88.1, he rejects the identification of the Bokopia with the meal of Herakles, which (citing Apollod. *Library* 2.118) he would move to Thermydron (identified by Hiller von Gaertringen, *Ath. Mitt.* 17 [1892] 316–18), since there is no farmland at the site of the Βοκόπια— but that is equally the case with the Attic Buphonia: we know nothing about the route of the sacrificial procession. Blinkenberg speaks of "vaches," yet fig. 8 M p. 905 depicts a bull. The βουζύγης on Lindos is mentioned by Lactantius *Inst.* 1.21.31; cf. Suda *s.v.*

32. *Appendix Proverbiorum* 1.61 (*Paroem. Gr.* 1 388) βουζύγης· ἐπὶ τῶν πολλὰ ἀρωμένων. Cf. Eupolis fr. 97 Kock: τί κέκραγας ὥσπερ βουζύγης ἀδικούμενος. Calling down a curse upon oneself in the διωμοσία played a large role in the court at the Palladion.

33. Ael. *Var. hist.* 5.14 calls the prohibition against killing the plow-ox an Attic custom, along with the command to bury a body, which the Scholia to S. *Antig.* 255 attribute to the Buzyges. In Aratus 131 f. the slaughter of the plow-ox is a primeval crime, and the Scholia refer to the Athenian Buphonia. On the taboo in connection with the plow-ox, see Aristoxenos fr. 29a W. (Pythagoras), Dion *Or.* 64.3 (Cyprus), Ael. *Hist. an.* 12.34 (Phrygians), Plin. *NH* 8.180 and Val. Max. 8.1 *Damn.* 8 (Rome).

34. This is what Ovid has Pythagoras demand, *Met.* 15.470. Adaios describes a Thessalian farmer acting in this way, *AP* 6.228: such peculiar behavior merited an epigram. Ovid thinks that the sacrifice of a bull was not allowed at the festival of Ceres (*Fast.* 4.413–16), but inscriptions at Eleusis testify to bull sacrifices "at the Mysteries" themselves (*IG* II/III² 1008.8, cf. 1006.10, 1011.8, etc.) even though Triptolemos's injunction ζῷα μὴ σίνεσθαι is right near by; cf. Porph. *Abst.* 4.22. Cf. the Old Testament passage in Lev. 17.3 f.: "If anyone of the house of Israel slaughters an ox or a lamb . . . and does not bring it to the entrance of the tent of meeting, to present it as an offering to the Lord before the tabernacle of the Lord, he shall be held guilty of bloodshed; he has shed blood." Slaughtering implies bloodguilt—it is permitted only in a sacral context.

35. The fundamental study is K. Meuli's "Griechische Opferbräuche," in *Phyllobolia, Festschr. P. Von der Mühll* (Basel, 1946) 185–288; cf. the author's "Greek tragedy and Sacrificial Ritual," *GRBS* 7 (1966) esp. 102–13; chapter 1 of this volume.

36. Deubner 158–74, Cook III 570–872, Meuli 275–77. The three "sacred plowings" mentioned by Plut. *Praec. coniug.* 144a, πρῶτον ἐπὶ Σκίρῳ . . . δεύτερον ἐν τῇ Ῥαρίᾳ, τρίτον ὑπὸ πόλιν τὸν καλούμενον Βουζύγιον, are perhaps divided up between the Skirophoria-Buphonia, the Mysteries or Proerosia, and Maimakterion. In the sequence in which Plutarch lists them, they would come between harvest-time and the end of sowing. The juxtaposition of Acropolis, Eleusis, and Βουζύγιος is presumably another instance of the "pluralistic" religious order of the polis. There are also references to Buzygai "from the Acropolis" (Ael. Arist., *Or.* 2.1.20 Dind.) and in Eleusis (Schol. Artist. II 473 Dind.).

37. Diphilus fr. 62 Kock. Antipatros *SVF* III 253=Cicero *Off.* 3.54, Clem. *Strom.* 2.139.1; cf. Ennius *Scen.* 398–400 V², Philo in Euseb. *Praep. ev.* 8.7.8; Toepffer 139; Nilsson 421.1; cf. n. 33 above.

5

DEMARATOS, ASTRABAKOS, AND HERAKLES: KINGSHIP, MYTH, AND POLITICS AT THE TIME OF THE PERSIAN WARS (HERODOTUS 6.67–69)

For the historian, legends are mostly a rank, disturbing overgrowth that scholarship clears away with a firm hand so that the facts can emerge. If, then, the *pater historiae* Herodotus fills his "investigation" with innumerable legends, the response is predictable: there is a certain indulgence for the irrepressible raconteur, a degree of openness to the charm of his tales, yet the historian does his best to get around Herodotus to the facts, while the philologist sees no need to move beyond formal and motif analysis to a consideration of the factual content of the narrative. Legends, however, do not always spring just from an arbitrary play of imagination, detached from all basis in fact. Their meaning may be quite precise, with a clear—if mediated—connection to reality. Fears and hopes, desires and disappointments, demands and complaints: legends can communicate, transmit, and imply more than what can be expressed in direct terms.

Demaratos, the deposed king who accompanied Xerxes on his campaign against Greece, plays a significant role in Herodotus. Not that he does anything particularly important. Rather Herodotus gleaned important information about the Persian expedition from the associates of Demaratos; he could, moreover, put this Spartan to good dramatic use at the Persian court as a figure of contrast, one who could interpret Greek character and warn against Asiatic blindness. That is why the events surrounding the banishment of Demaratos are described at length in the digression on Sparta in book 6. The factual circumstances emerge clearly: the two Spartan kings harbor feelings of enmity toward each other; their strife grows worse with the approach of the Persian conflict, when Demaratos stabs Kleomenes in the back during the action against Persian sympathizers on Aegina; then there are the intrigues of Kleomenes, who bribes the Delphic oracle to affirm the rumored doubts about Demaratos's royal ancestry.[1]

While there are novelistic touches in the tale of the deposed king's expo-

7

sure to his successor's scorn and consequent decision to go into exile, the narrative is on the whole realistic. Suddenly, however, it veers off toward the legendary, the mythic or fairytale-like: Demaratos's mother had had a divine encounter in the sanctuary of Helen at Therapne, whereupon she was transformed from the ugliest into the most beautiful girl in Sparta.[2] Demaratos turns to that same mother when he is deeply hurt and determined to break with Sparta. He sacrifices a cow to Zeus and, bidding her to touch the entrails of the sacrificial victim,[3] asks her with utmost solemnity, "by all the gods and by Zeus Herkeios," who his father truly is. King Ariston, of the line of the Eurypontidai, had remained childless in two marriages, and his third wife had given birth to Demaratos in an abnormally short time following the marriage. Now at last, his mother tells him "the whole truth" (*pan tōlēthes, ta alēthestata panta*), which she had previously not confided in him:

> On the third night after Ariston took me to his house as wife, I was visited by a phantom exactly resembling him. The phantom lay with me, and afterward took the wreaths it was wearing and put them on me. Then it vanished, and when Ariston came in later, he asked who had given me the wreaths. I said he had given them to me himself, but he denied it; then I protested with an oath that it was so, and reproached him for his denial, since so short a time before he had had me in his arms and given me the wreaths. Hearing me take my oath, Ariston realized that the hand of God was in this; moreover, the wreaths proved to have come from the Heröon by the courtyard gate, which is known as the shrine of Astrabakos, and when we questioned the diviners, they replied that it had been Astrabakos himself. There, my son; now you know everything you want to know. Either Astrabakos is your father, or Ariston; for that was the night when you were conceived.[4]

Amid the sharply delineated conflicts of Spartan politics, this story introduces the soft focus of a fairy tale, if only for a few moments. The legend has no sequel in Herodotus, although we have only a beginning that leaves everything open. Naturally, scholars have long noted the similarity with the myth of Amphitryon. Yet little is gained by establishing the influence, borrowing, or imitation of a motif. The question remains as to *why* there is a borrowing in this context, what function the motif can, and is meant to, perform. Now the story of the two Amphitryons is, in its origins, not the lighthearted stuff of comedy that it came to embody in world literature.

In great reliefs centrally located in the temple of Deir el Bahri is the depiction of how Amon, led by Thoth, sought out the queen, so that the future ruler Hatshepsut would be born. The hieroglyphic inscription adds the following explanation: "The glorious god Amon, lord of the throne of the two lands, came after having put on the shape of her husband. They found her resting in her beautiful palace."[5] For Hatshepsut, who built the temple to glorify herself, divine ancestry is the highest legitimation of her rule. Amenophis III had virtually the same text inscribed with almost identical images to promote his greater glory in the temple he built in Luxor.

Just how the Greek myth of Herakles came to be linked with the theology of Egyptian kingship can scarcely be determined in detail. But there can be no doubt that there *is* a connection. And maybe it is more than just an odd coincidence of names that precisely those pharaohs who chose to glorify themselves in this way resided in Thebes, and that Thebes was the birthplace of Herakles.[6] Yet there are so many possibilities of reciprocal contact in this complex of narrative motifs, iconographic tradition, and kingship ritual, that mere suppositions do not get us farther. What is clear is that the myth of Herakles' birth has the same significance as the Egyptian temple inscriptions: to legitimize kingship by reference to divine origins. Herakles is the ancestor of royal houses, in particular of the Lakedaimonian kings, who regard themselves as Heraklids. And in fact, it is the Spartans who carefully maintain the tradition of Herakles' divine birth. In the fifth century, Charon of Lampsakos attests that the Spartans preserved and displayed the goblet that Zeus had given as a gift to Alkmene. And an archaic stele leads us back still further in time, if it truly depicts Zeus and Alkmene.[7] Alexander, the king who ultimately succeeded the pharaohs and later sought divine honors from the Greeks as well, traced his lineage to another line of Heraklids; and legends of his birth likewise sprang up quickly, though not modeled on the myth of Herakles, but rather on the Dionysiac cult of his royal mother, Olympias.[8] By virtue of his legend, Demaratos stands between Herakles and Alexander the Great.

The fifth century was likewise the time when the myth of Herakles spread almost like a contagion in a different, if related, domain: The most successful athlete of his day was Theogenes, son of Timosthenes of Thasos, Olympic victor in 480 and 476 B.C. In later years he seems to have played a leading role in the politics of his native Thasos. The cult of "Herakles Thasios" was renewed around 450, a statue of Theogenes erected in the marketplace around 430. Theogenes wanted to compete with Herakles and Achilles. Accordingly there is a legend that may even have been part of   99 the official inscription in the marketplace: Not Timosthenes, but Herakles himself in the shape of his priest Timosthenes, visited his wife and begot Theogenes—a name suddenly filled with meaning.[9] The cult of Theogenes survived for centuries. For people of that time, the notion that a victor in the games was imbued with divine radiance was more than just a Pindaric metaphor. There was the story that Theogenes' most important rival, Euthymos of Lokris, was the son of a river god, and that he died no natural death; a votive offering bearing his name and a picture of the river god were discovered in Lokris.[10] Very ancient, aboriginal connections seem to persist here between kingship and victory in the agon. Thus the Olympic victor Kylon attempted his coup d'état at the time of the Olympic games; the great athlete Milon of Kroton led his fellow Krotonians into battle in the guise of Herakles, and his house became the gathering place for the Pythagorean brotherhood that ruled the city; the Sicilian tyrants, calling themselves kings, competed for victories in the Panhellenic games; and Demaratos—of all people—"was the only one of all the Spartan kings" who was victorious at Olympia in the four-horse chariot race (Hdt. 6.70).[11]

Now in the case of Demaratos the god involved is, strangely, not widely known nor recognized. His name remains a puzzle, even though it is solemnly invoked again later: *Astrabakos ho hērōs*, "the hero Astrabakos." With our limited knowledge, we may not be able to decipher its meaning. Yet the beginnings of a solution may be within our grasp.

One thing that is certain is that the name lends the story a decidedly Lakonic local coloring. The legend was created in this form either in Sparta or for Sparta, for only there could it be fully understood. The significance of Astrabakos thus lies in his link with the realities of cult: the Heröon existed,[12] and wreaths were deposited there—presumably on a regular basis. Heroes were at times more assiduously venerated in cult than were the great but distant gods of Homer and Hesiod.[13]

Another clue may be found in the detail that the Heröon's location was not far from the house of the king. Is it likely, however, that the legend would randomly select a hero who just happened to be the closest one at hand, just as the narrative was crossing into divine territory? Astrabakos has further been called "the tutelary demon of Ariston and probably of the entire royal house,"[14] but that contradicts the genealogy that connects Astrabakos with the other royal house instead, that of the Agiads (Paus. 3.16.9). There remains that small bit of cult legend transmitted by Pausanias, which links Astrabakos with one of the most important and famous cults in Sparta, the cult of Orthia. His Heröon, too must have been located near the sanctuary "in the Marshes," *en Limnais* (Paus. 3.16.6).

To be sure, plenty of other unsolved riddles are connected with the cult of Orthia. Ancient accounts focus on the bloody spectacle of the whipping of the youths, yet they include scarcely any details about the cult that could help elucidate this ritual. And excavations have exposed just how big the gaps in our knowledge really are.[15] Undoubtedly the cult consisted of more than just the *diamastigōsis*, "the whipping." But how the details fit together—the contests of various kinds, sickles as prizes, grotesque masks, dances performed by maidens—remains obscure. Regarding the *diamastigōsis*, there is at least a notice in Hesychius[16] that informs us that it was preceded by a time of preparation, a period of withdrawal and physical training, *sōmaskia*, outside the city, known as *phouaxir*, "the time of the fox" (?). And indeed, in the cult legend Astrabakos has a brother called Alopekos, "the fox." The whipping itself must originally have been a thieving game: the youths steal cheese from the altar of Orthia, while others defend it with whips.[17] Later on there is mention of a procession around the altar, or of keeping still beside the altar.[18] The legend of Astrabakos is linked with a more ancient, less regulated custom: "Astrabakos and Alopekos . . . discovered the statue of (Taurian) Artemis and at once went mad. At the sacrifice for Artemis, the Spartans from Limnai, Mesoa, Pitane, and Kynosura got into an argument which ended in blows and killing."[19] This calamity is resolved by an oracle commanding that the altar be sprinkled with human blood, which then becomes an annual occurrence. The madness of those who discover the statue, and the senseless and bloody argument between the participants from the four villages, may reflect the *diamastigōsis*-ritual: a state of extreme excitement, of even deadly madness, in the service of a barbarian goddess. Pausanias remains silent about what happened to those who discovered the statue. One may suspect that Astrabakos himself lost his life; thus his Heröon is located near the precinct of Orthia, where the tombs of other victims were likewise pointed out.[20] Astrabakos would thus be the one who both discovered the goddess and was her first victim, and as her victim he would be raised to the higher plane of a hero's existence.

Further confirmation for the pairing of Astrabakos and Artemis is provided from another source: in Karyai, it was not just the famous maiden choruses, the Karyatids, who danced for Artemis; according to etiological legends, the dancing maidens must have scattered in flight, while herdsmen, *boukoloi*, penetrated the sanctuary and sang their song. These "bucolic" songs, however, were called *astrabika*.[21] As with Orthia, we have maiden choruses and male interlopers; stories of bridal abduction linked both to the Karyatis-cult and to that of Orthia,[22] and once again a similar name that is, moreover, a "speaking" name: *astrabē*, the comfortable saddle for a mule, especially favored by women.[23] Yet what does a "mule rider" have to do with Artemis, and how does the delicate dance of the maidens converge with madness, blood, and death? All this remains a risky guessing game.

Just why the Demaratos legend would settle on Astrabakos in particular, then, only seems to grow more and more puzzling. Yet a solution might be in sight if we could set the *diamastigōsis* within a larger framework. Two observations are decisive in this regard: first, that different groups of boys or youths take sides against one another in conflict—this points toward the realm of brotherhoods, to *Knabenschaften* and *Männerbünden*; second, that each Spartiate between the time of childhood and manhood must submit to this ordeal—we are dealing, then, with an initiation ceremony comparable to widespread and amply documented rites of puberty.[24] The fact that this is preceded by a period of isolation, the "period of the fox," fits perfectly into the paradigm of the "rite of passage"; the fact, moreover, that a festive procession in long robes—known as the *Ludōn pompē*[25]—comes at the end, likewise establishes a close link to rites of transformation, where putting on new clothes is common. Community is built upon the shock of the anomalous, even the horrible. The newcomers, pushing their way into the society of their elders, are hit with a wave of aggression. Once that aggression is released, a new order can take shape. This is not the place to pursue the dark sides of human society expressed in the sanctified brutality of such rites. The goal is to establish a new life despite our destructive instincts. Precisely by undergoing the *diamastigōsis*, a new generation comes to the fore to take its place as equals in the *Männerbund*. Only he who has sacrificed his blood to Orthia can become a Spartiate. Initiation ritual is thus the source through which the community renews itself. And that source is linked in a unique way to Astrabakos and, through him, Demaratos. The intimate ties between kingship and the rites of the *Männerbund*, between initiation and enthronement, have been demonstrated by Alföldi.[26] We are dealing with a rite of passage, with the crossing of a boundary to a new and higher state of existence. Even if the esoteric details remain obscure to us, we can guess approximately what Astrabakos was meant to signify as father of Demaratos. When the Heraklids seized power in the Peloponnese, they were shown the way by someone driving a mule (Paus. 5.3.5), a certain Oxylos, inventor of the mule's saddle, *astrabē* (Schol. Pi. P. 5.10b).

At any rate the legend tells us that one of the *kreittones* (the higher powers) intervened here so that a child could be born; this child is thus destined for extraordinary things: it will exceed the bounds of normal human existence. The human alternative implicit in Demaratos's question to his mother—am I the son of a king or not?—is, in a startling way, raised to a new plane and canceled out in his mother's reply. If Demaratos is not a legitimate king, one of many, then he is more, indeed he is unique, comparable only with Herakles, whose descendants founded Sparta. Bribed or not, the Delphic oracle may have spoken truly: a hero for a father is not a consolation prize for one who has been deposed,[27] but rather the expression of his most exalted claim. Divinity here initiates a new beginning, full of unimagined possibilities.

That is what the Demaratos legend proclaims, inasmuch as it has a precise meaning. It stands thus in almost grotesque contrast to the historical reality. Demaratos accomplished nothing in his life that would put him on a par with Herakles and Alexander, or even with Theogenes or Euthymos. He died a Persian vassal, the petty prince of Teuthrania. And though his descendants bore the names of the original kings of Sparta, Eurysthenes and Prokles,[28] the Persians mocked his monarchic ambitions: "This diadem has no brain to sit upon."[29] There was a great gulf between claim and reality. The Astrabakos legend was certainly not created with Teuthrania in mind, especially given the clear references to Spartan cult. Yet there came a time in Sparta itself when Demaratos seemed about to accomplish something extraordinary: when Demaratos returned to Greece with Xerxes, when the Spartan contingent at Thermopylai had been annihilated and the huge army was driving inexorably southward, Xerxes might already have thought of himself as lord of Greece, and his government in exile stood poised to take power—that is to say, Demaratos. Reinstalled thus, Demaratos would in fact have been in a position in Sparta, and so in all of Greece, unlike that of any king before.[30] From this standpoint, the legends about Demaratos coalesce with the historical circumstances to form a meaningful, necessary, and indivisible whole. To start with, his mother was blessed by the gods; her son Demaratos, "prayed for by the people" (Hdt. 6.63), was begotten by the hero Astrabakos, for his was to be no ordinary destiny. To be sure, there was resistance, deposition, dishonor, exile; such is the fate of the chosen: his path is marked by a Passion.[31] But now he is returning to his hereditary homeland to take up his proper station, just as the higher powers, the *kreittones,* intended to judge his enemies, bring blessing to his friends. The Demaratos legend thus acquires a startlingly precise meaning: we are dealing with the myths that preceded Demaratos as propaganda in the year 480, outlining the policy of the government in exile. Even the form of the legend points to its semi-official origins: Demaratos learned of the secret of Astrabakos in a private conversation with his mother; if it was passed on to others, therefore, Demaratos himself must have made it known to his people.[32]

Only at this point does the meaning of a line in Herodotus become clear, which has caused interpreters great difficulty: when Demaratos suffers the insult that drives him into exile, he says that this act will be the start of either endless evil or endless good fortune for Sparta (6.67). While it is understandable that an injured party would threaten evil, what does he mean in the same breath with the words "endless good fortune"? Some have tried to explain them as a rhetorical antithesis, where only the first term is meant seriously.[33] But that is to despair of the words' own meaning. Others think that Demaratos—a prophet *malgré lui*—was predicting "endless good fortune" for his enemies if his attacks were to fail.[34] But this is implausible not just from a psychological standpoint; despite Plataea and Salamis, the Persian War was in Herodotus's view first and foremost an almost incalculable calamity (6.98). Yet if one takes the sentence in the context of that monarchic propaganda of the year 480, it acquires its natural sense and so confirms the interpretation of the legend: At this moment Demaratos had broken with his native city, with legality and legitimacy; now there was nothing for him but to fight against the established order, a ruthless fight—*muriē kakotēs,* "endless evil"; but if he were successful, if his homeland were to lie humbled at his feet, that would be the start of a whole new era, different and more glorious than anything that preceded it. This was the chance for that "endless good fortune," *muriē eudaimoniē.* And that is precisely the cue for the legend of Demaratos's "rejection"[35] of Ariston for the sake of a direct relationship with higher powers.

The political paradigm that the Demaratos legend hints at is tyranny. When Pausanias, the victor of Plataea, "wishing to become tyrant of Hellas" (*erōta schōn tēs Hellados turannos genesthai,* Hdt. 5.32), allows himself to be pushed down the very path that his victory had closed off to Demaratos, this only confirms how dangerously real that option was. We get a clear notion of how one part of that *muriē eudaimoniē* might have looked in Sparta when we learn that Pausanias contemplated liberating the Helots. It has often been noted that tyranny draws its support from the lower classes.

No wonder, then, that in the context of tyranny the most ancient religious forces break through to the surface, jubilation and almost chiliastic expectations about a divine king. Peisistratos had entered Athens with a divine escort (Hdt. 1.60), and plenty in Sparta as well would have been willing to cheer the return from abroad of the conquering savior king of mysterious divine origin; the enthronement of a king would in any case have been accompanied by choruses and sacrifice (Thuc. 5.16.6). His opponents, of course, made a joke of the legend: "son of the ass keeper"—that was the reply to the Astrabakos legend, as has long been recognized, a bit of counter-propaganda built right into Herodotus's narrative.[36]

One can appreciate from this perspective what the victory of the Greek *poleis* in the Persian war meant for the history of ideas. The "oriental" power that threatened the Greeks was something that lurked inside the Greeks themselves as an age-old legacy and dark potential. If the Classical age had not occurred, would Late Antiquity have started 400 years earlier? After Salamis and Plataea people woke up from their dreams of a savior king, and the measure of all things became man. Demaratos was thus transformed after the fact into a champion of things Greek. Herodotus exploits the tradition without falling prey to it: a few distancing remarks[37] allow us to suppose that Herodotus understood very well indeed the legend he so masterfully narrates. But even if people had awakened from the dream of this myth, its language still can touch the soul at its deepest levels. And the promise of *muriē eudaimoniē* offered by a tyrant retains its dangerous appeal.

NOTES

1. Cf. B. Niese, *RE* IV, 2029 f.; Th. Lenschau, *Klio* 31 (1938) 412–29; D. Hereward, "The flight of Demaratos," *RhM* 101 (1958) 238–49; G. Zeilhofer, *Sparta, Delphoi und die Amphiktyonen im 5. Jh. v. Chr.* (diss., Erlangen, 1959) 17 ff.; A. R. Burn, *Persia and the Greeks,* (London, 1962) 232 ff., 268. Demaratos's flight is usually dated to 491 (R. W. Macan, *Herodotus, The Fourth, Fifth, and Sixth Books,* II [London, 1895] 87; J. Beloch, *Griechische Geschichte* I 2² [Berlin, 1913] 182); Hereward pleads for 490, but this deviates from Herodotus. H. W. Parke, *CQ* 39 (1945) 106–12, suspects that the deposition followed the ritual described in Plut. *Agis* 11; against him, W. den Boer, *Laconian Studies* (1954) 211, Zeilhofer (*supra*) 17 n. 33, contradicted in turn by F. Kiechle, *Lakonien und Sparta* (Munich, 1963) 241 f. On the "Demaratos source," following H. Matzat, *Hermes* 6 (1872) 478 ff.; P. Trautwein, *Hermes* 25 (1890) 527 ff.; D. Mülder, *Klio* 13 (1913) 39 ff.; F. Jacoby, *RE* Suppl. II, 404, 412 f., 442 f., 476; consult also H. Hignett, *Xerxes' Invasion of Greece* (1963) 31 n. 3. On the Demaratos scenes in Hdt. (7.3.101 ff., 209, 235), see H. Bischoff, *Der Warner bei Herodot* (diss., Marburg, 1932); R. Lattimore, "The Wise Adviser in Herodotus," *CP* 34 (1939) 24–35.

2. Hdt. 6.61.

3. On this rite, see P. Stengel, *Griechische Kultusaltertümer*³ (Munich, 1920) 136 f.

4. Hdt. 6.69. The Codices ABCP have Ἀστρόβακος, as opposed to Ἀστράβακος, in DRSV, Clem. *Protr.* 2.40.2 (based ultimately on Hdt.) and Paus. 3.16.6, 9.

5. For the reliefs from Deir El Bahri, see E. Naville, *The Temple of Deir El Bahari* II (London, 1894) pl. 47, cf. p. 14. For the German translation of the hieroglyphic text, see S. Schott, *Altägyptische Liebeslieder* (Zurich, 1950) 89 f. Cf. the English translation in J. H. Breasted, *Ancient Records of Egypt* II (Chicago, 1906) #196; H. Frankfort, *Kingship and the Gods* (Chicago, 1948) 45. For the reliefs from Luxor, see A. Gayet, *Le temple de Louxor* (Paris, 1894) pl. 63, cf. pp. 98 ff.; on the text, see Breasted (*supra*) #841. Scholars compare the speech of Ptah to Ramses II in the temple of Abu Simbel (Breasted, III #400): "I assumed my form as the Ram, Lord of Mendes, and begat thee in thy august mother." The same text appears in the temple of Ramses III at Medinet Habu (Breasted III p. 175 n. b). Cf. also the "Märchen des Papyrus Westcar" (ed. A. Erman [Berlin, 1890]; Erman, *Die Literatur de Ägypter* [Leipzig, 1923] 72 f.; Schott [*supra*] 183), which describes how Re begets the first kings of the Fifth Dynasty with the wife of the high priest of Heliopolis. See also F. Daumas, *Les mammisis des temples égyptiens* (Paris, 1958). The whole pictorial and textual material can now be found in H. Brunner, *Die Geburt des Gottkönigs* (Wiesbaden, 1964); we see, however, just how remote the Egyptologist is from the Greek tradition in the assessment of the Amphitryon story as the product of a "hellenistisch[sic]-ägyptischen Mischkultur mit ihrem unsauberen Lachen" (214).

6. There is remarkably little comment on these connections among Hellenists, even though the similarity of the Egyptian representations to the Amphitryon myth had already been noted by Gayet, *Le temple* 99. To be sure, A. Wiedemann, *Herodots 2. Buch* (Leipzig, 1890) 268 had drawn attention to Luxor, and following him cf., e.g., R. Reitzenstein, *Poimandres* (Leipzig, 1904) 139, R. Merkelbach, *Die Quellen des griechischen Alexanderromans* (Munich, 1954) 58 n. Yet there is no refrence to Egypt in either the comprehensive treatments of the Herakles saga by O. Gruppe (*RE* Suppl. III [1918] 1015 f.) and C. Robert (*Griechische Heldensage*[4] [Berlin, 1921] 612), or in the more recent mythological lexika of H. Hunger (Vienna, 1953) or H. J. Rose (London, 1928). The myth of Herakles differs in three characteristic details from the usual Greek myths about divine paternity: (1) The transformation into the husband's shape, whereby the miraculous event is made to fit with everyday experience of marriage; in addition to Demaratos and Theogenes, this motif appears in the story of Zeus-Phoinix-Kassiopeia (Clem. Rom. *Hom.* 5.13.6, and compare Satyros *P.Oxy.* 2465, Schol. Stat. *Theb.* 1.463); occasionally we find that god and mortal husband visit the woman during the same night, e.g., in the story of Poseidon-Aigeus-Aithra (Apollod. 3.15.7.1). (2) The god is accompanied by Hermes-Thoth, while the gods (including Zeus) otherwise go to their polygamous trysts alone. (3) Hera nursing Herakles, a quite unusual detail from the Greek perspective (see most recently M. Renard, "Hercule allaité par Junon," *Hommages J. Bayet* [Brussels, 1964] 611–18; L. Preller and C. Robert, *Griechische Mythologie* [Berlin, 1894–1926] 427); in the Egyptian reliefs we find depictions and descriptions of goddesses nursing the royal newborn. Note, too, that Egyptian Thebes is known as early as Homer (*Il.* 9.381 f., *Od.* 4.126), and that H. L. Lorimer, *Homer and the Monuments* (London, 1950) 95 ff., is inclined to see in these passages one of the clearest reminiscences of the time of Amenophis III, while Gruppe establishes with respect to Greek Thebes that Herakles was "a stranger" there ([*supra*] 936). It is assumed that there were pre-Dorian, Mycenaean remnants connected with Spartan kingship (Kiechle, *Lakonien* 160 f.). Problems remain, not least of all why the Greeks called that Egyptian city "Thebes" despite its entirely different Egyptian name (see A. Bonnet, *Reallexikon der ägyptischen Religionsgeschichte* [Berlin, 1952] 792 f.). The "Amphitryon" version of the kingship legend cannot be traced back earlier than Hatshepsut (Frankfort, *Kingship* 44 f.).

DEMARATOS, ASTRABAKOS, AND HERAKLES

7. Charon, *FGrHist* 262 F 2. G. Loeschcke, *Über die Reliefs der altspartanischen Basis* (Progr. Dorpat, 1879) thought he could recognize the encounter of Zeus and Alkmene on the Spartan stele (G. Lippold, *Griechische Plastik* [Munich, 1950] 31 n. 9: prior to 600), with reference to the depiction on the chest of Kypselos (Paus. 5.18.3). His interpretation is accepted by Bethe (*RE* II, 1792), but Möbius thought of Menelaus and Helen (*RE* III A, 2311), Lippold tentatively of Zeus and Hera. Since the male hands the female a wreath, not a δέπας, the interpretation remains uncertain. On the legend, see Pherekydes, *FGrHist* 3 F 13 with Jacoby ad loc.; it is ignored in *Od.* 11.266 ff., but hinted at in (Hes.) *Scutum* 3=Hes. fr. 195 M.-W.

8. For the legend of Alexander's birth, see Plut. *Alex.* 2; W. W. Tarn, *Alexander the Great* II (Cambridge, 1950) 347 ff.; Merkelbach (*Quellen* 57 f.). For the descent of the Macedonian royal house from the Heraklids, see Hdt. 8.137; there are Macedonian coins depicting Herakles as early as the 5th century. The Mysteries of Andania were considered the "legacy of Aristomenes" (Paus. 4.26.4), and thus Aristomenes' conception was linked with these Mysteries (Paus. 4.14.7). See also O. Weinreich, *Der Trug des Nektanebos* (Leipzig, 1911).

9. Paus. 6.11; on the chronology 6.6.5 f.; Dion. *Or.* 31.95 ff.; *SIG*³ 36. For an exhaustive treatment on the basis of new finds, J. Pouilloux, *Recherches sur l'histoire et les cultes de Thasos* I (Paris, 1954) 62–105. In the literary tradition the name is transmitted as Theagenes, in inscriptions ΘΕΟΓΕΝΗΣ and ΘΕΥΓΕΝΗΣ. For the legend of his birth, see Paus. 6.11.2, and on a Thasian inscription that may relate to it, see Pouilloux (*supra*) 82 f. It is doubtful whether the legend assumes a hieros-gamos rite in the Thasian cult of Herakles; against this, see M. Launcy, *Rev. arch.* 18 (1941) 22 ff., A. D. Nock, *AJA* 52 (1948) 301, and Pouilloux (*supra*) 66. On Theogenes' emulation of Herakles, Pouilloux (*supra*) 200: Herakles had been victorious at Olympia simultaneously in πάλη and παγκράτιον (Paus. 5.8.4), and Theogenes wanted to win simultaneously in πυγμή and παγκράτιον (Paus. 6.6.5); for emulation of Achilles, Paus. 6.11.5.

10. On Euthymos, Callim. fr. 98/99 Pf., Paus. 6.6.4-11, Hiller v. Gaertringen, *RE* VI, 1514; for the votive offering from Lokris, *Not. Scav.* (1946) 144 fig. 10, cf. 146 f. (Hellenistic).

11. For Kylon as Olympic victor, Thuc. 1.126; for Milon as Herakles, D. S. 12.9.6; for the gathering of the Pythagoreans ἐν τῇ Μίλωνος οἰκίᾳ, Aristoxenos fr. 18 Wehrli. The relationship between agon and kingship was treated in a sometimes overly bold, but largely accurate manner by F. M. Cornford in J. Harrison, *Themis* (Cambridge, 1912) 212 ff.

12. Cf. Paus. 3.16.6; S. Wide, *Lakonische Kulte* (Leipzig, 1893) 279 f.

13. "It is striking how rarely Herakles appears in local Lakonian saga and cult," Wide, *Lakonische Kulte*, 302. The Lokrians did not assign one of the Olympians to be the father of "their" Euthymos, but rather a local river god.

14. Wide, *Lakonische Kulte*, 280, following E. Rohde, *Psyche*² (Leipzig, 1898) 196 f., considers Astrabakos a ἥρως ἐπὶ προθύρῳ.

15. The fundamental study of the Orthia cult is by M. P. Nilsson, *Griechische Feste* (Leipzig, 1906) 190 ff.; for the excavation report, R. M. Dawkins, *The Sanctuary of Artemis Orthia* (London, 1929), in which see 399–407 for H. J. Rose on the cult; cf. also Ziehen, *RE* III A, 1465–71; K. M. T. Chrimes, *Ancient Sparta* (Manchester, 1949) 248–71; E. Kirsten and W. Kraiker, *Griechenlandkunde*⁴ (Heidelberg, 1962) 406 ff.; on the chronology, J. Boardman, *BSA* 58 (1963) 1–7. For discussion of the Partheneion by Alkman, I refer to D. L. Page, *Alcman, The Partheneion* (Oxford, 1951) 71 ff.; for the dance of the maidens and their rape, Plut. *Thes.* 31. It is quite unclear into which of the various Spartan age groups (on which H. I. Marrou, *REA* 48 [1946] 216–30) the διαμαστίγωσις belongs: παῖδες, Plut. *Inst. Lac.* 239c, Nikolaos, *FGrHist* 90 F 103 z 11; *pueri*, Cic. *Tusc.* 2.34; *impuberes pueri*, Schol. Stat. *Theb.* 8.437; otherwise mostly ἔφηβοι. For finds from a sanctuary of Artemis Orthia in Messene (late Hellenistic): Ἔργον (1962) 122 ff., with votive inscriptions of the priestess who "keeps the cult statue"

(βρέτας κρατοῦσα), just as the Spartan priestess keeps the shrouded cult statue (Paus. 3.16.11, Schol. Plato *Leg.* 633b); the Dioskouroi abduct the Leukippides from Messene, and on the Meidias vase (*Wiener Vorlegebl.* IV 1; *ARV*² 1313) this happens beside the statue of a goddess who is holding something shrouded in her arm.

16. Hsch. φούαξιρ (φουαέξιερ cod.)· ἡ ἐπὶ τῆς χώρας σωμασκία τῶν μελλόντων μαστιγοῦσθαι. φουάδδει· σωμασκεῖ. φοῦαι· ἀλώπεκες. Cf. Justin 3.3.6 f: *pueros puberes . . . in agrum deduci . . . neque prius in urbem redire quam viri facti essent.*

17. Xen. *Lak. Pol.* 2.9 (a passage first taken seriously by Nilsson, *Griechische Feste;* still athetized in Marchant's edition [Oxford, 1920]); hinted at in Plato *Leg.* 633b; cf. also the etiological legend in Plut., *Arist.* 17. The connection with the goddess's "lion's cheese" in Alkman fr. 56 Page is obscure: there the festival is "on the mountain tops," not ἐν Λίμναις. Ritual theft and whipping dances were more frequent than we might think; see L. Lawler, *TAPA* 75 (1944) 26 citing Poll. 4.5 etc. One may also compare the theft of the sacrificial meat by the *hirpi Sorani* (Serv. *in Aen.* 11.785), and further the Delian rite in Callim. *Hymn* 4.316 ff. with Schol. (Lawler [supra]).

18. Nikolaos, *FGrHist* 90 F 103 z 11: οἱ δὲ παῖδες νομίμως περί τινα βωμὸν περιιόντες μαστιγοῦνται; and Schol. Hor. *C.* 1.7.10: *ut iuvenis aras ascenderet, superimponeret manus et tamdiu loris caederetur ab alio iuvene, quamdiu sanguis de vibicibus in aram manaret;* as well as Serv. *in Aen.* 2.116: *aris superpositi;* and Schol. Plato *Leg.* 633 b: κινεῖν . . . τὰς χεῖρας οὐκ ἐτόλμα, ἔχων ταύτας ἐπὶ τῆς κεφαλῆς.

19. Cf. Paus. 3.16.9. It is notable that the four original villages are mentioned, with the exception of Amyklai. From the mention of these villages, we may perhaps conclude that attackers and whip-bearers in the thieving game came, respectively, from different villages: spilling your "neighbor's" blood was not permitted. It is regularly emphasized that blood must flow on the altar, according to Philostr. *VA* 6.10, among others. The genealogy cited in Paus. makes Astrabakos (fifth generation after Agis) a contemporary of Lykurgos (ἕκτος ἀπὸ Προκλέους according to Ephoros, *FGrHist* 70 F 149.18), who is credited with the introduction of the rite. F. Altheim (*Griechische Götter im alten Rom* [Giessen, 1930] 124) connects the name of the father of Astrabakos and Alopekos, Ἴρβος, with the Lakonian river Virbius (Vib. Seq. *Geogr.* p. 152.6), as well as with the Virbius in the cult of Diana of Aricia.

20. Luc. *Anachr.* 38, and compare Plut. *Lyc.* 18; Cic. *Tusc.* 2.34; the ceremony sank to the level of a gladiatorial game; as late as the third century A.D. a theater was built for spectators; the ritual, however, is always jutified through its "holiness" (Philostr. *VA* 6.10); the claim that in earlier times the ritual was "relatively harmless" (Ziehen, *RE* III A, 1468) is nonetheless unfounded; cf. n. 24 below.

21. C. Wendel collected the different versions of the legend concerning the origins of bucolic poetry in his edition of the Theocr. Schol. (Leipzig, 1912) 2 ff. The name *astrabicon* appears only in Probus III 2 p. 324, 20 Thilo-Hagen=p. 14, 11 Wendel. Yet Nilsson, *Griechische Feste* 199, is right to consider it an old tradition. The maidens' flight is also mentioned by Schol. Stat. *Theb.* 4.225. Besides Nilsson 196 ff., cf. also v. Geisau, *RE* X, 2245 f.

22. For the rape of the maidens in Karyai, Paus. 4.16.9. It is strange that the Dioskouroi—themselves notorious abductors of girls—are supposed to have taught *karyatizein;* see Luc. *Salt.* 10. Cf. n. 15.

23. Mau, *RE* II, 1792 f.; the meaning "wagon" (Probus [above, n. 21], cf. Herodian *Gramm. Gr.* III 1, 308; Tzetzes *Chil.* 9.854 f.) is secondary and rare. Formally, Ἀστράβακος is related to *ἀστράβαξ as Ἀλώπεκος is to ἀλώπηξ and can be seen as a κ-expansion (Schwyzer, *Griechische Grammatik* I 497) of ἀστράβη: "the fellow with the mule saddle." The connection of Astrabakos with ἀστράβη is confirmed by the ὀνοφορβός story; cf. n. 36. Wide, *Lakonische Kulte,* 280, detects a resemblance between the "mule rider" and Dionysus. Yet

one must ask why Dionysus in particular—and above all Hephaistos—are portrayed as mule riders.

24. Set in this context by J. G. Frazer, *Pausanias* III (1898) 341 f.; cf. H. Jeanmaire, *Couroi et Courètes* (Lille, 1939) 511 f., 514–23; Nilsson, *Griechische Feste* 192 cites Frazer approvingly but thinks that one needs to look farther for a specific purpose in the whipping, which he then finds—together with A. Thomsen, *ARW* 9 (1906) 397 ff.—in the idea of a "blow with the rod of life" (*Lebensrute*); in a similar direction, cf. F. Schwenn, *Die Menschenopfer bei den Griechen und Römern* (Giessen, 1915) 53 ff.: a communion with the god. In that case, one must hypothesize that λύγος-branches were initially used, and only secondarily the whips that are always referred to. Today, however, there is greater readiness to admit that such rites do not arise from conscious "ideas," and therefore that they have no well-considered "purpose"—magical explanations are every bit as etiological as historical explanations—they are rather an outcropping of the soul's deeper layers. Yet the rite does have a psychological meaning and a social function. For an attempt to interpret initiation ritual in light of father-son conflicts, see M. Zeller, *Die Knabenweihen* (diss., Bern, 1923); A. E. Jensen, *Beschneidung und Reifezeremonien bei Naturvölkern* (Stuttgart, 1933) 167 ff.; at Sparta, of course, youths take sides against youths (*ab alio iuvene*, n. 18 above, cf. nn. 17 and 19). In any case the Greeks were not entirely off the mark in believing that διαμαστίγωσις had replaced human sacrifice; one must simply take their belief in a psychological rather than a historical sense. For Nilsson, the blood-obsession of the rite was degenerate; it had "lost its religious significance" (193) although its sacredness is its true justification. There are fatalities even in primitive initiation ceremonies (cf. n. 20). On initiation generally, A. van Gennep, *Les rites de passage* (Paris, 1909) and M. Eliade, *Das Mysterium der Wiedergeburt* (Zurich, 1961).

25. Plut. *Arist.* 17; H. Diels, *Hermes* 31 (1896) 361 f.

26. A. Alföldi, "Königsweihe und Männerbund bei den Achämeniden," *Schweiz. Arch. f. Volksk.* 47 (1951) 11 ff.; cf. G. Binder, *Die Aussetzung des Königskindes* (Meisenheim, 1964) esp. 29 ff. One further detail is worth noting: the λύγος-tree plays a large role in the cult of Orthia (Paus. 3.16.11); the statue of Λυγοδέσμα was found in a λύγος-shrub. Comparable stories circulated about the statue of Hera of Samos (Menodotos, *FGrHist* 541 F 1): a λύγος-tree served as cult monument in the Samian sanctuary of Hera (the stump was discovered in the German excavations of 1963). When the Samians voted divine honors for Lysander at the end of the Peloponnesian War, his cult was merged with the festival of Hera: τὰ παρ' αὐτοῖς Ἡραῖα Λυσάνδρεια καλεῖν ἐψηφίσαντο (Duris, *FGrHist* 76 F 71, cf. F 26; Ch. Habicht, *Gottmenschentum und griechische Städte* [Munich, 1956] 3 ff.). To be sure, the Heraia happened to be the main festival of Samos. But if a simple name change sufficed for the festival of the goddess to absorb the ruler cult, then the cult of the goddess with the λύγος must already have possessed a meaning that pointed in this direction. To state it as a preliminary hypothesis: the cult of the great goddess belongs in the context of "*Männerbund* and *Königsweihe.*" Cf. no. 8 above on Andania.

27. Macan, *Herodotus* II 87 thinks that the story's intent is "to justify the practical result, even while glorifying the true descent of the disposed king." Mülder (above, n. 1) 57 f. suspects that the Astrabakos legend was circulated by Delphi following the bribery scandal (n. 1 above). The narrative form, however, cannot be traced to oracles, quite apart from the question of whether divine descent is compatible with the Delphic injunction γνῶθι σαυτόν.

28. On Demaratos's descendants, Xen., *Hell.* 3.1.6, *An.* 2.1.3; 7.8.17; Ath. 1.29 f.; Sext. Emp. *Math.* 1.258; Plut., *Q. conv.* 677b; Hellanikos, *FGrHist* 4 F 116, considered Eurysthenes and Prokles as founders of the Spartan constitution, rather than Lykurgos.

29. Plut. *Them.* 29; Sen. *Ben.* 6.31.12.

30. Thus already Macan, *Herodotus* (on 6.70): "If Xerxes had been victorious, presumably

Demaratos would have returned to Sparta as 'Tyrant' of Lakedaimon, perhaps as Satrap of Peloponnese or of Hellas." Cf. Burn, *Persia* 393 f.

31. Banishment and return have belonged to royal legend, from the "return" of the Heraklids and the legend of the Macedonian kings (Hdt. 8.137 f.), to the "flight into Egypt" and the "return" of Dietrich von Bern.

32. "One might think that one is hearing Demaratos himself in the final sentence of 69," Jacoby, *RE* Suppl. II, 442. Perhaps there is a connection here with the story of the message Demaratos is supposed to have sent to Sparta before Xerxes' invasion (Hdt. 7.239); the Demaratos-source used by Herodotus would have claimed that Demaratos wanted to warn Sparta—a claim that seemed implausible, however, to Herodotus.

33. H. Stein, *Herodotus*, 5th ed. (Berlin, 1894) ad loc., but his parallels break down (*Il.* 9.78; Hdt. 5.89; 7.8 γ; 8.68 γ). W. W. How and J. Wells, *A Commentary on Herodotus*, 2 vols. (Oxford, 1912) and Ph. E. Legrand, *Hérodote*, 9 vols. (Paris, 1946–54) follow Stein.

34. This "prophetic alternative" is considered already by Macan, *Herodotus*; cf. the thorough treatment of A. Dovatour, "La menace de Démarate," *REG* 50 (1937) 464–69, who recognizes the "invraisemblance psychologique" of this explanation; similarly B. A. van Groningen *Herodotus' Historien* (Leiden, 1945) ad loc.

35. Cf. the words of Kleitos against Alexander: . . . ὥστ᾽ Ἄμμωνι σαυτὸν εἰσποιεῖν ἀπειπάμενος Φίλιππον (Plut. *Alex.* 50.11).

36. Cf. Wide, *Lakonische Kulte*, 279 f.; Macan, How-Wells, Legrand, van Groningen ad loc.

37. Hdt. 6.61: Demaratos hinders Kleomenes, κοινὰ τῇ Ἑλλάδι ἀγαθὰ προεργαζόμενον . . . διέβαλε—this is, moreover, the first sentence of the entire digression on Demaratos; see also 7.239, n. 32 above.